How Accountants Lost Their Balance

How the profession has drifted away from reality and must adapt to an intangible world.

By
Nick A. Shepherd

EduVision Inc.

ISBN 978-1-7775703-0-9

Books by the same author
"Variance Analysis for Cost Performance Measurement"
"Governance, Accountability and Sustainable Development: An agenda for the 21st Century"
"The Controllers Handbook" (2nd edition)
"Reflective Leaders & High Performance Organizations" (jointly with Dr. Peter Smyth)

Dedication

To all the accountants that I have had the pleasure to work with over the years; especially to the thousands who I was privileged to have attend my professional development workshops. Thanks for the support, ideas, thoughts, and criticisms. Thanks also to all the people in the professional associations, clients and employers who all added to my learning experiences.

Especially thanks to my wife and family for their patience and support over the years, and to my son, David who joined the ranks of the professional accountants.

How Accountants Lost their Balance

Contents

Foreword

Accountants have an important role in society because in many cases they keep track of other people's money. They also provide these records, and their advice about what they mean, to decision makers who then decide how to spend this money. Good decision making is critical - even a sacred trust. Accurate records are also critical.

In the last 50 years, the way that people and organizations spend money has changed significantly. In the industrial age it was all about tangible assets - property, plant, and equipment. Today, there are many organizations that have almost no tangible assets but have poured massive amounts of money into creating a business model where its' underlying capacity to sell services and earn profits comes from intangibles.

My entire career has involved living and working through this period of change. I was part of what happened (and some of the stories about life before the internet and mobile phones amuse my grandchildren).

We spent millions in building business processes that were cost effective, replicable, and delivered products and services when required. We spent millions on developing human resources who became the driving force for innovation and creativity. We spent millions of developing leaders who would lead the workforce and create a business environment where people could be "the best they could be." We spent millions on partnering with key suppliers and other 3rd parties who became part of our business model and who we could not operate without. We spent millions of doing a better job of getting to know our marketplace and our customers so that we could be more customer focused, more responsive and build our brand and reputation. We also spent millions in adapting to new technologies that totally changed the way we did business. We also tried to encourage and participate in local community activities. In recent times business has invested millions to improve their operations so as to reduce and eventually eliminate their negative impact of the environment.

All of these activities cost money. Money that flowed through our expense statements yet, strangely money that then disappeared. Complying with accounting standards, these investments we were making, were not creating assets for the business but had to be written off against current revenues; as a result, they either reduced profits or created losses and reduced our shareholders equity in the business.

The real world DID value these investments though. The accounting assets became a smaller and smaller proportion of an organizations value in the marketplace, to the level where today only a small proportion of assets are in the accounting records. Audits no longer verify and protect a shareholder's value, because accounting records do not record most of that value. Yet these individual investors were buying into these organizations at values that far exceeded their accounting value. Organizations are also prepared to pay significant premiums to acquire these "asset light" businesses. When this happens, accounting has to do something with the premium being paid and creates "goodwill" to account for the difference. The result is that in many organizations, goodwill is now their largest asset on the balance sheet. Without the goodwill there would be negative shareholder equity.

This book looks at how we arrived at this point and suggests that the accounting profession must change to align with the realities of an intangible world. Accounting will remain important as cash is "the life blood" that feeds the creation of the intangibles, but supplemental accountability and reporting frameworks are proliferating to provide information about the intangibles that now form the largest share of an organizations business model. Yet there appears to be a limited link between accounting and these intangible assets that have become so important.

I think it is time that we started answering the questions "where did the money go?" It is time that these aspects of accounting were considered material and included as a key aspect of sustainability as a going concern. Without some changes we will continue to have organizations that fail after they have been given a clean bill of health by the auditors. We will see scandals and failures as poor decision making is made by misleading financial information. We will see fraud, misrepresentation and misappropriation as internal controls continue to fail because of unexpected human behaviour.

It is the dawn of a new and exciting age for accounting. The profession needs to build on the strength of its' history but adopt new and supplemental approaches to embrace intangibles.

1.　**The Balance of Accounting**

"Life is like accounting; everything must be balanced." – Unknown.

The inside joke is, of course that accounting is all about balance - about "balancing the books." When this is achieved everything appears good. But Bob Newhart, who started to become an accountants at one point, tells this story about the pain accountants go through to achieve "balance" when he talks about the task of reconciling accounts:

"as long as you got within two or three bucks of it, you were all right. But that didn't catch on ... At the end of the day I had to balance the petty cash with the slips—every time you give out money you had to get a slip. It had to balance. Well, I'd be there for three or four hours tying to figure out where the last dollar or dime went to. So finally I'd just take it out of my pocket and I'd put it in. If there were two dollars leftover, I'd take it out ... And they told me you can't do that. You gotta find it. I said, "you're paying me five dollars an hour to find two cents—it doesn't make sense." So I wasn't a very good accountant."

Beyond balancing the books accountants face the real challenge of trying to apply what is perceived to be an exact science in an inexact world of business. For accountants working in business, balance is about ensuring the required level of compliance with risk. Too much control and the required level of innovation and creativity is stifled; too little control and the organization is open to fraud and potential failure. While quarterly and annual accounts require an accurate portioning of costs and revenues, and the resulting profit into a calendar, that is not the way the business runs. Organizations are "perpetual motion machines," constantly shifting, moving, and changing course to respond to a changing marketplace as well as changing laws, standards, and regulations. Annual accounts are at best a snapshot in time.

Auditors are in a worse position; they are expected to spend time in an organization, as outsiders, and provide an accurate assessment that the organization has presented its financial information in a true and fair way, and that the organizations is a going concern as it moves forward. In an increasingly fast moving and complex world this might appear an impossibility. It has been often proved, that boards of directors, executives and other employees can effectively conceal accounting issues and control problems from auditors, who, months or even years later are criticized for not finding the problems. It has often been said that an auditor should be a "watchdog and not a bloodhound." But has the world changed to the degree that a watchdog is not enough anymore? The Chairman of the National Finance Reporting Authority in India, referred to this as "…a serious misconception." He went on to say, "this misconception has very far reaching consequences."

The reason for audit was originally to provide an "independent and objective" view of the accounts, but this proves more challenging as organizations grow and become global in scope which needs to be matched by an equivalent scale of capability by audit forms. More oversight and increased legislation might have made some difference but there remains a growing gap between expectations of audit reliance and the ability to deliver. To increase effectiveness, auditors need to understand their client's business - yet if they spend time outside the audit trying to do this, it potentially seriously impacts their independence.

Accountants are also supposed to achieve balance in serving the public and "the collective well being of the community" as well as their clients. As global organizations strive to optimize international tax planning, accountants are often placed in an ethical dilemma, where to serve the clients interest, they will effectively disadvantage the citizens of a state or nation. Codes of ethics seek to provide guidance for accountants as they navigate the changing world but, as a professional development workshop, that I once taught and delivered was called, ethics are "Black and White and Sometimes Grey." Guidance on ethics certainly exists - but the International Federation of Accountants "minimum" level of code runs to 254 pages.

Has the balance in accounting been lost? As the world has changed, has the accounting profession kept pace or is it falling behind and becoming irrelevant? In the pages and chapters that follow, we will discuss all the changes in the real context behind the work of accountants, and hopefully arrive at a point where the apparent problems that currently exist can be used as a springboard to a professional renewal.

2.   Introduction

Is there really a problem here? After all, accounting information forms a cornerstone of corporate information and reporting. I remember being taught that the value in accounting comes from distilling everything down to a simple common denominator - money. I also remember being taught that accountants and economists live in totally different worlds. Economic value and accounting value are NOT the same. Since I was taught these things over 50 years ago, I have had a career in business that has involved turning the academic "learnings" into practical experience.

What I have learned is that I have become increasingly uncomfortable with the gap between what my chosen profession presents to both internal and external users and the reality that it is supposed to reflect. I believe there is a problem because the world has changed immensely over the last 50 years, but accounting has been slow to adapt.

For a significant portion of my career, I developed and taught professional development programs for accountants. Participants seemed to enjoy them, and I earned a few rewards and recognitions for my work. I also tended to steer away from programs around traditional areas of accounting and often developed programmes around evolving areas of interest.

Some who have been around a few years may remember some of these subjects - standard costing and variance analysis; zero based budgeting; activity based costing; the balanced score card; sustainability and even one program about the future of the profession. I remember this was around the 1990's and I suggested that there was no future for a "general accountant" and that jobs would become much more specialized as automation took over.

How Accountants Lost their Balance

For those readers that get this far and say "Ah Ha - an academic; those who can do, those who can't teach" - let me be quick to add that I had 10 years of business experience before I seriously moved into accounting and I had almost 20 years of line experience in accounting, financial and general management BEFORE I started my own consulting and professional development company! This included being VP Finance of two company's as well as 3 years as President of a large distribution business.

So, I do not consider myself academically biased! I was also an early adopter of management innovations earlier in my career - quality management, service management, teams and team development, open book management and many others. All of this interest helped me maintain an awareness of the changing world within which business operates and, while often creating discomfort with the challenges of change, it also made me increasingly aware of how the world was changing and how I felt my chosen profession needed to adapt. This also led me to concerns about of profession and its adaptability to change.

The marketplace is a great driver of the need to change and here again I believe that there have been many signs that our profession is "challenged." Increasingly there are problems with financial reporting and the integrity of "the numbers." The marketplace tends to have less faith in placing broad reliance on accounting information as the search is on for a more comprehensive "report card" on business performance.

There have been scandals about business failures that should have been apparent, but which did not get revealed by advanced warnings during audits. There have been failures of financial controls leading to misappropriation of funds - sometimes causing the failure of a business. There have been unethical practices around the use of company funds; there have also been questionable approaches to tax planning that have ended with both clients and their financial advisors in court. The accounting definition of value has come under scrutiny as the gap between an organization economic or market value has expanded exponentially to a situation where the book value presented by accounting statements have little relationship.

For the last 30 years or more, external users of financial reports such as ratings agencies, regulators and investors have faced increasing risk through a lack of transparency and have sought new information to supplement and complement financial data. Supplemental reporting systems have been developed to fill this gap, which include information on non-financial data - however in many cases these supplemental reports only address the impact of these changes on financial reporting in a very minor way.

Many of these initiatives attempt to increase visibility into corporate value, yet most fail to expand the role of financial management in this new environment. The major changes that have faced the accounting profession and impacted users of financial reports was the shift towards internationally agreed accounting standards; the goal was to provide users of financial reports with better, more consistent financial information. In many cases the impact of applying these new standards has been an increase in audit costs and greater complexity in assessing comparative performance. Have these helped?

Internal users are also not receiving the level of support they need - in particular in telling the story of how they are using shareholders resources to create a sustainable business. In many situations, by following accounting standards on how costs should be treated, managers are faced with explaining why they are decreasing profits and depleting shareholders equity when they are in fact making the right business decisions and investing in areas that will ensure value creation.

There has in fact been a long-term trend in the scepticism of internal financial reporting and good decision making. Management accountants developed a whole profession around this area, but solutions offered have been hard to apply; new tools that more closely align expenditures with the real driver of resources (aka ABC or Activity Based Costing) have, in general not gained the understanding and traction that they deserve.

The role of accountants in helping and supporting other managers in making good decisions on resource allocation has also been less than effective; operations managers seeking to invest in quality management often faced a demand to know "where is the return on investment" because accountants failed to demonstrate what the absence of quality was costing their business. Human resources professionals, cognisant of their growing importance of a trained and motivated workforce have faced challenges in trying to demonstrate what the lack of a trained work force is costing in lost productivity. IT professionals have found it hard to justify expenditures to enhance technology, because accountants are unable to demonstrate what the costs of poor, out of date systems are to those who are using them. More currently the "climate" or culture in a business is being recognized as a core driver in competitive advantage yet accountants are not at the head of the line in explaining what the "cost of a por culture" is in financial terms.

I have often suggested that our profession is "getting better and better at what is less and less relevant" - in particular with our focus on standards, audits, and compliance. If the accounting profession is to survive and be relevant in the future, it will need to deliver value. Many practitioners have already recognized this and have tried to move their accounting practice away from its reliance on compliance activities to a focus on delivering client value. Many financial managers are trying to push the boundaries on how financial information is presented and how they support internal decision making - but there remains a gap and an area for concern. However, in order to align the profession more closely with changing business and social trends a great deal of change will be needed.

We need to do a better job of explaining the link between financial management and value creation and enterprise sustainability - not just by the use of non-financial indicators but by explaining how financial resources are being deployed - and need to be deployed in an "asset light" world. We need to be leaders in the need to align the work of our profession and the changing social expectations of more effectively "acceptable social behaviour." We need to embrace concepts such as brand value and a whole series of "intangibles" as these are the things that managers are spending money to develop and sustain, which, in turn are critical components of a "going concern."

This issue of intangibles is at the heart of the changes and problems that will be discussed. The intangible world has grown as the service and knowledge economies have grown and organizations have adapted to this reality. We will discuss the reality that in 2020 many major organizations have goodwill as their greatest asset - in fact without goodwill, many organizations would have negative equity. We will discuss the fact that since 1975, when an average of about 85% of an organizations value was depicted on its financial balance sheet, by 2020 this number reversed so that today over 85% of an organizations value is NOT on the balance sheet - yet still holds "value" for the investor.

Underlying this shift is the diversion of billions of dollars into building intangible operational capability. Yet both the spending and the resulting "asset" are nowhere to be seen in financial reporting. Non-financial reporting is evolving to create some level of transparency into these "non financial" capabilities within the business model, but the link to finance and the money invested is nowhere to be seen. This has had major impacts on financial accounting and reporting, management accounting, auditing and risk and internal controls; if there was any doubt this chart from a 2020 survey[1] should reinforce the challenge:

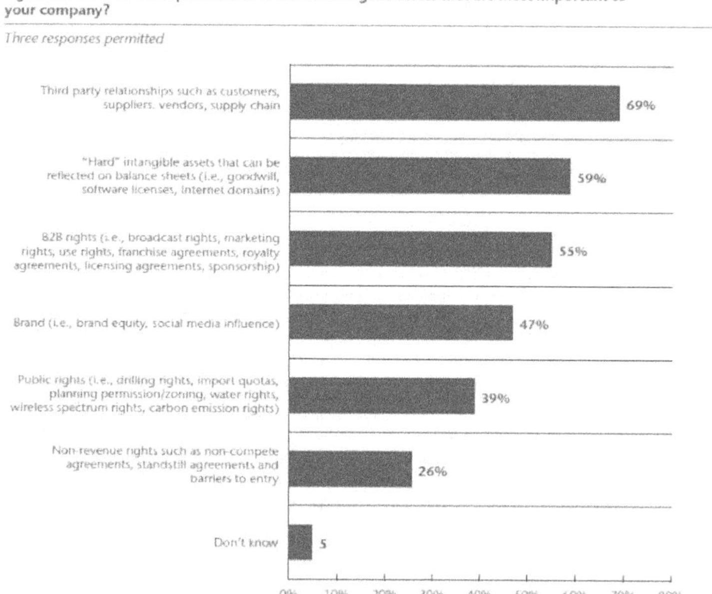

The cost of creating most of these important intangibles is buried in expenses. There is no asset to verify. No audit can assess the impact of the

---

[1] ©2020 Aon plc/Ponemon Institute LLC 2020. Financial Impact of Intellectual Property & Cyber Assets Report, GLOBAL EDITION 2020

quality of these assets for an ability to be a going concern. They are not considered "material." In short, the financial impact of the ntangible revolution has been ignored by accounting.

In the pages that follow I will try and take readers on a journey from where we came from, why it got us to where we are today; what the challenges are today and finally some solutions for us to move forward. I do not profess to have all the answers, but I do have a window on a changing world and if I can provoke some thoughts and ideas, then my job is started. I do not expect total agreement - but I do ask for an open mind together with some innovation and creativity (and who knows, maybe some action?).

As we take our journey, I have tried to place milestones at what I consider significant events; what is important is to question where the next milestone may be? Do we have some pointers to suggest that the time may be right for another change? Bear in mind this has been a LONG journey and I spend some time "setting the stage" to reflect how the world has changed during this period, before I discuss how the profession might respond.

3.   Why we are here and how we arrived.

This is not going to be a "complete history of accounting;" that would probably be quite boring, and many readers will already have some level of appreciation to the background. However, this first section is to provide a foundation for our thinking as we move forward. The following statement is probably familiar to many:

> '"Those who cannot remember the past are condemned to repeat it."
> *The quote is most likely due to writer and philosopher George Santayana,*

> It may be common sense that all of the good things and all of the bad things about people, and the way that we organize ourselves, are simply going to breed patterns as we continue to make history as a species. It may be that we are simply given to a certain irrationality which leads us down paths, some disastrous, again and again.

This was quoted in a great short article about Nicholas Clairmont in an article in "Big Think" blog on 31st July 2013; I also like what he went on to say:

It is true that as a species we do kind of "muddle along" doing the best we can; however, awareness of both the changes going on around us and our history can provide some context as to where we are today and how we might move forward. The challenge with progress is that the reasons and need for change are often really clear afterwards, but not so much at the time. As a friend used to say, "planning is great, but it's best done ahead of time."

3.1 A short reflection

Bear in mind two things; conceptually accounting is simple, and it has been around a long time. The reason our profession is often referred to as "bean counters" is because that is what we do - we count beans. Our profession came about because people wanted to track things, initially being exchanged through the barter system. Before currency, the medium of exchange was goods - such as potatoes, wheat, corn, beans, or chickens; someone needed to keep track of what "deals" were agreed - this was especially true if I agreed to do something for you in exchange for those chickens that was delivered at a later date. This is talking thousands of years ago - so we really are an OLD profession. The concept of "ledgers" was developed which were nothing more than a record of the transactions. As trading goods and services developed, and the challenge of establishing a common "value" for things increased in importance, currencies were introduced, and these become a means of exchange.

In the 15th century an Italian named Luca Bartolomeo de Pacioli developed a system of double entry bookkeeping which remains the foundation of accounting today - some 500 years later. Many accountants never actually get to see a ledger anymore or in fact actually see a double entry because the process of accounting is computerized and generally "invisible" - but more of that later. It is interesting that Pacioli was a Franciscan friar and a mathematician (and also collaborated with Leonardo da Vinci). Maybe this tells us something about ethics and creativity as foundations for accounting? Again, more about these subjects later.

From the beginnings there were two sides to every transaction - a buyer and a seller; someone gave something, and someone got something. Today's accounting concepts and double entry bookkeeping reflect this. To be "in balance" both sides of the transaction have to "add up." In modern terms an initial investor in a business will provide cash and in exchange will get a share of the business ownership represented by "shares;" or they might put in cash in the form of a loan and receive a commitment from the borrower to pay back the loan at some future date. After this transaction, to be "in balance" my accounting will show that I have the money in the bank, and I have a debt of an equivalent amount that I owe the lender. Simple right?

While all sorts of complexities have arisen that call for all sorts of defined "standards" as to how transactions are handled, in essence it all rests on this principle. As we will discuss later in more detail, some of the complexity starts to occur when the money that the initial investor put in, is now worth more once the business is operating; this is where "market value" comes in. Remember - we are trying to keep it simple at this stage!

MILESTONE

Through the work of Pacioli the foundations of modern accounting were established being the "double entry" system. This remains the underlying principle upon which all accounting records are maintained.

To understand the evolution of accounting we have to understand history in particular the evolution of trade. As early as 2,000 BC trade existed between the middle east and far east and as trade developed so the concept of the barter system and record keeping developed. Trade development is not a new issue but the level of integration, in particular through communications, mobility and education, so that trade, both for goods and services is now done around the world between and among different societies. Historically as trade developed each group developed its own interpretations of record keeping and their own systems of how things would be done in their society.

Key events occur in history that are often referred to as "sea changes;" these are when a whole series of small changes combine to bring about a major change and an upheaval in "the way things are done." One could suggest that Pacioli was a "sea change" in the world of accounting, however for our discussion, we will not trace the changes from 2,000 BC up to today; we will focus on only the more recent changes because these have a more significant impact on the approaches, systems and standards that exists today that most of the profession is familiar with. Change occurs when existing approaches are no longer "fit for purpose."

To understand this concept, we can consider a simple analogy. A race car is not used for shopping (usually) as it is not fit for purpose. In my career I have seen many changes because what was in place was not fit for purpose; as an example, in the "quality revolution" of the 1970's many manufacturing organizations has to completely change their internal process they used to manufacture products because the systems that they had could not be improved to a level where they were "fit for purpose." They had to be trashed and re-designed.

One specific example I clearly remember was from a time when I was VP Finance of a major computer company; in those days' computers were all "main frame's" that were expensive, large, and mostly hand built. Typically, clients placed an order for a mainframe and expected to wait until it was scheduled to be built; this wait could often be several months. The pressure started when minicomputers were introduced that were less expensive, smaller, assembled from pre-built modules and often available within weeks. Then came the personal computer that was typically available "off the shelf." When a buyer purchased a PC, they expected short term delivery - even available on the same day maybe?

One key problem for us was that it took several weeks to process a customer order for a computer and it quickly became clear that we needed to streamline the process - so we set up a team to improve it. Could not do it. We had to dump the whole system and build a new one. (One of the key financial implications here of course is that as technology changed quickly, past "investments" in administrative systems that had been intended to deliver benefits over many years - and were often "still working" had to be replaced as being "not fit for purpose." When we are faced with spending resources to replace something that is still working is created heartburn for accountants).

3.2 Evolution of accounting

Accounting in its' most basic terms is bookkeeping but has developed over the years as changes in society have taken place. The original accountants "kept the records" for those having goods and services to trade and later for those investing monies in ventures such as the developing trade between individuals and societies. The main communications took place either between those employing the bookkeeper to track their activities and other bookkeepers. The profession was rarely seen and as Charles Dickens portrayed in The Christmas Carol, did their work in dimly lit backrooms, rarely interacting with others. In fact, many initial "accountants" keeping records were in fact the money lenders themselves.

Whilst accounting has been around a long time, the role of auditing evolved somewhat differently; early records suggest that activities closest to "audits" took place as early as 500 BC in ancient Persia where spies acted as "the Kings ears" in checking up on the activities of provincial governors[2]; it is unfortunate and maybe an historical burden the profession still carries in that, at that time these people were considered spies!

More closely related to current auditing was the work of public officials charged with oversight of public financial records. The "Audit of the Exchequer," in England in 1314; the establishment of the "Auditors of the Imprest" by Queen Elizabeth in 1559 and in 1780 the appointment of the "Commissioners for auditing the Public Accounts" to control the issuance of funds to the government[3]. Modern auditing occurred after 1844 when the Joint Stock Companies Act was passed by the British government; this required that directors report to shareholders by way of a balance sheet that essentially outlined what assets and liabilities existed and how much the shareholders "net worth" had changed (pretty minimal insight). Professional training as an accountant and independence were not required until the Companies Act was passed in Britain in 1900. It was this evolution that started the rise of the accounting profession as it is known today.

So, by early 1900 we had the start of an organized accounting profession and the activities of bookkeeping and auditing. Financial transactions had historically not involved the public at large and the communication of financial information was focused on shareholders who were typically people who understood financial information and were involved in their business activities so were close to, and understood the risks involved. But, under the surface some major changes were taking place in society and these would lead to the first major shift in importance of the accounting profession.

3.3 The development of a profession

One small piece of background that is helpful in "context setting" is to consider the social development of professions and how accounting fitted into this. There is an interesting story that.

back in the 16th century, the term profession was used for, and limited to medicine, law, the divinity. These were the so-called learned professions and they differed significantly from the development of "the trades" - although as

---

[2] "A brief history of Accounting" published May 12th 2017, Audit Monk
[3] Wikipedia "Financial audit"

we will see, professions, as they developed did adopt some of the organizational features of the trades. They were called "learned" professions because they were reserved for people who had "learning" - at a time when education and literacy was limited to the wealthy and religious institutions.

In the 16th century, professions were mainly members of the privileged class who had been educated in universities - the oldest being Oxford in 1096 (originally established by religious). It was said[4] that *"...having a profession provided a social location in life for the second, third, and fourth sons of aristocrats..."* who did not inherit portions of their father's estate which went exclusively to the eldest son. As children of the aristocracy, should not have to work for a living and thus submit to the vulgarities of the marketplace. The professions *"...provided the great families with an honorable social location for their surplus gentlemen."*

It follows, therefore, that the respect bestowed upon professions flowed in part from the education required and the value of their services which tended to be supplied to other aristocrats. More important, their status stemmed from the privileged births of their members. It is worth noting that "the religious" played a key role and many young men went on to become ministers in the Church; this fact supports the fact that many social records in England prior to 1832 were kept by the parishes - such as all births, baptism, marriages, and deaths.

From this privileged and learned beginning, the character of the professions only changed slowly, over the generations that followed. With the onset of the Renaissance and the development of the middle class, increasing numbers of people—especially in England—entered occupations that more and more resembled the traditional professions. These "new professionals" also wanted to be looked upon as members of a profession rather than as a tradesman who typically did not share the same social background.

Members of the would-be professions formed associations, or guilds to ensure survival - in some cases seeking exclusivity through methods such as applications for Royal Charter. Over the course of generations, they took whatever was necessary to establish their credibility. For example, it was

---

[4] Dr. William F. May, Southern Methodist University, Dallas, Texas

essential that adequate training leading to recognized "credentialing and / or a license to practise" was required and made available for aspiring professionals. Their goal, in other words, was to restrict the practice of their particular occupation to members of their group.

They also understood that they would not be taken seriously unless they demonstrated that they could provide dedicated service, administered with a sense of integrity. For many years, in fact up to fairly recent times, those seeking to become accountants would have to "article" to another individual or firm of professionals, in order to obtain the required training. In many cases the pay was minimal and for many years' applicants had to pay an initiation fee and have their expenses subsidized by their family. In this was they reflected the trades in terms of exclusivity, training, and indentured apprenticeships.

While this was the pattern for the development of professions in England, it also served as the prototype for the United States. In both countries, each hopeful and aspiring occupation launched its own process for gaining credibility, reputation, and exclusiveness in the marketplace.

<table>
<tr><td>

MILESTONE

The founding of universities after 1,000, and the evolution of education and literacy among the privileged, set the basis for the founding of the professions especially after the 1600's. Professions sought to restrict entry to, and the practise of their particular specialization through a process of training and licensing

</td></tr>
</table>

3.4 Economic evolution

Accounting exists in a world of economic activity - the world of business; as outlined earlier, this business activity goes back a long way and involved "markets" where products (and later services) were traded first locally, then regionally, nationally, and internationally. Accounting has always played a support role in documenting the activities that take place in the market between buyers and sellers. Buyers and sellers in markets traditionally did business on the basis of trust and there was an "understood" commitment to ethical behaviour. As commerce developed so did the need for places where buyers and sellers could meet and "trade." In terms of modern financial markets, the stock exchanges would be the current focus of that evolution where buyers and sellers trade shares (and other financial "instruments").

The role of accountants was traditionally to keep records of the transactions. As London (and New York and other commercial centres) grew, formal markets or exchanges (places of exchange) were established; in London, The Royal Exchange established in the mid 1500's primarily as a place to buy and sell commodities. As we shall see, when "stocks" started to be traded in the early 1600's, brokers who sold these stocks were not allowed into the London Exchange as they were considered "rough and rude" and as a result much of the early stock trading was done in London's coffee houses that surrounded the Royal Exchange.

"Sea changes" often take place when social or technological shifts take place. In the last century or so the speed of change has increased as has the breadth. We talked earlier about developments in trade and these have been a key part of the need for changes in activities that support commerce. Maritime trade that developed in the 15th and 16th centuries was a core driver of international commercial development and awareness; business became international as larger quantities of goods moved to more distant locations. Initially maritime exploration had been funded mainly by royalty in the name of their nation; additionally, early trade development was for "the good of the nation" through "charters" that created international trading companies such as the East India Company, The Hudson Bay Company, and others; historically, these activities formed a core aspect of imperialism and were established by Spanish, Dutch, French, and British countries.

These trading ventures often made a lot of money and individuals outside government wanted to "get in on the act" and make some money. This led to the creation of the early joint stock companies that sold "shares" to people willing to put up the money for trade "missions" who hoped to receive a share of the profits. Experienced traders who understood the risks involved in sea voyages expected a "win some, lose some" reality; trading was often speculative, but the potential rewards were significant so investors, some with little real knowledge of the business, clamoured for shares in the hope of windfall profits. (Many of these "deals" matching buyers and sellers happened in the coffee houses in London - and this location relates to the creation and rise of Lloyds of London in Tower Street in about 1686 to "underwrite" maritime risks.).

One of the early organizations to "cash in" on the opportunity to match buyers and sellers was the South Seas Company which was granted a similar charter to the East India Company; their ability to raise funds was so successful and the built plush offices in the better parts of London with the money raised. This potential to make money quickly caught the attention of other "businessmen" who started to offer shares for non-maritime investments which were quickly bought up. Alas, the bubble burst when South Seas Company failed to pay dividends and the investors ultimately lost their money. As a result, the British government outlawed the issue of shares until 1825.

There are some early ingredients of the foundations of financial failure in this experience; inadequate oversight and regulation of the markets; inadequate understanding of risk; speculation and the opportunity for wealth creation (by "just" investing); trust in promoters offering promises of great returns and a lack of independent and objective advice. Additionally, trust was a key factor between experienced buyers and sellers. The "South Sea Bubble" bursting was to be a repeated occurrence as the economy developed - much of it related to human behaviour and the issue of "adequate information."

In the 16th and 17th centuries economics changed and manufacturing trade developed; by the 18th century automation of both agricultural and manufacturing processes started in earnest. During this period record keeping developed although the foundations remained bookkeeping, based on double entry. Accounting was of little interest to the general public until they had money available to spend and invest. Traditionally the people who had money such as landowners and later traders and industrialists generally understood the basics of record keeping and managing debts. Our interest in this evolution becomes more important at the end of the 18th and into the 19th century. It was at this point that "scale" became important. Mechanization increased, and labour became available as it was freed up from areas like agriculture and this, in part gave rise to the entrepreneurs, who were able to able to exploit their ideas and innovate in creating new businesses.

Individuals began to move beyond their lives being tied to the "feudal" economy and being subservient to landowners. It became apparent that many of these entrepreneurs had ideas but often lacked money, so they searched for investors willing to put money into their ventures. Raising money from investors continued to be an important source of financing and although the British government had outlawed the sale of shares after the South Sea Bubble burst, the later 1825 financial crisis resulted in the resumption of share issuance and trading. The British government continued to make changes to regulate commerce and the financial industry through the 1800's, hoping to improve the populations understanding of the financial system and to provide better regulation to the increasingly important world of "corporate finance."

Meanwhile, around the world, in particular in the United States, new and less regulated markets were emerging and opportunity for investment expanded exponentially. The US stock market was established in 1792, but the New York Stock Exchange had been formally established in 1817 and started trading stocks from its first day in business; similar exchanges opened up in many countries around the world reflecting the growing importance of the trading of shares in both national and international organizations. The US stock exchange as befits an emerging nation at the same, had its share of ups and downs: in 1812 cotton prices collapsed causing a number of bank failures; in 1837 the wheat crop failed and a number of US brokerage firms failed - the market again recovered by the end of the 1840's.

In 1857 Ohio Life Insurance and Trust Company failed due to losses on railroad securities causing the market to drop and 900 firms to lose liquidity - the market took 2 years to recover. Jay Cooke and Company, another heavy investor in railroads went bankrupt causing the market to drop, a 5 year recession, 3 million out of work and a drop in food prices; in 1893 the market collapsed again with mass sell-off's; there was a credit crisis, 16,000 businesses failed and one in six Americans lost their job. What this clearly illustrates is that the financial markets increasingly impacting the lives of individuals especially those who put their money and their faith into the market in the hope of wealth creation and security.

3.5 Accounting comes "out of the shadows."

By the end of the 19th century two things had happened; the "good times" had arrived for many with the growth in the "working class" and the gradual development of a middle class; this increased the money that was available combined with the availability of credit to an individual. Secondly, during the 1800's, major areas of investment were requiring significant amounts of money for their development. Steel Mills, chemical plants, railroads, shipping; many of the owners of these businesses raised money by raising capital both privately as well as through "joint stock" companies that had been formed and whose shares traded on public markets. This combination led to increased consumerism which drove investment in many areas which in turn created a continuing demand for capital. Although the US entered the first world war in 1917 as it was coming to an end, it had been a significant supplier of equipment to its allies which again increased demand and factory activity.

As often happens it seemed the good times would roll on; although the federal reserve had warned about a growing level of speculation in the markets, people felt the good times would roll on and the market would continue to climb. Margin buying had become popular but when the slide began in the spring of 1929, investors started to sell to cover their borrowings. Eventually after some up's and down's the market took a dive in September and October 1929 and then continued to adjust, until, by July 1932 the index had lost over 89% of its value over 3 years since the decline started. As Wikipedia reports:

The crash followed a speculative boom that had taken hold in the late 1920s. During the latter half of the 1920s, steel production, building construction, retail turnover, automobiles registered, and even railway receipts advanced from record to record. The combined net profits of 536 manufacturing and trading companies showed an increase, in the first six months of 1929, of 36.6% over 1928, itself a record half-year. Iron and steel led the way with doubled gains. Such figures set up a crescendo of stock-exchange speculation that led hundreds of thousands of Americans to invest heavily in the stock market. A significant number of them were borrowing money to buy more stocks. By August 1929, brokers were routinely lending small investors more than two-thirds of the face value of the stocks they were buying. Over $8.5 billion was out on loan, more than the entire amount of currency circulating in the U.S. at the time.

How Accountants Lost their Balance

In Britain, the market not only reacted to what was happening in New York but had its own problems when a prominent investor, Clarence Hatry and many of his associates were jailed for fraud and forgery. Hatry was a typical entrepreneur; starting as an insurance clerk and starting t make money in the silk market; he then flipped an insurance company making significant profits. He used WW1 as a basis to profit and by the end of 1921 he was a director of 15 corporations. Although frequently going bankrupt he somehow always came out richer and as his reputation for creating wealth grew, many people invested in his ventures. However, in 1929, just as he was about to consummate a merger of steel companies, the SEC caught him committing fraud and his empire collapsed.

The collapse of the investment market set off similar contractions around the world and is often seen as partly responsible for the "Great Depression" that followed. What ever the cause of the depression that followed it had significant impact on the population; industrial production in the US dropped 46%, wholesale prices 32%, International trade 70% and unemployment grew 607% - a devastating blow to families. In the UK, the drops were not quite as significant but still had a social impact. Suddenly the good times had gone; as humans we often look for someone to blame. Politicians tend to look for answers so that they can respond; a senate commission was set up in 1932 and as a result, the Glass-Steagall Act was enacted in 1933 that changed banking regulations to separate commercial banking and investment banking. This was a start, but more was needed. Prior to the Wall Street crash most securities regulation in the US had been state based - such as the "Blue Sky Laws."

In theory, these investors were protected by the Blue Sky Laws (first enacted in Kansas in 1911). As Investopedia explains:

These state laws were meant to protect investors from worthless securities issued by unscrupulous companies and pumped by promoters. They are basic disclosure laws that require a company to provide a prospectus in which the promoters (sellers/issuers) state how much interest they are getting. Then, the investor is left to decide whether to buy. Although this disclosure was helpful to investors, there were no laws to prevent issuers from selling a security with unfair terms as long as they "informed" potential investors about it.

The Blue Sky Laws were weak in both terms and enforcement. Companies wanting to avoid full disclosure for one reason, or another offered shares by mail to out-of-state investors. Even the validity of the in-state disclosures was not thoroughly checked by the state regulators.

Regulatory oversight was not keeping pace with the rapid development of "the markets." It was soon again to become evident that changes were needed. When events happen that impact individuals in society, politicians start to take notice. It was clear following the great depression that many people across the world had been impacted through loss of jobs as well as shortages of food and shelter. Times were hard and people wanted to know why the "system" had failed them. People blamed Wall Street speculators, bankers, the Hoover administration and by 1932 there were food riots and protest marches. In England changes proposed by the Prime Minister caused a revolt by backbenchers from his Labour government but while he remained in power this only happened through the creation of a coalition "national party" government. Changes had to be made.

Soon after, the US passed the Securities Act that strengthened the concepts of the Blue Sky Acts at the Federal level and in 1934 the Securities Exchange Act was created that had a major impact on the accounting profession. Changes in the UK were slower but came about in 1948 with the Companies Act that clearly laid out the responsibilities of directors.

MILESTONE

With the impact on people's lives and the importance of improved oversight, accountants became part of the structure for financial integrity and reporting under statute. From this developed GAAP and accounting standards including what is known today as FASB in the US; this ensured a consistent approach to what must be reported and how it is to be prepared as well as mandatory audits for public organizations.

Essentially these changes affected the role of the accounting profession and started its journey as a key player in oversight and reporting. Although the accounting had existed for many years and started to develop as a profession in the late 1800's it was now seen as having a key role. Up until the great crash companies had used their own approaches as to prepare and report financial information which created a spectrum of disclosure from extremely poor to exceptionally good - however there was no minimum standard. In the 1930's in the US the American Institute of Accountants together with the New York Stock Exchange formed a committee which recommended broad foundational principles going forward which included enhanced disclosure including the submission of audited financial statements.

At this point the issue was about money - the investors had often been ill informed about how their investment was to be spent and often remained unaware of what the company had done with their money. There was a degree of "trust me, your money is in good hands and you can see from my past performance (or from my promises) that you will receive a significant payback." While professional investors understood the risks, many small investors who had entered the market, using their newfound wealth in order to not lose out of the profits that were being made, were often poorly informed. Although one can argue it was "caveat emptor" (or let the buyer beware especially in the free-wheeling US marketplace) the "losers did not see it this way and protested loudly about the need for better disclosure which politicians responded to.

Historically, accountants had little responsibility to report on the activities of organizations for whom they kept the accounting records, and although there were in fact organizations that had instituted voluntary audits because they saw it as a "responsible thing to do" many organizations provided little independent insight to outsiders including investors. From this point forward we saw the development of GAAP and accounting standards, defining how accounts would be kept and presented to ensure consistency, and what mandatory "financial statements" were to be produced. At this point the approach was mainly national in nature with national standards bodies. Additionally, the prime area of interest was financial accountability - answering the question "where is my money?" These standards were initially applied to all public companies but later were, in many cases embedded in legal and taxation legislation requiring all companies to adopt GAAP of Generally Accepted Accounting Principles. One might illustrate the hierarchy:

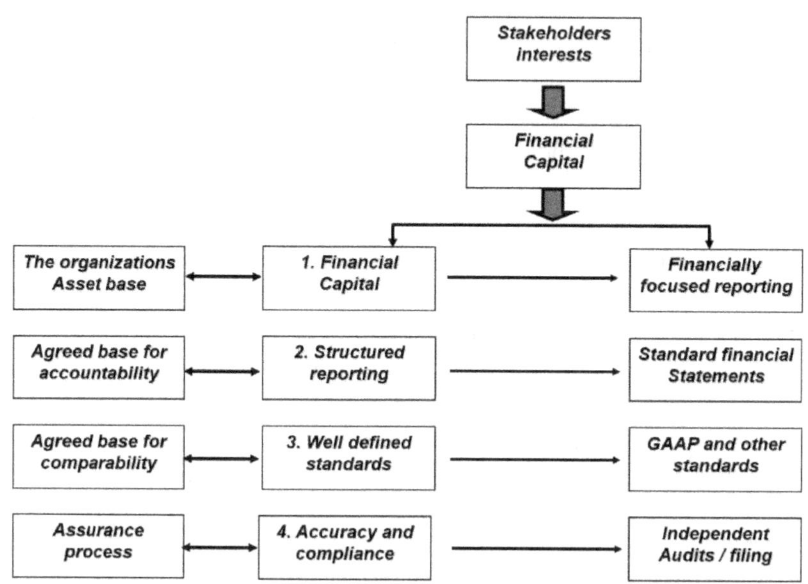

The shareholders interests had to be protected and what was at stake was financial capital, as this formed the base of the assets of the company (1) - as a result the focus was on financial reporting. What was needed, so as to ensure consistency and comparability was some form of structured reporting (2) and this included several requirements but specifically focused on a balance sheet showing assets and liabilities, an income statement showing the results of trading, and a cash flow statement. These statements had to be created using a standard approach to how each transaction and type of activity as to be treated and so developed accounting principles and supporting standards (3).

Finally oversight and compliance were of primary importance so there must be some level of both independent checking of the financial statements and compliance with the production of the required reports (4). This formed the basis of both SEC filing requirements (and equivalents in other nations) together with an independent 3rd party audit by an accredited accountant. At this point accountants not only became more visible, but they started to be seen as providing "assurance" to users of financial reports that all was well.

This foundation enhanced the growth and evolution of the accounting profession. In the US around 1915 the demand for accountants had already started to grow as a result of the imposition of income taxes and this new requirement for standards, auditing and reporting cemented the future. Around this time the AICPA had about 1150 members and the UK based ICAEW when established in 1880 had some 600 members. In the UK, although "the profession" dated back further its' development reflected the same type of growth - including demand in the early 1900's for responding to implementation by governments of taxation. Accountants had worked hard to develop a professional reputation, and, in many ways, this was crystallized with the embedding of mandatory roles for the profession in the legislation following the depression.

A key component of ensuring that this trust was well placed was the (general) acceptance as part of being given either a Royal Charter (as in the UK) or recognition under law as in other jurisdictions, that the professional accountants would hold themselves to a level of ethical standards, in addition to compliance with the law and their own accounting standards. In cases where a member was found to not behave ethically, they could be expelled from the profession. We will return to this area as it is a key challenge to the profession in today's reality. This exclusivity had some negative connotations - as an example in 1904 eight accountants in the UK formed themselves into the London Association of Accountants in order to allow broader access to the profession than was being allowed by the Chartered Accountants.

These two bodies continue to exist in the UK marketplace together with a third management accounting body (that we discuss later). The London Association went on to become the ACCA, originally standing for the Association of Certified and Corporate Accountants because their membership focuses on both audits, as well as providing financial advice and support internally to organizations. Today they have also received a Royal Charter and the title has been amended to be the Association of Chartered Certified Accountants.

While this may not have been a milestone it was an important step in building the public's expectations for the work of the accountant. The profession had been honoured by being placed in a position of oversight and trust.

INDEPENDENT, OBJECTIVE AND TO BE TRUSTED

While some may disagree, this elevation placed accountants in a unique position of trust. The public and the whole banking and investment community were "assured" that if accountants had approved the financial statements, they could be trusted to follow the rules and ensure compliance with both the word and the intent of standards. It was also assumed they were, as a profession objective and independent of the organizations that they were auditing. This expectation extended to taxation authorities who were able to rely on professionally prepared financial statements.

Gradually after the great depression things improved but this was again interrupted by the second world war. At this point we can look at the next major event or change that impacted the profession.

3.6 The Emerging Role of Management Accounting

Before going further, we must not forget that another significant change took place in the accounting profession in the late 1800, early 1900's in parallel to scientific management. This accompanied the progress of the industrial revolution and in particular the development of large scale, complex organizations. This was particularly true in the development of the manufacturing sector. Accounting for resources had historically focused on record keeping and reporting - mainly to external users but as management developed, so did the need for accounting information tailored to those managing organizations.

Management accounting was to fill this need; its' focus is on understand the financial implications of management decisions, and with helping management decision making by providing relevant analysis. If traditional accounting was "big picture" reflecting the income statement, balance sheet and cash flow, management accounting was to focus on the decision making "behind the numbers."

As traditional accounting - often referred to as financial accounting developed based on the economic realities of the times, so did management accounting. In the early years this branch of the profession was called cost accounting as that was the focus. Managers needed to understand why costs were being incurred and what purpose they served; much of early development of cost accounting centred on understanding manufacturing costs as that was a predominant consumer of financial resources. In total, owners and managers knew that there were major regular outlays for payrolls and for payments to suppliers, but for decision making they needed to know these costs at a much more granular level.

Who is incurring these costs? Why? What products are they associated with? Once managers understand these costs being incurred, they can start to manage them more effectively. Additionally, major funding was going towards the purchase of expensive plant and equipment. Was this justified? How long would it last? How would the costs be recovered in terms of what the equipment is used for? What does this equipment cost to operate? What is the expected return on the investment for these expenditures? All of these questions needed answers and the accountant, who understood the numbers, was faced with integrating their knowledge of accounting with the operational reality of the organization.

This era produced many of the foundations of cost accounting; the concepts of variable, semi-variable and fixed costs; the concept of direct and indirect costs; overheads and allocation of costs; responsibility accounting; general ledger collection and reporting of costs by type of expenses - (labour, materials, supplies etc.) and department. Interesting that in England one of the early accounting bodies was the Association of Cost and Works Accountants (ACWA) founded in 1919, that eventually became the Chartered Institute of Management Accountants (CIMA). In the same year, The National Association of Cost Accountants was established in the USA that became the Institute of Management Accountants (IMA).

The training of management accountants followed a different track to those who focused on financial accounting and as the social and economic reality changed during the 1900's, so did the application of management accounting approaches. However, the fundamental changes that have been taking place in recent years have also impacted management accountants.

3.7 Early Signs of Valuation Problems

After the second world war, the focus was on re-building and reconstruction; this led to the start of the "post war boom." Returning service people wanted to settle down and get their lives "back to normal" and many married shortly after the war creating a baby boom. Significant investments were being poured into re-building homes, factories, roads, ports railways and other infrastructure and goods were beginning to flow again for consumers. There was also the start of a technological boom as many innovations had occurred during the war that would continue to be developed in peace time impacting areas such as communications, travel, and many others. Women, who had taken over many of the roles of the men who were conscripted for war had experienced the workplace and justifiably expected a place in the recovery. This drove economic activity and this in turn drove the continued growth in employment in accounting.

While double entry bookkeeping remains a foundation of accounting, so does the concept of "cost." Accounting has always tended to try and reflect accuracy in the numbers they record, and many of the accounting standards that have been developed focus on the adoption as cost as the measure of value. What something "costs" has traditionally been what has been recorded in the accounts. When one strays away from costs the attribution of what something is worth becomes difficult. This is why accountants and economists live in different worlds. Value is important to the economist but for accountants, cost has always been the assured foundation for value. Comparing each we see:

In accounting the term "cost" refers to the monetary value of expenditures at a point when a transaction takes place (i.e., using money as the basis of exchange - how much was exchanged in the transaction?)

How Accountants Lost their Balance

In economic terms, "cost" is defined by the market value at any point in time (i.e., what a willing seller and buyer arrive at in terms of a value for a specific exchange; today's cost can be different from tomorrows)

What are the implications here? For accountants, if an organization pays $100,000 for a piece of equipment, then that is the value recorded in the accounts; likewise, if an organization pays the same amount for a building or a piece of land, under traditional accounting approaches, those are the values that will be recorded in the accounts. My "asset" (land, building, machinery) on the balance sheet will reflect what I paid for it. In times of price stability, the accountant's definition of costs will result in financial statements reflecting the value of the organization; however, if market prices are changing then the value as portrayed by traditional accounts will soon be out of date and inaccurate to assess the "worth" of an organization. This was to come to a head in the late 1960's and early 1970's when the word inflation became known to the average consumer.

For the early part of the 1960's inflation - the rise in prices, remained low. In the US between 1960 and 1965 the average inflation rate was 1.1% but rose to an average annual rate of over 4% in the latter years. Many factors contributed to the rising inflation, but it also started to create social discontent. In Britain, a similar series of events occurred for different reasons and with different responses. The period saw governments try and control the situation by implementing wage and price controls which only further distorted the situation; changes to the international finance system also required economic re-adjustments. Another major event that occurred in the early 1970's was the "energy crisis." There were several aspects to this but coming at a time when most western economies were already in weak shape, it made things worse.

The outcome of the "slow down" in the late 1960's and the resulting government actions created soaring inflation that brought with it, social chaos. It was a period of major industrial strife in the UK. Why was this important to accounting? To answer that we have to return to the foundation of using cost as a basis for "value" in accounting records. The following table illustrates what happened when inflation rose in the 1970's in both the UK and the US (and many other nations).

How Accountants Lost their Balance

This shows how significantly inflation became as a result of failed monetary policy. This created major issues, especially with the genera public.

	UK CPI	US CPI	UK prices	US prices
Base			100	100
1970	6.40%	5.80%	106	106
1971	9.40%	4.30%	116	110
1972	7.10%	3.30%	125	114
1973	9.20%	6.20%	136	121
1974	16.00%	11.10%	158	134
1975	24.20%	9.10%	196	147
1976	16.60%	5.70%	229	155
1977	15.80%	6.50%	265	165
1978	8.30%	7.60%	287	178
1979	13.40%	11.30%	325	198

In accounting terms this meant that in the UK, an asset that was purchased in 1969 for £100 would, in all probability, have cost £325 to replace by the end of the decade. Had it been equipment, subject to 10 years use, this might not have been important but if it was property, then a substantial "hidden" gain had occurred. A similar picture would have occurred in the US although the price rise was less - only double. Entrepreneurs and true capitalist realized that many organizations, according to their "book value" appeared to be worth far less than their now underlying value in the marketplace. Also, as the stock market was depressed for a significant period of the 1970's even market prices did not reflect the true value of these organizations. So "asset heavy" organizations became acquisition targets, not for their business but for the underlying assets that were then sold.

There was a growing question as to accountants were not able to accurately reflect the values of a business and as a result rules were brought in that allowed organizations to re-value their assets and create an equity increase on their balance sheets. What was important was that this was the beginning of the debate about "fair value accounting." It had become obvious that the gap between values in the marketplace and accounting records was becoming a concern. It also created an unhealthy management accounting situation; the practise of depreciating or amortizing the purchase cost of a piece of equipment over its useful life was called into question. If a company had purchased and asset for $100, and then amortised it over 10 years to recover the initial cost - that would work well in times of stable pricing. However, if the same asset costs double or more to replace, then prices need to be increased to retain adequate earnings to help fund the replacement equipment. This would add to inflationary pressure.

While this was not a major event, it did damage confidence in the profession of accounting and its ability to present a "true and fair view" of an organizations financial state of affairs. Accountancy Age, the UK magazine wrote[5]:

> *As a period of political turbulence, it also marked the beginning of fundamental change in the accountancy profession. The 1970s accountant was rather like the actuary of today. It was a profession unused to public scrutiny, confident in its own beliefs and practices, which had gradually drifted out of touch with a changing public mood.*
>
> *Following a series of mishaps, it (the survey) found that the public's perception of the profession and what it should do, was far removed from the image it had of itself and what it thought its purpose was.*
>
> *Like actuaries today, accountants were summoned to the Treasury and told in no uncertain terms to clean up their act….. but while that was the way the tide was flowing, it was often hard to see because of the squalls, of which the biggest was inflation accounting.*

Up until this point the work of accountants had gone on in the back rooms and audits and audit opinions were the subject of investor and regulator interest. In fact, between the 1940's and 1970's the "scandal index[6]" in the UK declined and plateaued, but this was to change once financial turmoil hit again in the late 1960's and into the 1970's (it always seems that when economics tighten up, many people start "pushing the financial boundaries" at which point the accountant's role comes under increased scrutiny).

---

[5] "AA in the 1970's - demands for change," Anthony Hilton, November 17th 2004, Accountancy Age

[6] Steve Toms, Leeds University report to UK ICAEW in 2019 - see Financial Times, January 9th, 2019

MILESTONE

Inflationary pressures in the 1960's and 1970's started to demonstrate the challenges of cost based accounting, as market prices increased and the gap between book and market prices began to widen. Questions started to be asked about the use of cost, and why couldn't some approach of "fair value" accounting be adopted? Financial scandals also brought the role of accountants "into the light" and open to scrutiny.

A similar study[7] around the same time that looked at profits and pay in the financial sector and revealed that the "…size of finance and financiers pay packets had rocketed up." This was to be an "early warning indicator" of future challenges not just from a technical perspective but more importantly, from the perspective of (as David Maister[8] calls it) the "trusted advisor."

The economic turmoil of the late 1960's and into the 1970's was a precursor to a significant shift in the foundation of trade and broad based economics. Between 1970 and the end of the millennium, seismic shifts took place that impacted the very foundations of financial accounting and with it, management accounting.

3.8 Paths of Divergence and Losing Balance

While the valuation issues of the 1970's and the resulting changes in government approaches to economic policy had a minimal initial effect of the accounting profession, it marked the beginning of an era where the traditions of accounting would be challenged as never before. While the traditional activities of accounting continued it was like a ship heading into stormy sea. A number of underlying themes started to evolve, each of which has its own unique impact on the economy, and the world of finance within which the accounting profession operates. Legislation was introduced as governments

---

[7] Thomas Philippon, New York Economist
[8] "The Trusted Advisor" David Maister, 2001

responded to the impact of these changes, and the practise of accounting also evolved in response; however, there were two major "seismic" changes that gradually grew in importance and which started and continue to create growing problems for the profession and its credibility.

The first theme is the emergence of intangibles as drivers of value creation. This has become a growing issue for accounting for four main reasons, all of which have contributed to the lack of a "balanced view" of an organization as depicted by financial reporting.

First, being a conservative profession and not wanting to depict something as an asset unless it is *"easily identified, owned, can be accurately valued, and can be shown to be of extended value"*, accountants have always been reluctant to treat intangibles as assets and to show them as a balance sheet item i.e., part of the accounting "book value."

Second, because the increasing cash flow being directed to the creation and nurturing of intangibles is buried as an operating expense (because it is not creating an "asset), earnings and equity are being inaccurately depleted, and the financial impact is invisible.

Third, because of the growth of intangibles, mergers and acquisitions now give rise to the creation of a large goodwill amount, (because intangibles exceed book values by a factor of more than 10 times on average). This creates both valuation issues, identification, measurement, and management issues, and often leads to impairment write-off's in the buyer's books.

Finally, as alternative reporting frameworks have developed that reflect changing drivers of value creation and social changes and expectations for corporate accountability, there is almost no financial link between the evolving importance of non-financial, value creating "assets" and financial reporting.

This shift to, and growth of intangibles has been gradual as the real economy has transitioned. First the "service economy" grew and developed; this was followed by changes brought about by the broad application of new technology, both eventually leading to what can be referred to as "asset light" organizations - those where intangibles have become the principal drivers of an organizations ability to create value for its owners. What we have learned, and still not solved is that the world of intangibles (the "asset light economy" as Warren Buffett calls it) is volatile, hard to value and hard to monitor, measure and report. It is also extremely hard to audit.

The second theme that contributed to seismic change was a foundational aspect of capitalism - human behaviour. Two aspects are critical for the effective functioning of the system and both have changed considerably. The first is expectation of compliance with the law plus behaviour that reflects social expectations as a member of the society within which the organization operates.

The second is the role of labour that shifted as the knowledge economy developed, from "passive" providers of a commodity (manual labour) to the contribution of "brain power." This shift became more important as it was realized that human capital could only be fully optimized when the management systems moved from "command and control" to inclusive and participative. As the world of intangibles has grown, so have the challenges of internal control, ethical behaviour (by both leaders and employees), corporate management and reporting, and the understanding of risk.

For accountants, these two themes have left the profession "out of balance" with the needs of society. Firstly, unacceptable human behaviour has led to a growing challenge for audits as well as for internal control systems. Not just the role of human capital in the capitalistic model has changed, but economists have also changed their opinion as to the potential for people to behave in a rational manner. This has led to a growing inability of auditors to identify and highlight behavioural risks and has highlighted the impact of personal values on corporate behaviour and sustainability. Secondly, the creation, growth and sustaining of corporate intangibles now consumes a major portion of financial resources which is invisible to users of accounting information internally and externally as it falls outside traditional accounting standards.

This has led to a growing gap between market values of organizations and the financial value reflected by accounting. This in turn has led to growing issues with the accounting treatment of goodwill after mergers and acquisitions, plus significant losses from impairment of intangibles post-merger. In the next two chapters we will track how both these themes evolved. In the next three chapters we will explore each of these aspects - intangible growth, behavioural issues, and valuation and goodwill.

4.   Sucking Cash: The Rise of Intangibles

The growth of intangibles has taken place over almost fifty years; one of the better depictions of this shift is the following chart[9] that shows the evolution of underlying valuation for the S&P 500 since 1975. As discussed, the 1970's were the era of "tangible and fair market value challenges", mainly caused by inflation, but these were centred on tangible assets. As the service economy started to grow including especially financial services the 85% portion of value attributed to tangible assets gradually declined to less than 10%. Put another way, on average $0.10 of corporate "value" is represented by a financial balance sheet and 90% by "something else" that owners attribute some level of value to.

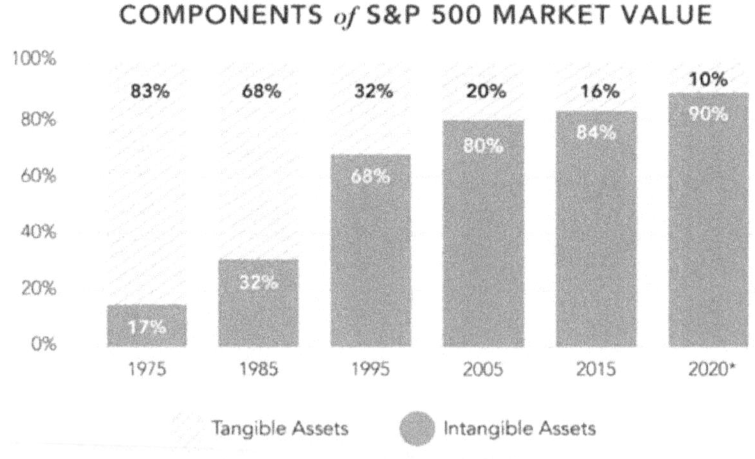

---

[9] Ocean Tomo

One has to be careful of these numbers; when the overall economy takes a dip, typically overall market values decline but book values stay the same - thus these percentages are more valuable as a trend than as an absolute number. But the trend is clear.

Another way to look at these numbers is to consider what is behind the S&P 500; the numbers reflect the average. While of the organizations making up the S&P 500 have remained the same[10], in 1969, 166 of the 500 companies on the index, a full 33%, were industrials, but by 2019 there were only 70 represented.

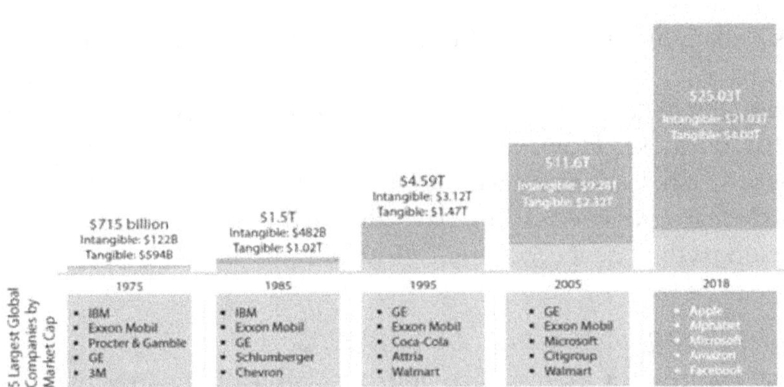

However, in 1969, there were only 16 Information Technology companies on the index, by 2019, there were 68 technology companies represented on the index, representing a 425% growth since 1969. This depicts both the shift of investment and the underlying importance of technology. The following chart[11]

---

[10] History of Companies and Industries Listed on the S&P 500, Extract from QAD blog, Caleb Finch -October 3, 2019

[11] ©2019 Aon plc/Ponemon Institute LLC 2019 Intangible Assets Financial Statement Impact Comparison Report.

illustrates the shift on a global basis and illustrates the leading role that high-technology stocks have evolved in to:

Note that the leading tech stocks are often referred to as the FAANG stocks - Facebook, Apple, Amazon, Netflix, and Google (Alphabet). As can be seen from the chart, these changes have added over $24 trillion in value. Were our approaches to accounting, oversight and reporting keeping pace with these changes?

What has been happening since 1975 that has required such a massive diversion of resources into intangibles? Did people know it was happening and if so, why wasn't it reported? What outcomes were created that drove such a significant growth in organizational value? As history books tell us "things were different then." Sometimes it is hard to remember what did not exist then, that is commonplace today - things which required investment.

Essentially it has been the functioning of the capitalist system that drove these changes, mainly through innovation and creativity in new products and services, global competition, and the application of technology to almost every facet of business. How was this financed? By the one thing that remains constant - cash. Cash that accountants have failed to track, monitor, and report. Cash that progressive CEO's have directed towards initiatives necessary to transition to the "new economy." How did this all take place?

4.1 Changing Economic Foundations

Frameworks for governance and oversight are created by legislation and regulations that are put in place at certain times that are relevant to the reality of the world at that time. So, it was after the great depression when much of the founding governance legislation, still being used today, was put in place extending through until the 1950's. The challenge for legislators and regulators is that "times change." What was adequate and relevant in the 1930's needs to be changed and adapted as the world changes. This is critical to understanding the shifting "adequacy" of accounting information.

Accounting became embedded as a core component of corporate oversight during this period because tracking financial information, principally based on cash flows and tangible assets was, at that point, valid. The changes that were made in the 1930's was important because the world had changed both from a more agrarian economy into the middle stages of an industrial economy.

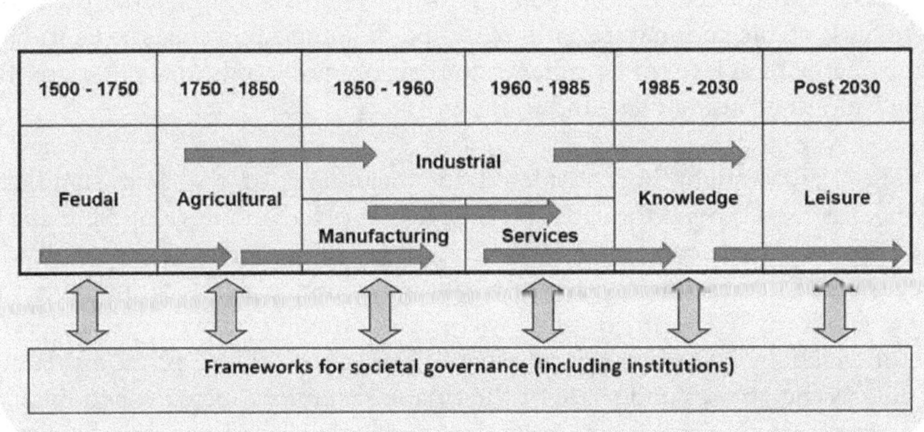

For the sake of our journey, especially since around 1975, and as a basis for the phases and terminology, the chart might be helpful in providing some context and to see when significant changes in oversight and regulatory frameworks and needed. (These times frames are not absolutes and each era transitions into the next one and remains as an aspect of activity e.g., agriculture is still a significant activity but as part of the complexity of social and economic life, it is a far smaller portion than it used to be).

The systems and structures of feudal times gave way to new approaches for the next era and so on. When the industrial age started to mature, especially after the 1929 financial crisis, it became evident that new approaches to accounting, accountability, and reporting were needed, and this is what happened in the 1930's. As the underlying transitions were taking place, with the creation of the SEC and formation of what is now FASB, accounting was seen as a profession that could be relied upon as independent and objective and which could be relied upon to assess and deliver objective opinions about the affairs of organizations that had obtained and was using money belonging to others.

The profession was held in a position of trust; however, the underlying approaches to accounting remained heavily based on the "industrial age." Most assets were tangible and book values represented over 90% of market values. Capital was provided by fairly straightforward financial instruments; internal processes and procedures, including costing systems and industrial processes were fairly stable and mature, and the scope of audits allowed auditors to have a reasonably high level of confidence in their opinions of both a "true and fair view" and of a "going concern."

The 1970's might be considered the beginning of the next significant change; as time moved forward and business evolved and developed, many of the approaches to accounting and oversight began to "creak and groan" with the strain of having to provide information, assurance and accountability to a "new economy." The major shift was the continuing growth of the service sector which, by 2020, comprised over 68% of the overall US economy; largest of all was the growth and share of the financial services sector which by 2020 was almost double the size of manufacturing, which had declined by almost 50%, from about 23% of GDP in 1970 to about 11% by 2020.

Other large growth areas within the service sector were financial services (including insurance and real estate) and "trade" at almost 15%. This shift saw a significant growth in knowledge workers as well as a major streamlining of manufacturing; additionally, technology impacted all sectors including trade where the whole underlying business model changed. While these changes are illustrated by US statistics, the shift was global. Politicians were also trying to adapt economic policies to stimulate growth and take advantage of the business opportunities that were developing. So, let us start with the impact of financial markets on the rise of intangibles.

4.2 Growth in Financial Services and Deregulation

Financial services have grown to be a major component of the economy, almost double the size of US manufacturing share of GDP. Revisions to economic thinking, which had been spurred by changes following the inflationary period in the 1970's and early 1980's continued, as efforts were made to "free up" the markets. This included the desire to both privatize organizations previously run by governments and also to limit regulations and controls in the marketplace. The same agenda was being pursued across the Atlantic in the US and, to a degree in Canada. It was felt that once government "got out of the way" of the free market, growth, innovation, and creativity would rebound. The availability of "cash" would help this transition. One factor that will be discussed in the next chapter is that creativity is not limited to manufacturing and technology but can be applied to almost everything (sometimes where it is not wanted). There is a great quote on the website that keeps track of many of the financial scandals of the period that states[12]:

"Bankers who hire money hungry geniuses should not always express surprise and amazement when some of them turn around with brilliant, creative, and illegal means of making money."

We will also discuss some of the side effects from the growth in the financial services sector in the next chapter however for now we will focus on the growth of the sector itself. Banking at the time in many ways was a mature market, but organizations are always searching for new products and services that offer the opportunity for profit and market share. This is not a new phenomenon, nor has it stopped. In the 1970's in the US, there was a growing belief that the financial industry needed a "shake up" to make it more innovative and Congress passed a number of Acts that removed several areas of financial limitation relative to how banks could operate - as well as extending the opportunity to offer some banking services to organizations that had previously not been able to offer these.

The first changes focused on expanding the role of the "thrifts" or savings and loan institutions; these were typically smaller scale, localized financial institutions that provided financial services such as loans and mortgages. These changes allowed thrifts to offer a wider range of savings products and reduced regulatory oversight. The intent was to allow S&Ls to "grow" out of their "market limitation." Other changes included authorizing the use of more lenient accounting rules and the elimination on the minimum numbers of stockholders. (These changes, combined with an overall decline in regulatory

---

[12] Quote by Linda Davies
https://projects.exeter.ac.uk/RDavies/arian/scandals/classic.html

oversight, would later be cited as factors in the later collapse of the thrift industry).

It seemed to be working; between 1982 and 1985, S&L assets grew by 56% (compared to growth in commercial banks of 24%). However much of the growth came from financially weaker institutions which could only attract deposits by offering remarkably high rates and which could only afford those rates by investing in high-yield, risky investments, and loans. By the late 1980s and into the 1990s there was the failure of 1,043 out of the 3,234 savings and loan associations (S&Ls) in the United States which ultimately cost $160 billion to resolve of which $132 billion came from the taxpayer.

While not directly being an accounting profession "issue" it occurred in the "finance world" and in many cases involved problems with accounting, financial regulation, and reporting. The changes in the banking industry were somewhat different and slower to take effect; in the early 1980's there were some 15,000 banking organizations in the US but, through consolidations, mergers and acquisitions, this had dropped to below 8,000 within the next twenty years or so. By 1999 the banks would be allowed to offer both banking services and insurance and investments. These strategic shifts set the ground for another financial crisis some years later. It did however affect accountants because it created more service employment, and, as regulatory oversight was weakened to spur innovation, audits became even more important.

What it did do was to encourage banks to become more active in the areas of "fee based" financial services and high on the list were services in encouraging, facilitating, and supporting mergers and acquisitions in the marketplace. Innovative products such as "leveraged buyouts" were encouraged where banks would facilitate the sale and purchases of businesses through heavily debt financed debt structures; the buyer would be saddled by high interest payments but would be able to meet these by wringing economies out of the acquired business. Through this period of time many people were impacted by closure of facilities or "down-sizing."

The growth in fee based services, both in retail and commercial banking, together with advisory services in areas like initial public offerings (IPO's), mergers and acquisitions brought with it a major increase in "knowledge workers;" historically banks had employed a large number of tellers and clerical workers, but as these positions decreased, especially as automation was introduced, they were more than replaced by individuals whose "tacit knowledge" made them valuable as an "asset" to the business. As competition for "base banking services" grew, banks competitive edge no longer came from its ability to make money on loans but to be innovative, and creative both in the creation of new products and services as well as alternative approaches to "doing a deal."

Other financial services were also experiencing an increase in knowledge workers - financial advisors, wealth management counsellors, insurance underwriters, investment strategists and advisors and many others. This growth in knowledge workers resulted in large numbers of MBA graduates entering the financial services industry; additionally, "competition for talent" became significant and the potential for large earnings provided an even greater incentive to be innovative and creative. The growth in the financial services required a commitment of significant cash flow into the creation of new services with the underlying processes and people skills to support them. Additionally, as technology developed, supported by global data and voice communications, financial services quickly became a global operation supported by complex IT and human networks.

4.3 Streamlining and "reinvention" of Manufacturing and Service

While it remains important, manufacturing almost halved as a share of US GDP after the 1970's; this decline is reflected in most western economies as the sector became more global and many "direct labour" jobs migrated to lower labour cost locations. This period was marked by significant changes and restructuring which included major investments in automation and other improvements - after all there are only two ways to reduce cost; lower labour rates or automate. These changes greatly reduced the numbers of less skilled workers but grew the number of semi-skilled and knowledge workers. One of the most significant changes that has occurred has been driven by the "opening up of global markets." However, our first stop on the journey, in the 1970's was where many of the early investments in intangibles started to take place.

How Accountants Lost their Balance

In 1973 and again in 1979 North America and many other industrialized countries suffered an "energy crisis." Between 1973 and 1974, the world price of oil had risen nearly 300%, from US$3 per barrel to nearly $12 globally; this first event was due to an oil export embargo imposed by OPEC in retaliation against the west for its support of Israel. This event is often called the first "oil shock." The second shock in 1979 was caused by a shortage of oil caused by the Iranian revolution; prices more than doubled. While oil prices have risen and fallen (as any global commodity) they came at a time when many economies - especially the USA were "energy hungry." Not only were most cars "gas guzzlers" but much of society had been built around cheap and abundant energy. The 1973 oil shock also occurred at a time when the Japanese were finally starting to develop and sell competitive products globally as they rebuilt their economy after the second world war.

This period created a significant increase in the sales of more energy efficient cars, and also increased the price of many items. North American auto manufacturers in particular (the big 3, GM, Ford and Chrysler) were hit by a wave of Japanese imports into the US market, which were not only more fuel efficient, but their quality was also superior; as a result, the market share of domestic manufacturers declined in the west - especially the USA where the "Big 3" market share had been about 90% in the 1960's, had dropped to about 80% by the 1970's and declined to around 50% thereafter.

This in turn sparked a major renewal in approaches to manufacturing. Several initiatives started in the auto manufacturers but were quickly driven down into their supply chain. While there were many "programs" that tended to be a diversion and not create long term benefits, there were many new approaches adopted that changed the "way of doing business" and almost every area of the manufacturing business model was impacted.

Consumer electronics and technology was also growing in the 1970's although PC's were not widely available, there were early video gaming systems like the Atari. Also popular were audio cassette tapes and recorders; 8 track audio systems were still available; the video cassette recorder was introduced. Colour televisions were also starting to be available. Historically the US and many other western countries had been involved in consumer electronics manufacturing; as an example, in the 1950's over 90 American companies designed, made and sold television sets.

This came to an end in 1995 when Zenith Electronics Corporation sold control to LG of South Korea. By the 1970's the integrated circuit or computer chip started to be produced in volume and at prices that would allow it to replace existing electronics; there was growing fear in the US that once again overseas manufacturers would eventually develop capacity in this area and the US would lose its production capability. So, in 1972 CAM-I was created; although it still exists, when originally formed it was a consortium that was to focus on innovative and creative ways to run organizations so as to remain globally competitive. Similar work to seek out "best practices" had started back in the 1950's under the title of "reverse engineering." Organizations would buy competitors products and take them apart to understand what new approaches and advances were being implemented.

In the 1970's reverse engineering developed into what is more commonly known as benchmarking; this started with competitive benchmarking. One of the earliest leaders in applying these ideas was Xerox. For many years Xerox was the king of copy machine manufacturing (years before PC's, scanners, e-mail, and electronic documents!), but they found themselves in a precarious position because their Japanese competitors appeared to be able to manufacture higher quality copy machines for far less. Xerox saw their market share dropping significantly, so they went on a quest to determine how their competitors were able to accomplish quality and operational efficiencies. These efforts to look outside, especially at foreign manufacturers revealed major changes were needed.

By the early 1980s, the focus of benchmarking switched to process benchmarking. Where competitive benchmarking focused on the direct competition, as the name indicates, process benchmarking encouraged companies to look beyond their own industry segment and investigate best practices in other industries. As an example, Xerox examined warehousing processes at L. L. Bean., which, at that time, was regarded as having the best warehousing procedures in the retail industry. Xerox was able to incorporate these best practices and create efficiencies in their warehousing operations. The focus on process benchmarking continued, but in the late 1980s two new phases emerged - strategic and global benchmarking.

In strategic benchmarking a company focused on processes but also examines the entire way others are doing business; this sometimes revealed that the overall corporate structure and organization was restricting a company from reaching optimal levels. The final phase was global benchmarking, which involves examining standards on a global scale including international trade, cultural and business processes.

The first "learning" by the automotive industry and others who became involved in benchmarking was the vastly different approach to quality management. Successful organizations appeared to rely less on product inspection and more of the design and development of the underlying products and processes and managing their business system "as a whole." While the goal was to achieve enhanced levels of quality as well as reduce costs, few organizations really understood the cost impact of poor quality and many were reluctant to spend money on things like process development and people development that would just add to overheads. The payback was often not clear. At this point we might make a small detour.

The cost of poor quality was never really understood by CEO's, and the quality department, which, at the time focused on inspection, was seen as an overhead cost (to be minimized). This led to a major challenge for organizations as they moved to change their approach to quality; accountants were of almost no help. While typical general ledgers identified excess cost areas like rework, return and scrap they completely failed in identifying the major true cost of poor quality.

When the US government realized that they were paying for the costs of poor quality that were buried in the costs being charged on government contracts - especially in the defence industry, they mandated that all these costs be identified and segregated. This was the start of understanding the real costs of poor quality - not just the visible ones like rework, repairs and returns. With its' focus on mass production, growth and output, organizations would often "keep producing" to keep their production lines operating, even when it was known that defects existed. These would show up later as scrap and customer returns - but the problem was that the cost and impact of this was not really understood.

In a landmark publication at the time, Phil Crosby[13] the author identified the various stages of awareness of the true costs of poor quality. What he was saying was that management were completely unaware of buried costs that probably exceeded 20% of total operating costs. This was without "costing" the negative impacts on brand, loyalty, margins, and lost capacity.

Category	Uncertainty	Awakening	Enlightened	Wisdom	Certainty
Characteristics	Minimal or no understanding	Focus on doing better, such as motivational talks	Develop and implement multi stage "holistic" improvement programs	Embedding programs and focus on continuity of improvement	Quality is an embedded value in everything we do
Actual excess costs as a % of sales	~ 20%	~ 18%	~ 12%	~ 8%	~ 2.5%
Reported or known excess costs	0%	3%	8%	6.5%	2.5%

One of the indicators of the change in approach to "managing for quality" was the emergence of national awards for quality management. These awards were based on government wanting to encourage the changes required in how organizations operated with a goal of becoming more competitive on the global stage. Implementing the concepts was strategic and involved moving to a more balanced approach, that maintained the focus from optimization of fixed assets - production equipment, which had historically been seen as a driver of manufacturing profitability but was to include all of the aspects of "the system" that surrounded the actual manufacturing activity.

A typical framework for organizational excellence was the US Baldrige Award; The award was established by Congress as "The Malcolm Baldrige National Quality Improvement Act of 1987 (Public Law 100-107). The goal to

---

[13] "Quality is Free," Phil Crosby, 1979.

promote improved quality of goods and services in U.S. companies and organizations, so as to enhance the competitiveness of U.S. businesses.

There was an equivalent Canadian Award, an Australian version, a European version, and several others include US State versions. A composite of the typical aspects as they were at the time, is shown below (while several of these awards still exist, many of the internal structures and categories have since evolved and changed - however this illustrates the scope of "strategic re-alignment":

Core Factors	Baldrige (USA)	NQI (Canada)	EFEM (Europe)	ABEF (Australia)
Leadership	Leadership	Leadership	Leadership	Leadership & innovation
Customer / Citizen	Customer focus	Citizen / Client focus	Yes	Customer & market focus
Employees	Workforce focus	People focus	People	People
Planning	Strategic planning	Planning	Strategy	Strategy & planning process
Process	Process management	Process management	Processes, products and services	Processes, products & services
Partners / Suppliers	Yes	Supplier / partner focus	Partnerships & resources	Yes
Results	Results	Organizational performance	People results, customer results, society results, key results	Business results
	Measurement, analysis & knowledge mgmt.			Data information & knowledge

The core factors attempt to identify what were the main themes common to all models. Then, under each model the specific section within that model that supports the common theme is shown.

4.3.1 Excellence in processes

Typically, the first areas of investment were in enhanced approaches to process management; major cash flow was directed towards understanding, documenting, and improving organizational processes, starting with the core design, development and manufacturing areas and eventually migrating to all other core processes through which input were converted to outputs. Because this work created no tangible asset, all this expense was charged against current earnings _yet in most organizations it established a foundation of knowledge which then became a permanent intangible asset_, forming the "system" through which work was performed.

As success was seen in manufacturing, so this enhanced approach to process management was also applied to the service aspects of manufacturing and then migrated across to the service industry. Organizations that designed and documented effective business processes not only improved their quality, they were also able to plan more effectively, predict key schedules and delivery times and reduce cost. These changes enhanced the "value" of the enterprise and made it more competitive.

Early on, it was identified that the functional "silo based" approach to organizational management detracted from the process approach. Silo based hierarchies (vertical management) built around functional specialties, contradicted effective process concepts that were built around horizontal concepts, with processes cutting across many departments. One of the earliest examples was between design and development and manufacturing. In the 1970's it was normal that the design and development team would create new products and then "throw them over the wall" to operations or production who would then start to figure out how to make it.

This sequential and linear approach to work management resulted in faster design but much slower "productization" because manufacturing could only start planning once designs were competed. Additionally, when production came to figuring out how to make things, they would often find problems, causing designs to be changed. This "backwards and forwards" approach significantly increased time frames, resulting in poorer quality and slower "take to market" cycle times; often production compromises were being made to "get the product out the door." This realization spawned both the introduction of much more structured and rigorous process around the "total" process including integration required for seamless operations between departments, as well as the impact that people in the workforce had on the process.

Managing processes, once they had been understood, developed, documented and employees trained would also require significantly improved management. This gave rise to the application of SPC (Statistical Process Control) and many of the process management and problem solving techniques that are in use today. These changes also link to changes to the business management system and the implementation of non-financial performance indicators. Another example of the creation of a "permanent capability" would be the development of a "6 Sigma Black Belt" capability within an organization. A group of people are specially trained as specialists in process improvement and are then used internally as a resource for process improvement. In some cases, organizations may have even gone through a "make / buy" analysis to decide whether to hire consultants or train internally; the advantage with internal training is once again an "ongoing capability." These process focused activities consumed significant expenditures, created key, permanent capabilities in value creation and enhanced the value and earnings potential of the business. However, there was no asset or trace of how the money was spent, and what the value of the investment had been.

4.3.2 Excellence in supplier relationships

Process improvement was also applied to supplier activity; incoming materials were one of the major costs of any manufacturer and so historically management goals was to "buy on price." Benchmarking soon uncovered the reality that the lowest price was often NOT the lowest cost; suppliers who "low bid" for materials often had delivery delays, paperwork problems, quality issues and other issues that impacted the buying organization. Again, these failures were causing part of the buyer's quality issues so the activities aimed at quality improvement that had started internally, were "pushed down" the supply chain. However - one key problem existed. The goal of buying on price had often resulted in thousands of suppliers most of which were kept at "arms length." This meant the buyer would send out "requests for quotation" together with supporting drawings and specifications and then seek out what appeared to be the best vendor who offered the lowest price.

Once buyers started to talk with suppliers, they often realized that there were quality improvement and cost savings opportunities that already existed that the vendor as aware of but had been unable or unwilling to share with buyers. This led to two core strategies; first a significant reduction in the number of suppliers based on a much broader based qualification process than just price. Second, suppliers and buyers started to develop "working partnerships" where designs and manufacturing could be mutually improved, and all other areas of cost could be investigated for savings.

At this time, vast numbers of employees were engaged in clerical and support activities "processing paperwork" for all the transactions between buyers and sellers and many other activities. Benchmarking once again started to demonstrate that there were large gaps between the administrative performance of best practise organizations and others. As an example, the Ford Motor Company became a shareholder in Mazda in the 1970's and Mazda helped Ford with its transition to smaller cars and engines and advised on many of the process improvements (that became known as lean manufacturing). One area that Ford benchmarked with Mazda was accounts payable; Ford had thousands of employees processing invoices in accounting and was looking for a significant reduction maybe in the region of 20%; however, when they looked at Mazda it was realized that they were able to process at least four times as many documents per person than Ford - a 75% (minimum) reduction. This led to a complete re-engineering of one key support activity and included the application of newly developing technology, called EDI or Electronic Data Interchange (prior to the internet) through which paperwork between the companies would be eliminated and relaced by electronic transfer of transaction information. This one change alone generated millions in savings.

Suppliers became more closely related to buyers and the "supply chain" became a critical aspect of value adding, which considered the total cost of doing business and not just the price. Included in these efforts, especially now that quality and predictability of supply had been enhanced, was the goal of improving inventory by removing "safety stocks" (or "just in case" inventory) and moving to a JIT or "Just in Time" approach where deliveries were made to the buyers' production line exactly when needed. This was a significant saving in working capital and also allowed for the streamlining of production space and the elimination of warehousing.

As we will further discuss in trade and transportation, these relationships and the underlying processes, relationships and capabilities became an even more complex and important aspect of the business model as major aspects of supply went "offshore." Buyers and sellers became "invested" in each other with the goal of mutual survival; in many cases this change in relationships also included "co habitation" with the supplier located on the buyer's production campus. _These changes required significant resources both in people costs and IT systems to create these operational capabilities which once again became a key intangible asset, that created value in terms of a successful business model._ Building and sustaining these intangibles had become and key underlying aspect of "the system."

4.3.3 Excellence in managing the workforce

As organizations started to improve processes and become more organized and to change their relationships with suppliers there was a growing recognition that traditional approaches to human resource management also had to change. While this journey is still in progress, there was significant investment made, again reflected in expenses in both changing the mix of the workforce and "up-skilling." It was an interesting side effect that during this period, union membership flattened and then declined as management paid more attention to its people. Early in the process improvement process, many organizations realized that a large part of their operational knowledge and competence was held as tacit knowledge in the heads of the employees. Little was written down so "on the job" training relied on the right skills being passed on - which sometimes changed from person to person.

As efforts began to define operational processes more clearly, there was a level of backlash as employees sometimes felt that once they released the knowledge they had about their job and shared it with others, especially when it was committed to documented processes, their job would be at risk. They were therefore reluctant to share and be involved. This became a greater problem, as it was soon realized that the people in the organization often had ideas about how things might be improved but had both given up trying to get their supervisors to listen, and eventually just stopped contributing. Loyalty was low, especially in the early 1970's and early 1980's, as economic growth, and change, including the early development of technology, was creating a high demand for workers. The traditional role of looking after employees was referred to as personnel management and mainly involved ensuring pay and benefits programs were in place, employment standards, including health and safety (and employment equity and others) were being complied with, and that people were available when needed.

The combination of the growing need for involvement and engagement of employees, in order to improve processes and build key relationships with partners like suppliers, combined with a "seller's market" for labour, resulted in a move to improve "personnel management" into a broader strategic role a "human resources management." Many organizations referred to their people as their "most important asset" yet in many cases the infrastructure to deliver on these words was missing. Once again effective process management had to be implemented in HR to ensure the fair and consistent treatment of employees, and investment to develop these had to be made. Compensation and benefits approaches had to be clearly defined and linked to roles, qualifications, employee training, development, and performance. Opportunities had to be identified for advancement in order to retain key talent in the organization. All of these HR management processes and structures had to be put in place as an investment and to be maintained. Organizations that did this well, enhanced loyalty and improved involvement and cooperation, as well as opening up opportunities for continual improvement in the way work was to be done. This made the workforce an asset in the true sense, as it became a real element of adding value to the business model.

While these models for excellence were initially focused on manufacturing, they have since moved out across the service industries with, is some cases specialized awards for not-for-profits, health care, education, and others; in line with this the criteria for developing excellence in people management have also continued to develop. What has been especially important from an "accounting for intangibles" aspect, is that these shifts have taken place across the whole workforce, and as the service portion of the economy has grown, so has the importance of viewing the workforce as an intangible asset. In many service industries, as an example in consultative and advisory work, other fee based work, project work, health care, information technology and others, while processes can be an important aspect *the REAL value lies in the tacit knowledge of an individual who uses their knowledge base to create services and solutions for the individual unique needs of the clients.*

There has been a shift away from training and development on "hard skills" - which employees often bring with them as qualifications for the position, towards providing the soft skills required for an individual to effectively apply these skills as part of "a system." Orientation and "on-boarding," team building skills, cooperation and collaboration, effective problem solving, dispute resolution, communications skills - all of these are investments in a workforce designed for long term payback. As the Xerox example in strategic benchmarking demonstrated, "In strategic benchmarking a company focused on processes but also examines the entire way others are doing business; this sometimes revealed that the overall corporate structure and organization was restricting a company from reaching optimal levels."

One final change that would have significant effect was, as part of re-structuring, re-training, and responding to competitive pressures, as well as introducing new technology, the scope of individual responsibility and decision making expanded. This made the development of "corporate values" and a clear understanding of ethical behaviour and delegated responsibilities much more important. While many organizations included these responses as part of the changin human resources activity, and embedded initiatives like corporate values in their "on-boarding" programs, many either failed to address it, or implemented it ineffectively. While the expenditure to do this was part of building the human "assets" of the organization and should being long term value and benefit, the organizations that failed suffered heightened consequences as we shall see in the next chapter.

4.3.4 Excellence in customer relationships

If there was one area of continuity with the past this was probably it! Customer focus was already a buzzword and many organizations felt they were already customer oriented. After all they said, "we delivered on time and met the specifications." The problem was that organizations often "failed to hear the voice of the customer" and as a result a gap developed between what the customer REALLY wanted and what the supplier thought was needed. Additionally, it was often believed that looking after the customer was the job of the sales force, yet the whole organization was, in reality about serving the customer. While there is some value in believing that, as a leading edge supplier you provide the customer with what they need not what they want, this can lead to distance, arrogance and the destruction of brand value. To understand what a customer needs, one has to be close to them and listen to them.

Progressive organizations made significant investments in the implementation of approaches and practices that closed this gap. Clients became part of the planning process, contributing ideas towards product and service improvements; investments were made in understanding and planning for brand integrity - supporting and investing in aspects of the organization's products, services and support that responded to what drove customer loyalty and re-purchase decisions. Investments were also made in areas such as "contact management;" training all staff on customer relationships skills relevant to their role and position in the organization. _Client relationships started to be seen as investments_; it was realized that, for many organizations, the cost of obtaining a new customer was far greater than the cost involved to satisfy an unhappy customer (the number was at least 4:1 - 4 sales calls before you get the first order). This is reflected today with organizations like Amazon having an open returns policy, which also reflects the mantra of "make it easy for me to do business with you." Often organizations would develop their "customer facing" processes to optimize internal needs without worrying about the impact on the customer. These had to be re-thought and re-designed to minimize the customers effort to interact with the company. Investments in on-line capabilities are a continuation of this requirement.

Call centres were also a new area of investment to again help solve customer issues; these were often seen as a cost centre where the goal would be to get the client off the phone as fast as possible. However progressive organizations realized that these interactions with clients could be learning experiences that could lead to understanding and resolving issues that created the client call in the first place. This point of contact approach also led to the investment in CRM or Customer Relationship Management systems where anyone in an organization who had an interaction with a client could record that, so a knowledge base would gradually develop on every customer. _This again would be an intangible asset of much greater value than the traditional "customer list."_

Many organizations realized that, in getting to know customers better, that there were different groups with different needs. It was also realized that financially, some clients were more profitable than others, so approaches, such as market segmentation became popular. This then led to investments being made in areas such as joint promotions, development, and other mutually valuable investments. Key customers were seen as assets not just the result of a successful sales call, but of a continuing investment in the relationship in order to sustain the relationship.

4.3.5 Excellence in leadership

Part of leading the many changes that were taking place in building "excellence into organizations" was the developing importance of leadership. While the traditional importance of management roles of planning, organizing, staffing, leading, and controlling remained important as change was implemented, the leadership role was the one that faced the greatest challenge. Initially the greatest impact was on supervisors and middle managers; as the approach to organizing the day-to-day work changed, and processes were developed, it was this level whose role changed from a heavier emphasis on "planning and control" to a role of enabling, coaching, and supporting. Historically, organizations had promoted people into supervisory and leadership positions who were experienced in the work being done. As long as the workplace was stable this worked reasonably well but as the workplace evolved and changed, it was realized that some of the best "technical" people did not necessarily make the best managers.

Significant investment was directed towards the coaching, supporting, and developing of people who were groomed for management roles. To facilitate the skills of collaboration and cooperation needed for the process approach, supervisors played a leading role in "breaking down barriers" and working with other departments. The supervisor also played a key role in building trust with the employees, which was necessary as a basis for engagement and participation in process improvement. The traditional "command and control" hierarchy that many people had as a background before they were promoted to managers was no longer the preferred approach to supervision.

Changes were also required "at the top" to create a climate where the efforts of all employees were focused on and directed towards the vision and mission of the organization. This required a much greater effort in communications internally, introducing events such as "town hall meetings" as well as leadership that was visible, available, and approachable. Building trust in the organization also started at the top of the organization and was about demonstrating the commitment to collaboration and cooperation from the most senior levels of a leadership team.

In parallel to clarity of purpose, it also became much more important that a "common attitude" was developed within an organization; this was needed to meet customer goals such as "make it easy to do business with you" that extended beyond product issues into areas such as support and administration. It was also a critical aspect of the goal to develop and sustain relationships with developing partners such as suppliers whose role was changing from an "arms length" potentially adversarial relationship (win - lose) to a collaborative win - win; this often required an attitude change.

Finally, the ongoing growth and development often involved greater delegation of authority and it was critical that aspects such as ethical behaviour become the "norm" at all levels in the organization; this started with the most senior leadership positions. Again, there were investments required to both create and embed and then maintain these underlying structural approaches. *Once again, the investments in leadership development started to be a consumer of increasing cash flow, but the value of good leadership as a key enabler of the workforce was a key aspect of value creation.*

4.3.6 Excellence in planning and reporting

In order to support the changing business models that were developing, the approach to "managing the business" needed to change. Various models from countries like Japan were researched and, in some cases, implemented. These were, after all, the "crucible" within which all of the other changes were taking place. Planning and budgeting were key aspects that needed to be improved; traditional approaches to planning often failed to introduce and implement the changes that were known to be required such as quality and process improvements. People knew change had to happen but making it happen was one of the biggest challenges.

One widely adopted model was referred to as the PDCA or PDSA model (Plan, Do, Study (or Check) and Act.

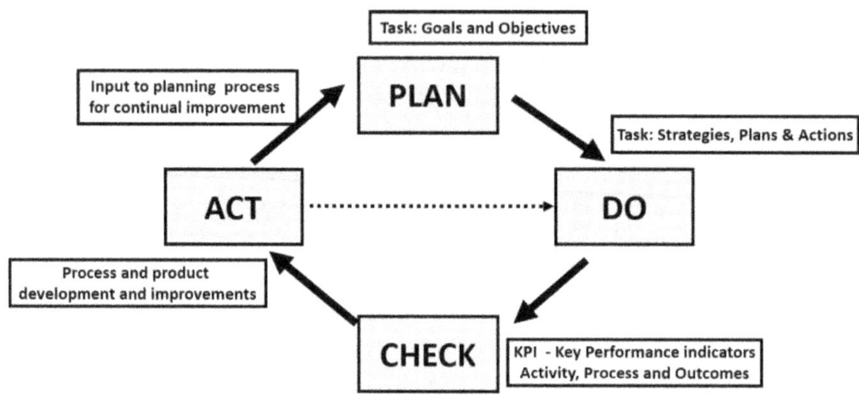

This approach was widely adopted by Japanese organizations and became widely adopted by western countries seeking management approaches to support the large number of operational changes being made. This model brought a strict regime to planning and attempted to change the traditional link between "DO" and "Act" that existed in many organizations into a more effective "think before you act" approach. This brought many requirements for re-training and the development of new processes and infrastructures that became part of "the management system" that was again an underlying intangible asset that if it were applied and followed could add value to an organization and lead to a competitive edge.

Another planning model was Hoshin-Kanri. This was adopted by organizations such as HP (Hewlett-Packard) and was reported to have provided them with a competitive edge in implementing real change.

Hoshin Plan Summary

Core Objectives	Management Owner	Goals		Implementation Strategies	Target		Improvement Focus			
		Short term	Long term		Short term	Long term	Quality	Cost	Cycle time	Safety

(●) Symbol indicates a strong relationship between improvement focus and a specific strategy

The Hoshin approach provided a fully integrated way of connecting high level goals and objectives to strategies, plans and action, as well as clarifying expected measurable outcomes and responsibilities. While the approach to planning changed so did the reporting frameworks, Organizations moved to implement non-financial indicators that included process performance, customer satisfaction, supplier performance, leadership performance, employee satisfaction and many others.

Once again this was the foundation of a whole "management control system" that was a key underpinning of an organization that had "value." It had implemented and was using a whole framework of intangible assets that had been developed to run the business. In effect these management systems and approaches, together with the improvements in underlying processes and other relationships formed the "capital assets" for the knowledge and intangible capabilities of an organization.

Changes were also taking place in accounting that tried to mirror these operational shifts. Costing started to change with the application of techniques such as quality costing and activity based costing. New budget approaches started such as ZBB and the BBRT (Beyond Budgeting Round Table) that advocated eliminating budgets. Internal management reporting expanded from its focus on financial management to include a broader base of non-financial indicators. Sadly, the one big change that was never implemented was an effort to explain and capture the diversion of financial assets (cash) that went into the creation of this whole range of capabilities that re-invented the way business operated, and formed the "enabling foundation" of organizational capability. What machines were to the industrial age, management systems are to the knowledge economy.

4.3.7 Information technology and communications

In parallel to this re-invention of the internal operations of a business were wound advances in computer and communications technology. Many of the base accounting tasks relative to bookkeeping had already been automated but as technology developed several changes took place. First, as personal computers and software advanced the traditional role of a "secretary" disappeared and managers started to manage their own communications. This required a totally new set of skills and capabilities but also the creation of an IT infrastructure that was able to support a broad base of individual users.

Secondly much of the analytical work of a business both in accounting but almost everywhere else, moved from manual, or manual plus electronic support (adding machines or calculators) to computerized. With the advent of everyday software tools such as spreadsheets, databases, word processors, presentation systems and many others, positions that had been essentially clerical were replaced by semi-skilled or skilled roles; many of these people had to be initially trained to use the tools but as the tools changed and developed ongoing training was needed. From an accounting perspective there was a period in the 80's and 90's where discussions centred on whether the tangible assets (computers) should be written off as expenses as they were now so cheap, and the expensive and valuable portion was now the human interface and interaction which actually created the value - essentially using the "dumb" computer in a way that created value. Some organizations actually started to provide this type of supplemental information in their annual reports because of the level of operating expenses being allocated to value creating activities (as opposed to work to support day-to-day transaction processing).

Also, computer technology and automation were extensively applied to operational processes, real time process monitoring, robotics, computer aided design and manufacturing, simulations, and many others. These again added to the tangible asset base but also created a growth in knowledge worker required to programme, operate, support, troubleshoot and maintain this equipment. _The "intangible capability" used in conjunction with the capital assets became a key strength and competitive advantage_. Anyone could spend the cash required to buy equipment, but the competitive edge came from the optimization of this equipment which in turn came from experience and tacit knowledge gained "on the job."

The combination of advances in communications technology also meant that employees were not "tethered" to the office by the need for communications; mobile phones and portable computers changed the way that people worked and again put power in the hands of the employees. As discussed in the supplier development area, and which also applied to relationships with customers, much of he "interaction capability" moved from paper based systems to "computer-to-computer."

Organizations needed to purchase the tangible assets to make these capabilities possible but again it required a re-skilling of the workforce. Once again, as these new tools were put in the hands of individuals, they identified opportunities for improvement and once again organizations developed a "value adding" knowledge base - often of tacit knowledge that gave a competitive advantage.

While IT systems themselves are often capitalized as an intangible asset and sometimes include internal labour associated with their development because they meet the accounting rules, there are many costs related to building the knowledge base that is then developed and makes the IT system of value that are not seen as an asset yet provide significant value.

4.3.8 Changes in the "trade and transportation" business model

Trade makes up almost 15% of US GDP comprised of retailing (5.5%, Wholesale trade (6.0%) and transportation and warehousing (3.2%). This was an area of the economy that moved from a tangible asset basis to an intangible, through their massive investment in computers and communications; once again these created tangible assets but also developed a key intangible in the knowledge base that allowed the systems to operate. Two examples demonstrate the importance of automated and integrated "logistics." Instant communications and the elimination of the majority of paperwork, combined with changes such as just in time deliveries made the transportation system a critical aspect of an organizations supply chain.

After the terrorist attacks in New York on 9/11 there was an immediate closure of all the American borders which particularly affected Canada and Mexico. Since the creation of NAFTA (North American Free Trade Agreement) manufacturing, particularly in the automotive sector became almost fully integrated between the three countries, much of this facilitated by fast cross border processing and the automation of documentation. Even if a supplier were in the US and an assembly plant in Mexico, parts would seamlessly flow cross the borders as part of a Just in Time delivery system. Within hours of the border closure a number of manufacturers were identifying shortages of parts and within days whole operations had been shut down. Technology and the people operating the system had become a critical asset in the business model for manufacturers. Creating the systems, training the staff from all organizations involved in using them, _integrating the various needs of governments, buyers, sellers, and others all together created a critical asset that was both a key part of the business model and also a major intangible asset_. Maintaining relationships with all those involved was also a critical aspect of sustaining these operations.

A second example of the capability that technology has created was for Maersk who was hit by a cyber attack in 2017. Maersk is the world's largest shipping line and operates 76 ports all of which are tied together through computer systems to its clients. Maersk is a key element of the supply chain infrastructure, but because of reliance on technology, the whole system became vulnerable to disruption:

"We can confirm that Maersk has been hit as part of a global cyber-attack named Petya on the 27 June 2017. IT systems are down across multiple sites and select business units…We have contained the issue and are working on a technical recovery plan with key IT-partners and global cyber security agencies".

While the IT system was probably a key tangible asset, the creation of an effective supporting human infrastructure was critical in ensuring its operational effectiveness. Providing this would have been creating a major intangible asset. However (at the time) one might question whether this investment had been made.

In its Crew Connectivity 2015 survey, Futurenautics found that, "Only 12% of crew had received any form of cyber security training. In addition, only 43% of crew were aware of any cyber-safe policy or cyber hygiene guidelines provided by their company for personal web-browsing or the use of removable media (USB memory sticks etc.). Perhaps unsurprisingly, given the above statistics, fully 43% of crew reported that they had sailed on a vessel that had become infected with a virus or malware".

This is not a criticism of Maersk - especially given that many other governments and organizations were being attacked in the same period and many were unprepared. What it does illustrate is the fiscal challenges involved in building an intangible infrastructure and maintaining it to ensure that the "system" is capable of value creation.

If we return to where we started this chapter, we identified the FAANG stocks - Facebook, Apple, Amazon, Netflix, and Google (Alphabet). The reason that these companies have such vast gaps between their market value is twofold. First, these organizations did not exist (except the early days of Apple) when the changes discussed in this chapter took place. These organizations looked at the emerging technology and built a major part of their business model on intangibles - thus their book values are minimal. They used sub-contractors a great deal (external workforce) as well as 3rd party suppliers. In many cases they leased buildings. They used 3rd party delivery services and, in many cases, sold through distributors and intermediaries OR they used e-commerce and focused on brand and reputation development and a growing network of "connected clients." In effect their whole operation was built on intangibles. If the stock market is at a high level then the gap would always appear greater, so the hard question is "what is the intangible value and how much of the value is "unsupportable, other than by future earnings or speculation?"

How Accountants Lost their Balance

Dec 31st 2019		Market Value	Brand Value	Book Value	Other Intangibles	Brand Value	Book Value	Other Intangibles
FB	Facebook	$647,840	$79,804	$105,306	$462,730	12.3%	16.3%	71.4%
AAPL	Apple	$1,581,000	$234,241	$78,423	$1,268,336	14.8%	5.0%	80.2%
AMZN	Amazon	$1,376,000	$220,791	$65,368	$1,089,841	16.0%	4.8%	79.2%
NFLX	Netflix	$200,680	$22,945	$9,334	$168,401	11.4%	4.7%	83.9%
GOOGL	Alphabet (Google)	$967,990	$167,713	$203,659	$596,618	17.3%	21.0%	61.6%
FAANG		$4,773,510	$725,494	$462,089	$3,585,927	15.2%	9.7%	75.1%

Facebook: book value of 16.3%, brand value of about 12.3% and the balance of "otherwise not defined intangibles" (ONDI) 71.4%. This would probably be considered to be the value of its' customer base (how much money did the company burn through to create a "critical mass" on its network?), its' processes and explicit knowledge base; its' implicit knowledge base of its employees; its' myriad relationships that enable it to operate and its' leadership and workforce that can work together to innovate and create new ideas and capabilities.

Apple: book value 5.0%, brand value 14.8% and ONDI of 80.2%. Certainly, the design and development capability - implicit and explicit knowledge, processes, supervision, external relationships but especially its' supply chain. It owns almost none of its productive capacity, so the channels and relationships are critical.

Amazon: book value 4.8%, brand value 16.0% and ONDI of 79.2%. Again, their systems and processes would be a core intangible as would their many relationships with suppliers and independent organizations that use their channels for sales and distribution; again its other external relationships. Happy customers, who find it "easy to do business" are key (and if they make problems ordering they are easy to fix). Their logistics and distribution network would also be key as a value component.

Netflix: book value 4.7%, brand value 11.4% and ONDI at 83.9%. Again, its network of users would be key - building a critical mass. Additionally, its relationships with production capabilities as well as its relationships with regulators in foreign markets that control its penetration. Its' financial results were suffering a few years ago when it was putting "expenses" into investing in growing its market as well as putting place media creation for non-English speaking markets. Its earnings were being affected and its equity depleted yet here was a clear case of building an intangible asset base.

Google: book value 21.1%, brand value 17.3% and ONDI 61.6% - a harder one because of its expansion into other ventures - but again its explicit and implicit knowledge base, ability to work together for creativity and innovation, its processes, and its client / user base. (A notable point might be the climate that leadership had created, that was initially an effective crucible for innovation, but in recent times, especially related to "corporate values" and the pursuit of government contracts, appears to have upset the workforce).

The financial reporting of these 5 organizations meets accounting requirements for a "true and fair" view and are also seen as a going concern. Yet from an audit perspective are the above issues, that make up its intangible "off the books" assets visible? Are these aspects of its activity "material" to its continuity? Are the actions of management building or depleting these intangibles? As long as they are making a profit the assumption is that things are working well. This chapter would not be complete without an observation that the answer to the above questions is that *we don't really know how to measure, manage, report and value*" knowledge based businesses where their asset are mostly intangible. At the time it happened it was in the early days of the technology revolution - the question is "what has changed?" Today many of the remaining technology companies are trading as massive multiples of price to earnings. It appears that valuation, using market prices, is leading us to the false conclusions of what these companies are really worth as a business system?

4.3.9 Dot-Com Bubble and Bust

In the late 1990's, while existing parts of the economy adapted technology into their operations and gradually became less "tangible" based and depended more on intangibles, a new field of economic endeavor was starting to develop - what we can refer to as a "pure play" technology business - these would include the FAANG stocks. Whereas traditional companies were diluting their balance sheets and employing greater intangibles to create value, these new companies accumulated an extremely limited level of tangible assets. They did however usually require large infusions of cash to fund their early operations. In many cases the concepts being developed were unproven and investors obviously hoped that a) they could make money eventually when the business became profitable or b) at some point there would be an opportunity for an IPO (Initial Public Offering) at which time their shares might be diluted but would be available to sell in the market at a value determined by what others were willing to pay for "a piece of the action."

Initial investors realized they were speculating as the venture may not work out, or would not be as great as they thought, or would never go public; however, if it did work out, the gains could be significant (and this attracted a lot of people who wanted a fast way to make money). However, the core question was "what is a company like this worth?" It certainly bore no relationship to any accounting values. As happened in the early 1900's when things were going well and "the average person" wanted to get a piece of the action, people who had cash or could borrow did not want to miss out on the opportunity for wealth creation. Those making money in this world of "high technology" started to get noticed as new start-ups blossomed, and some had spectacular success and increases in value - making some of the investors very rich.

Computers were not new and had been deployed in government and industry since the 1960's but what the technological advances of the 1970's brought, was the availability of computers to the individual principally through the mass production of memory and microprocessor chips. This was to be the beginning of a revolution that impacted work and social life. Previously computers had been mainframe or minicomputers which cost a significant amount of money and were out of the reach of the individual. However, as costs of the core computer components dropped, it encouraged the development of micro-computers together with the software to operate them and applications that could be used both for business and entertainment.

This spurred a whole industry of high technology "start up's" all of which focused on making money from this new world of technology. First among these was the Apple II in 1977 followed by several other approaches including the IBM PC in 1981.

In parallel to the development of computer hardware and software, computer services and communications were also changing rapidly. In the early

1960's data communications were developing initially between governments and universities based on the evolution from analogue to digital switching by the phone companies that shifted their systems from electro-mechanical to electronic. As technology developed so could more users' access "the network" and by 1983 the DNS (Domain Name System) was adopted as the number of computers attached to the evolving network spiralled.   that culminated in the publicly available internet. Individuals could access service providers using "dial up" phone lines where they could obtain all sorts of information. This eventually developed into the internet as it is known today.

There was an explosion of opportunity; hardware developers for business and personal computers and gaming machines as well as components, memory, storage, printers, and all sorts of peripherals; software development for both individual machine operating systems and networks; recreational and gaming software; business system software including packages for every conceivable business application including accounting. The number of new start-up's all needed cash and the money flowed.

Between 1996 and 2000 some of the highest levels of money ever flowed into the venture capital market[14]; those who were already "public" went for more money; those who were in the early stages looked at the capital appreciation that was happening in the market and went public. This pushed up the demand side and the "good times" for both opportunity and people, who could borrow against other assets, also jumped in. As often happens this led to both abuses of spending, as well as a proliferation of organizations that would, as many high-technology concepts do, failed to develop the intended capability or missed the market - or again as happens with technology, were overtaken by capabilities with greater potential.

---

[14] Value of venture capital investment in the United States from 1995 to 2019, Statistica

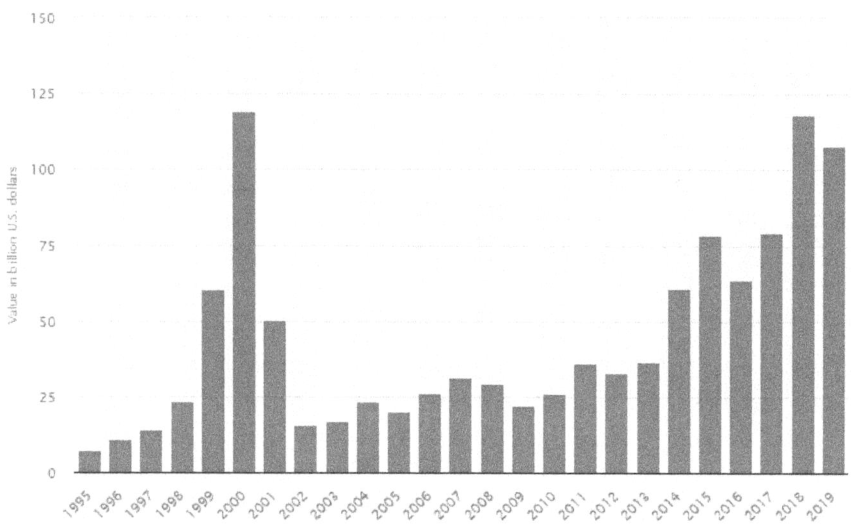

Between 1995 and 2000 the Nasdaq composite index rose over 400% with price / earnings ratio of over 200. For investors, the challenge was determining the risk. There were no underlying assets and in most cases the organizations were not yet showing a profit - any gain was based on expectations of share price increase and / or future earnings. In 2000 the bubble burst and the market crashed; several dot.com companies failed during this period and governments were starting to look at anti-trust issues - particularly at Microsoft. Investors got nervous and started selling.

Once again (like people after the 1929 crash) there were many "losers" who wondered why auditors had issued no warnings of impending disaster; one result was that attention focused on an organization "cash burn rate" - traditional financial statements meaning little. One problem was that there was limited exposure of "what the burn rate" was buying. Investors again were upset to find that in several cases their investment was not funding "go to market" development but items such as lavish offices and big pay packets. This extract is from the Wall Street Journal[15] following the crash:

---

[15] Wall Street Journal, February 9th 2001, Jonathan Weil

Look closely at nearly any company's annual financial statements, and you will notice an obscure yet important qualifier. They are prepared on the presumption that the company is a <u>"going concern"</u> -- that is, that it will continue as a business for at least another 12 months. And if an auditor has substantial doubt about a client's ability to continue as a going concern, it must say so in its report on the company's financial statements.

But what about last year's crop of failed dot-coms? Of the 10 publicly owned dot-coms whose financial problems forced them to cease operations or file bankruptcy-court proceedings, <u>only three had going-concern clauses</u> at the time they shut down. And one of those three did not have a going-concern clause in its annual report last spring, but instead got one from its auditor three months later -- after the stock had tanked. Among the flameouts that sported clean auditor opinions: Pets.com, Quepasa.com and MotherNature.com. All 10 were audited by Big Five accounting firms. (In addition to these 10 publicly traded companies, dozens of others that are still operating were delisted from stock exchanges, and many closely held dot-coms also filed for bankruptcy.)

I underlined the "going concern" phrase as we will return to this later. While changes have been made in accounting and auditing practise in the time since the bubble burst, society has continued to move to a technology based economy where tangible assets continued to decline. Another example of the inadequacy of traditional audits and financial reporting occurred much later. This example was not a high-technology company but one that had built its capability on intangible assets. The project management skills of its people; its relationships with customers and its' brand value; its internal processes and capabilities especially in the management of major construction initiatives; the tacit knowledge of its people in applying their expertise to specific types of projects such as public sector buildings; its outsourcing management capability. All of these intangibles created the intangible foundation and competitive capability, and yes - the value of this next company we will discuss.

4.3.10 The Carillion Collapse in the UK

This event was especially important for the accounting profession as it demonstrated the inability of the current oversight and reporting system to address the breadth of challenges related to being a "going concern;" for members of the public it again asked the question as to whether having the audit function report to management was a viable model (even with the FCA in place for oversight). The following headline in The Guardian newspaper said it all:

> # The Guardian
>
> ## Carillion fiasco shows why auditors must be accountable to parliament
>
> *Richard Brooks*
>
> Recklessness, hubris and greed were allowed to run riot because there was no incentive to blow the whistle
>
> Sun 20 May 2018 06.00 BST

This headline was followed by an equally scathing opening paragraph (and the whole article sums up and "feeds" growing public discontent):

Last week's verdict from the Parliamentary Committee on the collapse of construction and outsourcing company Carillion - "recklessness, hubris and greed" - marks the failure not just of a model for providing public services but of the system by which the businesses we all rely on are kept financially honest.

Some of the MP's strongest words were reserved for the accountants that should have acted as the company's financial watchdogs. The auditors from KPMG, earning around £1.5 m a year for vouching that Carillion accounts gave a "true and fair view" of its business, were in fact rubber-stamping figures that "misrepresented the reality of the business." In March 2017, the firm expressed no concern over reported profits of £150 m even though four months later these proved to be illusory."

The collapse of Carillion was predictable. The problem is that everyone was relying on the wrong information and missed the warning signals. No amount of hand-wringing, parliamentary enquiries or financial regulatory reviews will solve the problem - *which is that financial audits fail to disclose the health of any organization that is heavily reliant on non-financial assets for its business model.*

Many service organizations are "asset-light;" this means that their balance sheets fail to disclose the non-financial assets that drive their capacity and capability. Many organizations invest in and "grow" these intangible assets as part of building their business over the years. Accounting fails because these investments cannot be capitalized and shown as having a long-term value on the balance sheet and thus any expenditure incurred as part of this "capacity building" is a charge against equity – it appears to deplete shareholder net worth. For successful organizations that turn these investments into a growing revenue and income stream, investors notice and buy the stock. This drives the price up, which results in a growing gap between the "market value" that investors are willing to pay, and the worth of the organization as shown by the accounting records.

Successful service companies are typically judged by investors, on their revenue stream, order backlog, market share, brand value as well as their capability to deliver "no surprises" and deliver profits and dividends on an annual basis. Carillion was successful in doing just this. It delivered steady revenue growth, stable profitability and delivered an attractive and growing dividend to shareholders. Not surprisingly, Carillion investors were prepared to pay a premium for this, and the shares were trading higher than the book value; at year end 2016 the shares were trading at £2.26 versus a book value of £1.70 – a premium of £0.56 / share or about 33%. (As we will see later this was not an unusually high premium).

However much of Carillion's major growth did not come from growing its own capacity and capability but was the result of a spate of acquisitions. Typically, where a service business is acquired, the existing shareholders, whose investment value exceeds the book value as demonstrated above, expect to be paid by the purchaser based on the market value (probably plus a premium). As a result, the difference between the accounting value of the purchase price (assets minus liabilities) and the amount paid to the seller, creates an intangible asset called "goodwill" on the buyer's balance sheet. Thus, it becomes an asset to the purchaser – unlike if the buyer had built their capacity and capability, in which case there would be no asset on their balance sheet.

On December 30th, 2016, the last year end before the collapse, the goodwill carried on the Carillion balance sheet was a significant £1.5 billion pounds – about 35% of its TOTAL assets. At this point in time its shareholder equity – i.e., the book value of the business, was £701 million. Had this goodwill not existed, Carillion would have had a NEGATIVE equity and been essentially insolvent. Instead of trading at a 33% premium to book value, it would have been trading at "infinity" to book value. The impact of this reality was that Carillion's survival depended on sustaining its cash flow and profitability and optimizing the impact of the non-financial assets (i.e., the goodwill or capacity acquired for acquisitions) together with their own non-financial assets or "intangibles." It is interesting that the investment community had started to notice this problem as almost 30% of Carillion shares had been "shorted" – i.e., the marketplace was betting that Carillion stock value was in for a fall. A great example of how investors no longer think long term in their approach, but have become speculators profiting from future failure.

While audits typically do a reasonable job of assessing the integrity of financial assets – i.e., the processes behind sustaining profitability, the integrity of cash flow and the stated values of balance sheet assets and liabilities, as we have discussed, they provide little help in looking behind the numbers at the system of "capacity and capability" (sustainability) – other than a requirement to assess whether the stated goodwill on the balance sheet from prior acquisitions has been impaired. This "impairment assessment" is also fraught with problems as subsequent to acquiring these businesses their activities are usually integrated with the buyer's business system and any reasonable trace of the original intangibles has disappeared.

Adding to the Carillion problem was the significant risks that the company had started taking in order to sustain its cash flow. In particular, the practice of "reverse factoring" identified in 2015 through which significant amounts due to suppliers were being deferred and not shown on the balance sheet as a liability. (Interesting that it was this type of "off balance sheet financing" that was a core reason that Enron's financials were so misleading). This appears to be one of several warning indicators that management's efforts to sustain performance were venturing into risky and unethical territory (and it is clear from the 2016 accounts that the payables that were showing were already the largest source of ongoing funding for the business).

Getting new contract business and sustaining profitability were key issues for Carillion. Building magazine[16] gives an example of conduct in the

---

[16] https://www.building.co.uk/focus/analysis-carillion-by-numbers/5094583.article

marketplace that can spell future disaster. *"Carillion had bid £500m for the job, but that this was £50m too high for the client. Carillion's chief executive Richard Howson soon called him to say it would be doing the job for £450m after all, because the client would be giving them £16m in cash up front."* £100M drop in the price on a highly competitive contract?

Where were Carillion going to make that up? This is the type of problem that led to the disclosure, only six months after the 2016 year-end, and only about three months after KPMG signed off the accounts as representing a "true and fair view "of affairs, and being a "going concern," that Carillion faced contract losses of £845 million; one must question the integrity of a financial audit in assessing operating assumptions when this unknown and unplanned loss arose only months after KPMG signed off the accounts.

This amount was over 100 times the materiality that KPMG was using for evaluating Carillion accounts, 8 times Carillion annual profits and about 20% of annual revenues.

How could investors and others, been made more aware of what was happening? What information should have been available to supplement the financial reports to provide a better assessment of risk? How could the integrity of the underlying "integrated business system" have been evaluated to determine whether shareholders "value" and Carillion performance was at risk?

So, what have we seen? Business has changed materially; its financial assets remain important, but the application of cash flow has changed, from financing tangibles as the tools of value creation, to financing intangibles. This has depleted the value of the financial balance sheet as a representation of organizational value, yet little has developed to take its place.

The resources involved in creating these intangibles have been buried in operating expenses and have depleted equity when, in fact they are creating organizational value for the shareholder. These intangible capabilities are the drivers of value creation and sustaining them is critical to remaining a going concern.

These intangibles are material to the degree that they consume significant resources to create and to sustain; they are also critical if they become depleted and can cause the loss of capability. We have also learned that we do not know how to measure, assess, and report on the health of intangible based organizations and that audits cannot be relied upon to identify and report on issues related to the potential risk if and when these capabilities are being depleted. We have also learned that the bodies that have been put in place to oversee the work of auditors are not creating as much value as had been hoped.

5. Declining Control and Poor Behaviour

Corporate failures are a part of a dynamic and risk taking system although the goal is to avoid this "last resort" wherever possible. By the time an audit identifies a "going concern" issue it is probably too late anyway; financial reporting is a lagging indicator. Corporate scandals including unethical behaviour and fraud have again always been a part of the capitalist system - after all there is an underlying human behavioural trait of personal wealth creation that drives many entrepreneurs who take the risk of starting a business. However, it would appear that these types of corporate problems have seemed to escalate as the nature of business has changed over the last 50 years.

We have already discussed the challenges brought about by the major re-structuring of business and the shift to a service economy - but is there another issue that accountants have not kept pace with? Has the risk of "control failures" changed as the underlying economy has changed? If so, are traditional approaches, both to internal controls as well as the planning and execution of audits still doing the job of assessing risk? In this chapter we will look at the events of the past years.

5.1 Growing scandals and ethical challenges

Accountants achieved their prominent role in governance for two key reasons: the financial numbers represented a common denominator for the activities of an organization. Remember that in the early days, in fact up until the 1980's, tangible assets did indeed represent almost 95% of an organizations market value. If the balance sheet looked good, cash flows seemed to be in control and earnings met expectations, then the organizations should be solid. Rating agencies relied heavily on financial information to issue opinions on the quality of investing in corporations. Secondly, accountants are professionals and as such have been granted a position in society where they agree to abide by a code of ethics that reflects behaviour that not only fully adheres to the law, but "puts clients and society first." This is the basis of the trust that exists when working with a professional. No hidden agenda; independent and objective; not using ones' position for personal gain. Unethical conduct is not new - but situations now started to occur when the public trust in the profession would be further damaged.

The first wave of "modern day" financial problems started in the late 1960's and flowed into the 1970's; growth had started to slow, and policy makers believed that the system that had worked well in the past needed "stimulation." As discussed, there were waves of deregulation in areas like banking and financial services which extended to telecommunications, transportation, and other industries such as the energy markets. In countries like the UK this eventually gave rise to government selling off organizations that had been run by the government, and also getting out of services such as the building of social housing. In the US, it allowed the entry of new and innovative operators into fields that had previously been solid and stable.

It was also believed that efforts to grow international trade would "increase the size of the pie" and "raise all boats." In many situations this increased competition; manufacturing shifted from higher cost to lower cost countries; where a government "monopoly" had provided a certain service, now the private sector had the opportunity to do so and to earn a profit. Organizations responded in different ways, but one thing was common - competition was getting tougher. Accountants were impacted in number of ways; audits became more challenging as organizations sought more creative ways to generate and report earnings; additionally, audits became more complex as organizations became more global. New standards were being introduced to try and mirror changes in international trade and especially in financial markets.

Organizations relied more heavily on intangible assets for their business model. Internally, accountants were increasingly expected to suggest innovative and creative ideas to help expand profitability (whilst remaining ethical); these challenges extended to seeking out creative ways to minimize taxation while remaining in compliance with differing tax and legal systems around the world.

The pressure was on; oil prices continued to rise and between 2001 and 2011 they quadrupled from about \$25 / barrel to over \$100. It was not just the issues of the oil shock and energy crisis in the early 1970's. There were also significant changes and dislocations in the financial markets as international currency flows by multinational corporations started to exceed the value of small countries gross national products; these international trade flows had grown as communications, travel and shipping all became more important and cost effective.

Changes in world trade for each 10 year period in %			
1950 - 1960	109%	1960 - 1970	127%
1970 - 1980	67%	1980 - 1990	46%
1990 - 2000	86%	2000 - 2010	41%

Thus, in even the slowest ten year periods, international trade increased almost 50%. This brought with it, significant dislocations to organizations as they constantly adjusted to competitive pressures. In the financial markets, international trade had also grown significantly. Securities from any organization or country could now be traded throughout any 24 hour period by the technology that linked traders around the world. The challenge of effective oversight continued to grow and become more complex. There was a first wave of scandals and problems as these changes rolled through the economy, there were bank failures which, in a number of cases happened after auditors issued a clean bill of health[17]. There were a number of financial problems such as the following:

1967, Associated Electrical Industries (UK), misstatement of earnings.
1969, Pergamon Press / Leasco (UK), misstatement of earnings
1969, Continental Vending (USA), false certification of accounts by auditors
1970, Penn Central (USA), insolvency following merger / debt load.
1974, Herstatt Bank (Germany), insolvency after losses on currency trading

---

[17] As an example, I. W. Herstatt Bankhaus in Germany

How Accountants Lost their Balance

Some of these early failures were caused by organizations who had "over-extended" when conditions toughened up; others were "skating close to the wind" in using accounting standards and interpretations and were ultimately "called out" for it. Some of these were significant; as an example, Penn Central failure in 1970; the company was the result of the merger between New York Central and the Pennsylvania Railroads in 1968.

When it failed, defaulting on $87 billion of unsecured debt, it was the sixth largest industrial firm and the largest railroad in the USA; it controlled more than 20,000 miles of track on which travelled $1/8^{th}$ of the country's total freight. They controlled $6.5 billion in assets and at the time of the merger, significant "savings" were promised which would enhance the financial performance. However, according to Goldman Sachs after the merger *"…freight cars were lost, switchyards were jammed, and poor service and delays plagued both the passenger and freight lines. Penn Central had a highly complex corporate structure and experienced a number of management failures. As losses mounted, the dividend was cut, and the stock price plunged; Penn Central had to rely on issuing commercial paper at ever-increasing interest rates. After an unsuccessful government attempt to rescue the firm, Penn Central filed for bankruptcy on June 21, 1970."* (It should be noted that later investigations were critical of Goldman Sachs having profited significantly from the fees associated with putting some of these financial arrangements in place!)

Penn Central presents a classic case of cost-cutting as "the only way out" in a constrained industry, but this was not the only factor contributing to its demise. Other problems included poor foresight and long-term planning on behalf of both companies' management and boards, overly optimistic expectations for positive changes after the merger, culture clash, territorialism, and poor execution of plans to integrate the companies' differing processes and systems.

Not surprisingly there were concerns expressed by the public about these "governance failures" resulting in financial problems. Whilst the role of the accountants, both in managing the finances as well as those providing audit services had some role, the greatest impact was the start of a "loss in faith" of the expected oversight and security that was expected from the existing systems and reporting procedures. There were two distinct issues - the use of accounting cost versus "real" market value, and the awakening of the public to the fact that accountants review of financial reports did not offer 100% assurance that there were no underlying problems or issues. These may not have been major milestones, but they can be pointed out as events that impacted both the technical underpinnings of accounting as well as the perception of trust, independence, and objectivity.

In the 1970's and early 1980's these shifts focused mainly on governance challenges and the ability of directors to play a responsible role in the oversight of organizations. In several cases internal controls and the role of the board in reviewing annual audits appeared to be the problem. Some of the notable cases during this period included:

1970, National Student Marketing Corporation (USA), overstated earnings
1970, Four Seasons Nursing Centres, (USA), Overstated earnings, CPA partner indicted.
1973, IOS Fund of Funds (Canada), inflation of assets
1974, Slater Walker (UK), bankruptcy, overexpansion using debt.
1976, Lockheed (USA), payment of bribes to obtain contracts (led to US FCPA[18])
1980, Nugan Hank Bank (Australia), bank collapsed, violation of banking laws,
1983, Daiwa Bank / Toshihide Iguchi (Japan / USA), uncontrolled trading losses
1986, ESM Government Securities, (USA), failure after fraud; CPA partner bribed.
1988, Bankers Trust (USA), hid an $80 million mispricing loss.
1989, Livent (Canada), accounting fraud and forgery of records

Certain legislation was brought in during and after these types of failure, but the largest initiative was the creation of various commissions to investigate "governance failures" and recommend changes. The US Treadway Commission (USA), the Cadbury Commission (UK) and the King Report (South Africa) are among the best known. The Treadway Commission as an

---

[18] Foreign Corrupt Practices Act

example, reviewed financial reporting from 1985 - 1987 in the US and made several recommendations around governance changes; in particular the CoSo framework was developed that formed a mandatory base for risk assessment and internal controls in "listed" companies. One of the three stated goals was to enhance the "reliability of financial reports." The UK also responded with the creation of the FRC or Financial Reporting Council that was established to oversee corporate governance.

These "control" issues, while not all placed "at the door" of the accounting profession did continue to grow the feeling of unease about the reliability of public financial statements. While the profession moved to ensure that in its' audit reports it was made clear that significant reliance was always made of the "representations of management" there were still enough negative stories in the media, which left the public questioning the efficacy of the "clean audit report." The public was also starting to see stories about insolvent organizations failing yet senior managers receiving bonuses and pay packages that seemed "unreasonable."

This was again a governance, rather than an accounting issue but to many it continued to build scepticism of both "corporate capitalism" and the accounting profession that was seen as an intrinsic part of the system. It further developed social awareness as institutional investors started to call for greater transparency and exposure of financial information (in addition to other changes), which reinforced the efforts of the various commissions that were established to suggest ways for improvement. An article in The Atlantic[19] caught the tone:

"No one is laughing anymore about accounting practices intended to satisfy clients. Investors, regulators, politicians, and accountants themselves are asking how so many insolvent and fraud-riddled banks, savings-and-loan associations, insurance companies, and industrial corporations could have received clean audits from major firms shortly before they collapsed.

As the accountants hasten to point out, not all business failures are audit failures. Less than one percent of audits produce allegations of malpractice. Sometimes conditions deteriorate

---

[19] "Cooked Books," William Sternberg, January 1992, The Atlantic

rapidly after the audit is completed. Sometimes management is extremely clever in disguising illicit conduct. Markets can change in unpredictable ways, and the public can have unrealistic expectations about what auditors are supposed to do. But still: you have to wonder how twenty-eight of thirty savings-and-loans that failed in California in 1985 and 1986 could have received clean audits the year before they went belly up. How could Arthur Young have certified Vernon Savings & Loans when more than 90 percent of its loans were bad, or allowed Charles Keating to siphon money from Lincoln Savings & Loan? How could Deloitte, Haskins & Sells have okayed the books at CenTrust Savings Bank of Miami when its chairman was spending millions of dollars in insured deposits on Old Masters and other luxuries? How could Main Hurdman and then Touche Ross have signed off on the cooked books of the Wedtech Corporation, whose chief executive was mercurial and semi-literate? How could Ernst & Whinney have given a clean review report to ZZZZ Best, a California carpet-cleaning outfit run by a twenty-year-old whiz kid whose major contracts turned out to be nonexistent? How could Coopers & Lybrand have missed fraudulent activities and reckless management at the Los Angeles-based Mission Insurance Company? And how could Price Waterhouse have taken so long to blow the whistle on the Bank of Credit and Commerce International, known worldwide as the bank of crooks and criminals?

Some of the answers will no doubt emerge from a tidal wave of litigation that has engulfed the big accounting firms amid the wreckage of these and other failed enterprises. As of last May 1, federal banking regulators alone had thirty-two lawsuits pending against accounting firms, seeking $2.5 billion for damages to government insurance funds from accounting malpractice. This litigation could well be followed by billions of dollars more of derivative claims from piggybacking plaintiffs."

Two points to make on this commentary; the whole regulatory machinery also takes a large "hit" for these activities in fields like banking and savings and loans; secondly the phrase *"…Sometimes management is extremely clever in disguising illicit conduct"* as a reason for auditors failing to identify problems raises a number of underlying thoughts. Was a professional accountant involved internally with these transactions? If so, did they knowingly and willingly collude with their other senior managers? If so, are they guilty of ethical failure as well as potentially other illegal offences?

How effective can audits be when they are paid for by the company itself and thus is always time and resource constrained by the competitive pressures of audit as a mandatory service? This type of media article often appeared over a period of at least 20 years and gradually reduced public confidence in "the system" and the accounting profession that had been expected to provide "assurance.".

In spite of the increased attention to corporate governance, financial scandals continued throughout the 1990's. These followed a similar pattern and involved governance failures, fraud, false and misleading accounts and in some cases questionable audit and accounting practices. Examples include:

1991, BCCI (UK), Founded in 1972. By 1982 it was 7th largest private bank in the world with 400 branches in 78 countries and assets of over $20 billion. Investigation started in the 1980's and of 5th July 1991, regulators in 7 countries raided and locked down offices. A lawsuit was filed against Price Waterhouse and Ernst & Young which was settled for $175 million in 1998.

1995 Barings Bank, (UK) collapsed in 1995 from losses of over $1 billion caused by single rogue trader, Nick Leeson in Singapore; unhedged, unauthorized trading.

1997, Sybase (USA), overstatement of revenues by Japanese subsidiary; 5 executives fired, and earnings restated.

1998, Waste Management, (USA); restatement of 1992 - 1997 earnings by $1.7 billion, largest ever restatement in history following several and various fraudulent activities to meet earnings expectations; the SEC filed one of the first ever fraud charges against the company auditors and three individuals, which were settled out of court with no admission of wrongdoing for $7 million.

2000, Computer Associates (USA), kept books open after accounting period end in order to meet earnings expectations ($2.2 billion overstatement in 2002 and 2001); SEC filed fraud charges against officers. Company settled for $225 million.

It is important to remember that these settlements came out of shareholder equity so the interesting question would be as to whether even after the fines, investors owning shares in the company may have still been better off depending upon when they bought or sold their stocks?

Looking back, it would appear that problems had been building for many years towards "the perfect storm;" a combination of increasing competition, deregulation, global trade, technology, and the creation of new and innovative approaches to both accounting and financial market instruments, were together stretching the capabilities of executives and corporate financial managers including accounting, external auditors, audit firms, regulators, audit committees and others.

One can develop sympathy for the accounting profession as it struggled to sustain its role of financial oversight in the face of increased pressure. There was also the underlying "human risk" of the attractiveness of bonus and incentive schemes - especially those related to stock values, which could provide stress to those expected to "act in the public interest before their own" and to be independent and objective.

Leading up to the start of the new millennium there as a great deal of talk about the risk related to technology. The fear was that many legacy computer systems had been programmed without using the complete four digit date code; as a result, the fear was that when midnight on New Years eve was reached, computers would have no idea what year it was, and almost anything might happen. Power grids would fail; systems would shut down; errors would be made in payments; aircraft would be unable to fly; traffic signal and traffic control systems would fail and every imaginable problem. Computer resources were mobilized, and it is estimated that over $300 billion was spent in re-programming computers to be ready for Y2K (Year 2000). No one will ever know how large the risk was, but as the New Year rolled around a few problems were reported but overall, everything continued to operate. Heading into 2000 this risk was a centrepiece of attention but as it turned out the new millennium was to be a turning point in other ways.

The first challenge of the new millennium was in the technology sector; AOL (America Online) who was by this time one of the largest technology service companies, announced a merger with Time Warner - a move questioned by many financial analysts. This was to be followed by a "splurge of spending" by high tech companies on Super Bowl ad's; an article in Barron's that headlined "Burning Up; Warning: Internet companies are running out of cash - fast;" the failure of Yahoo! and eBay merger talks; the announcement of hikes in US interest rates; news that Japan had entered a recession; and a negative anti-trust ruling against Microsoft. By the end of 2000 some of the hyped high technology organizations started to fail as discussed in the previous chapter. These events together conspired to not only see the NASDAQ-100 drop 78% by the end of 2002 and an overall market loss of over $5 trillion. Once again this reinforced the fact that intangible based organizations are "hard to understand financially." But bigger issues were yet to come.

5.2 The Enron Saga

ENRON was a Houston based company formed in 1985 as an "energy powerhouse" growing as the result of mergers as well as the benefits from the de-regulation of the sale of natural gas. By the end of the 1990's it was a "stock market darling;" its stock had grown over the 1990's by over 300% which was only slightly higher than the overall market, but in 1999 the stock rose 56% and by 87% in 2000.

Readers can research all the background elsewhere but in summary the company collapsed as a result of fraudulent accounting activities which were only revealed once journalists, investors and others started asking questions about where the money was coming from. A period of financial restatements, investigations, executive departures, and debt downgrades all contributed to the final downfall of the company. Its' stock dropped from over $80 to $0.31 per share and in 2001 it filed for bankruptcy. A significant portion of the employee's pensions were invested in the company stock, so employees saw a massive personal loss, yet in the final days key executives had sold stock before it crashed and received significant bonuses.

Arthur Anderson was the auditor at ENRON and enjoyed a significant relationship with the company; in 2000 the practise earned $25 million in audit fees as well as $27 million in consulting fees. Many of the consulting initiatives involved the creation of the very accounting approaches that were questionable at best. However, when the problems started escalating it appears that

Andersons became part of the problem as it was later charged with the shredding of documents relative to ENRON affairs.

While the initial charges and conviction against Arthur Anderson by the SEC were eventually overturned by the US Supreme Court, the damage had been done. Anderson had to surrender its CPA license and 85,000 employees lost their jobs. Outsiders will never know the full story but the impact of both the ENRON failure and the role of Arthur Anderson combined to start further changes in corporate oversight as well as further erode public confidence in both capitalism and accounting.

ENRON was an interesting case because it combined both illegal activities with legal but unethical approaches; in a number of situations the underlying failure was to manipulate legal structures and approaches in a way that was not intended which brought about a call for improved ethical conduct both in corporations and by accountants. This "ethical versus illegality" challenge will be addressed again later. The second key issue is that the failure at Enron was one of several failures in the early 2000's that once again sparked political and regulatory change - similar to the activities after "the great crash." Some of the other major problems in the early 2000's included:

2002, Freddie Mac (USA), misstatement of earnings by about $5 billion; $125 million civil fine and four officers fired.

2002, Global Crossing (Bermuda / USA), "a child of dot.com" in 1999 was valued at $47 billion but never profitable; Q4 2001 company lost $3.4 billion on revenues of $793 million and filed for bankruptcy.

2002 Tyco International (Ireland / USA), improper accounting and fraud by senior executives.

2002, WorldCom (USA), misstatement of earnings amounting to over $4 billion followed by filing for bankruptcy.

2003, Parmalat (Italy), fraudulent transactions and misappropriation of funds; previous auditors paid $149 million in settlement; Bank of America $100 million; auditors $4.4 million.

2003, Nortel (Canada), misstatement of earnings and inappropriate bonus payments.

The US passed the Sarbanes-Oxley Act in order to improve corporate governance and oversight as these events were unfolding. This included the creation of the PCAOB (Public Company Accounting Oversight Board) that would oversee the accounting firms and profession relative to the performance of audits on public companies. This was a good indicator of the concern over the profession's ability to "self monitor" following the recent history of financial and business scandals. Similar enhancements in oversight took place in many other countries - in the UK as an example the FRC role was expanded to include the oversight of public audits and the accounting profession and its' role and funding was embedded in an update to the Companies Act in 2004.

While it took some time for these bodies to hire staff and get organized, it was clear that those tasked with building and running the PCAOB realized its importance[20]:

"I would like to talk with you today about the Board's responsibility to restore confidence in audited financial statements. Fundamentally, the Board's mission is not merely to register firms, to conduct inspections, to set standards, or to discipline those who fail to live up to their professional obligations -- although we will certainly be doing all of those things. At the most basic level, our job is to help the profession regain its capacity to furnish the service that most justifies its existence -- the ability to instill public confidence in financial reporting." "

.... Rather, the profession's reputation, re-built in the decades after McKesson & Robbins, was shattered largely as a result of fundamental changes in accounting firms and the environment in which they operate. Describing those changes and their impact on auditing could be the subject of several speeches. Let me simply list three factors that seem to have contributed to the erosion of trust in auditing:

First, the rise of non-audit, consulting, services......

Second, downward pressure on audit fees....

Third, reliance on more cost efficient means of auditing...

---

[20] Daniel L. Goelzer, Board Member PCAOB, Sept 15th 2003 speech to Investment Company Tax Conference,

One can argue that the speakers second and third points are really the same issue - one the problem and the second the response, but it is important to recognize that it is not just these issues that created the problem. One must step back and look at the context within which accountants and audit firms were operating in the reality of the start of the 21st century. High on the agenda were the following:

- The impact of "performance based incentive payments" to senior executives, that grew as high technology companies in particular, having limited cash, used to attract talent.
- The linking of compensation to market values through stock options - especially when focused on annual performance (which again grew in high technology organizations).
- The competitive business environment combined with organizations drive for market share following de-regulation and consolidation in the economy.
- Efforts to reduce government oversight by "cutting red tape" and reducing budgets as many oversight agencies.
- Complexity "across the board" both in the way organizations worked and in the complexity of financial tools available and used both by organizations and investors.

While these changes in oversight were clearly required and important, one has to ask whether they addressed the root causes of the underlying shift in commercial activity as has been outlined. Or was this just a case of "re-arranging the deck chairs on the Titanic?" In many of the situations the start of the problem was in the behaviour of leaders who allowed, even encouraged such problems to be created. ENRON was a classic example of not only questionable leadership values and action but an almost "dictatorial approach" to anyone who disagreed or questioned.

The CoSo framework for risk management and internal control assessment tool that was later adopted by the PCAOB provides a good "reality check." Risk is defined by "the tone at the top" - but to what degree can auditors really assess human behaviour in an organization? Again, ENRON demonstrated a solid lesson on ethics and ethical management. The company had a detailed Code of Conduct issued in July 2000, runs to 65 pages, and was signed by Kenneth Lay. After the bankruptcy, Lay was indicted in a 65 page document.

"…for his role in the company's failure. Lay was charged, with 11 counts of securities fraud, wire fraud, and making false and misleading statements. Lay insisted that Enron's collapse was due to a conspiracy waged by short sellers, rogue executives, and the news media. On May 25, 2006, Lay was found guilty on six counts of conspiracy and fraud by the jury. In a separate bench trial, Judge Lake ruled that Lay was guilty of four additional counts of fraud and making false statements. Sentencing was scheduled for September 11, 2006 and rescheduled for October 23, 2006 (but before this could happen Lay died).

How big a "hit" did the accounting profession take after ENRON? The headlines in national newspapers seemed to believe that the ENRON failure had occurred within a context of accountants finding it harder to serving client and the public or society. This piece from the New York Times was typical[21]:

ENRON'S COLLAPSE: THE AUDITORS

ENRON'S COLLAPSE: THE AUDITORS; Who's Keeping the Accountants Accountable?

The article sets out by placing the ENRON scandal in an historical context saying, *"After decades in which accountants managed to convince the public of their ability to bless the books of corporate America with virtually no regulatory oversight, there is growing skepticism about whether accountants can continue to police themselves."* The article continues to link the failure of the company with the impact on both employees and investors - society. *"In a way that no previous accounting scandal has -- and there have been plenty of late -- the collapse of Enron and the role of its auditor, Arthur Andersen & Company, have galvanized a discussion in the profession, among regulators and within Congress over the future of the industry. Investors, including thousands of Enron's own employees, poured billions of dollars into Enron as it reported strong profits, only to see their*

---

[21] Reed Abelson and Jonathan D. Glater, NY Times, January 15th, 2002

stock dwindle to nearly nothing amid doubts about the reliability of the company's financial statements."

The article touches on key points of sensitivity which both reinforces historical reality, but also reflect the way in which the media, reporting these incidents, impact public opinion. *"In recent years, concerns have mounted about whether auditors are truly independent of their clients."* And then a developing problem: *"…Accountants have always been paid by their clients for their role in reviewing their books, and critics have also argued that auditors are increasingly reluctant to alienate a big client that may contribute a significant portion of its revenue."*

The problem is made worse because of the "inter-mingling" between past employees of the auditing firms who are hired by the clients. (It should be noted that this is not an issue unique to ENRON, many personal relationships between audit partners and clients lead to the partner being hired away in a very senior role, as well as staff at all levels). *"Many companies also hire former auditors, making the relationships between the accountants and the companies particularly cozy."* Finally, a link back to the issue of "balance" between legislation and regulation and the belief in the effective working of a less restricted marketplace. *"Over the last 10 years, the legal threat that kept auditors honest has been greatly diminished,"*

The ENRON issue and the problems that it had raised continued to be on the mind of the public - an interesting example being an article published[22] in 2006 with the headline:

Perceptions Of Accountants:
What Are They After Enron
And WorldCom?

While the study was limited and this the conclusions possibly open to question, the article summarizes as follows:

---

[22] Perceptions Of Accountants: What Are They After Enron And WorldCom? Gwendolen B. White, November 2006, Journal of College Teaching & Learning

The results of the current study indicate that accountants were rated highly on the evaluation (goodness) dimension but not on the potency (power) or activity (engagement) dimensions. The results from the evaluation dimension of this study are consistent with the results of a 2005 Gallup poll taken with members of the business community (AICPA, 2005). Accountants were given a 45% positive rating. This is good news for the accounting profession. They are perceived as having more trustworthiness and honesty than any of the six occupations rated. Yet a more interesting result is how accountants were rated on potency and activity.

The profession clearly states and reinforces its reliance on both the opinions of management as well as the approach to internal controls and the business as a "going concern." This is important (and accurate as accountants, in the short time allowed for an audit are limited n what can be achieved).

Thinking back to Enron, how valuable was this Code of Conduct in terms of an auditor's ability to rely on "the tone at the top?" Clearly, management was doing the right things. No amount of regulation, audits or oversight can change the way in which an organization is managed. This, with, as the PCAO speaker indicated, the reductions in audit fees leaves auditors with an almost impossible task when it comes to assessing the overall health of an organization. And here we have the link to a phrase used before "a going concern." We will return to this.

5.3 Fraud, Restatements and Ponzi schemes

One of the larger issues frauds was American International Group (AIG) in 2005. Massive accounting fraud of $39 billion was alleged, through recording loans (assets) as revenues (income); manipulation of sales to those who would pay commissions to AIG; deals with traders to inflate AIG stock price and others. Settlements included over $1.5 billion to the SEC, $115 million with a Louisiana pension fund, and $725 million to three Ohio pension funds.

In an agreement between the board, internal and external auditors and the SEC, AIG also made the decision to restate its financial statements for the years ended December 31, 2003, 2002, 2001 and 2000, the quarters ended March 31, June 30, and September 30, 2004 and 2003 and the quarter ended December 31, 2003. On November 9, 2005, the company was said to have delayed its third-quarter earnings report because it had to restate earlier financial results, to correct accounting errors. There were a number of key issues here that once again tarnished the profession and the system within which they operate:

"Tone at the Top" was clear - fraud, but this did not appear to have been detected.

Financial audits (external auditors / accountants) did not reveal the problems as earnings dating back several years were re-stated.

Internal audit (internal accounting personnel) also appears to have either "been blind" to the problem or been aware of it but not escalated it.

The board did not appear aware of it, so governance, especially the role of the audit committee was ineffective.

The CEO was fired but no criminal charges were laid.

Clearly unethical and even illegal behaviour was taking place.

The company continued in business (and readers may wish to connect this behaviour with the part AIG played in the major financial meltdown a few years later).

Another clear case of "public exploitation" that occurred in 2008 was the "Bernie Madoff scandal." This was a classic "Ponzi" scheme that depended always on bringing new investors with new cash that would then be used to pay high "returns" to previous investors. The investment scandal was a case of stock and securities fraud. Bernie Madoff was the former NASDAQ chairman and founder of the Wall Street firm Bernard L. Madoff Investment Securities LLC. When the scheme was discovered, Madoff admitted that the wealth management arm of his business was an elaborate multi-billion-dollar Ponzi scheme.

Madoff had originally founded Bernard L. Madoff Investment Securities LLC in 1960 and was its chairman until his arrest in 2008. The firm employed Madoff's brother Peter as senior managing director and chief compliance officer, Peter's daughter Shana Madoff as rules and compliance officer and attorney, and Madoff's sons Mark and Andrew. Alerted by his sons, federal authorities arrested Madoff on December 11, 2008. On March 12, 2009, Madoff pleaded guilty to 11 federal crimes and admitted to operating the largest private Ponzi scheme in history. Sadly, Peter was sentenced to 10 years in prison, and Mark died by suicide exactly two years after his father's arrest.

On June 29, 2009, Bernie Madoff was sentenced to 150 years in prison with restitution of $170 billion. Prosecutors estimated the size of the fraud to be $64.8 billion, based on the amounts in the accounts of Madoff's 4,800 clients as of November 30, 2008. Harry Markopolos, Madoff's repeated (and obviously ignored) whistleblower, estimated that at least $35 billion of the money Madoff was accused to have stolen never really existed, but was simply fictional profits he reported to his clients. Half of Madoff's direct investors lost no money. The U.S. Securities and Exchange Commission (SEC) was criticized for not investigating Madoff more thoroughly; part of the reason may have been that the legitimate trading arm of Madoff's business that was run by his two sons and was one of the top market makers on Wall Street, and in 2008 was the sixth-largest. Questions about his firm were raised as early as 1999.

Madoff's personal and business asset freeze created a great deal of publicity as well as causing a chain reaction throughout the world's business and philanthropic community. Accountants had been involved with Madoff since the earliest days and several concerns were raised, especially about the capability of the 2 person audit firm involved - as being totally inadequate for the task. Once more the public heard about these issues through the media and for many it was further erosion of the level of trust both in the profession, in oversight and in corporate leadership and ethics. Both these cases raise the challenges of trying to conduct in-depth audits in situations where there is such as significant driver for personal wealth creation in the very people whose opinions are being relied upon by auditors.

5.4 Making it through the financial apocalypse

Accountants operate as a key part of the financial system as advisors, specialists, auditors and also in many executive and management roles. While the BIG financial melt-down that occurred between 2008 and 2010 cannot be placed "at the door" of the accounting profession, it did have a significant impact on both the credibility of audits and the perceived integrity of the profession overall. It also demonstrates how challenging it can be for accountants, in the age of asset light organizations, to assess the effectiveness of internal controls when human behaviour is the driving force behind noncompliance or unethical conduct.

The annual reports that accountants prepare, and auditors verify and certify are designed to provide an independent and objective opinion that the results published present a "true and fair view" of the financial affairs of the company. In a similar way, the financial market has rating agencies that are intended to be independent and objective in their assessment of the risk associated with different financial "products." Most people are familiar with the "ratings agencies" that use a numeric scale to rank their opinions about certain investments. The financial downturn of 2007-2008 and the resulting cascade effect which included the apparent "failure" of the ratings agencies, added another dimension to the erosion of trust in professional oversight bodies.

There have been many discussions and reasons for the 2007 - 2011 market and financial collapse, which was the first time that something equivalent to the great depression had occurred. It was like the collapse of a house of cards which was founded on trust; once it became clear that certain areas had failed this cascaded to other areas and soon the whole system was near collapse. The reader can find much more detailed explanations than will be covered here - however it would appear hat the key aspects of he collapses which started in the USA but impacted the globe had the following factors:

Housing ownership had been promoted and encouraged in the USA in the early 2000's.

Potential buyers were encouraged to purchase homes with almost zero down and at discounted interest rates, on mortgages that would come due for adjustment to "market rates" within 12 months (that many, clearly could not afford).

As demand increased so did prices, encouraging owners who had equity in their property to borrow against the increased value, and spend the proceeds on "consumables."

As interest rates rose, some of those facing renewal of mortgages after the initial term, could not afford the payments and were unable to refinance.

This stopped the increase in prices, which then started to drop as more properties became available.

Those who had borrowed against their property as house prices went up, were now "under water" with their mortgage larger than the value of the property.

The people who initially sold the mortgages had then packaged them up and sold them as "investment grade" securities to banks and other financial institutions (insurance companies, trusts etc.).

The rating agencies had provided assurances that these packages of mortgages were secure and had given then attractive ratings, encouraging investors to buy them.

When people started defaulting on the mortgages it was discovered that the packages of securities were in fact closer to "junk ratings."

The buyers of the securities had also purchased insurance to cover any potential losses on these items.

As the property market continued to decline more and more property foreclosures started.

Financial institutions, who now had to recognize major losses on their holdings of these investments, started to have liquidity problems and then started to fail.

The stock market suffered significant declines which then precipitated the calling up of loans secured against stocks, but these stocks were now often worth less than the loans leading to further liquidity problems.

Massive liquidity problems, insurance policies that could not be honoured, the collapse of the property and credit markets all contributed to a "melt down" of the whole financial system, and central banks supported by governments had to step in and offer both guarantees and bailouts.

The financial failure cascaded through the economy, causing reduced factory output, and increasing unemployment.

in a 2018 article, The Washington Post, looked back at the 2007 - 2011 crisis and, with the benefit of hindsight, summarized it as follows:

The crisis was the worst U.S. economic disaster since the Great Depression. In the United States, the stock market plummeted, wiping out nearly $8 trillion in value between late 2007 and 2009. Unemployment climbed, peaking at 10 percent in October 2009. Americans lost $9.8 trillion in wealth as their home values plummeted and their retirement accounts vaporized.

How Accountants Lost their Balance

In all, the Great Recession led to a loss of more than $2 trillion in global economic growth, or a drop of nearly 4 percent, between the pre-recession peak in the second quarter of 2008 and the low hit in the first quarter of 2009, according to Moody's Analytics.

Two key - points: first the impact on people relative to their homes, employment, and pensions. Second the underlying questions about "how could this happen in the financial system - where was the oversight? Who was protecting the interest of the public?" The Washington Post goes on to discuss the aftermath:

The U.S. economy has largely recovered. In late August (2018), the U.S. stock market set a record for the longest-running upswing in its history, replenishing the retirement accounts of workers who stayed invested through bouts of volatility. Home prices have also rebounded, pushing total housing wealth to top the levels seen in the pre-recession peak. Unemployment is low, at 3.9 percent in July.

Still, the recovery has not buoyed all consumers equally. Many workers have struggled to land jobs that paid as well as the positions they had before the recession. That shift, combined with the time spent out of work and other drops in productivity since the crisis, has led to a loss of about $70,000 in lifetime income for every American, according to an estimate from the Federal Reserve Bank of San Francisco. At the end of 2017, 4.4 million homeowners were underwater on their mortgage, meaning they owed more than their homes were worth, according to the real estate company Zillow.

So again, we can see that in the aftermath, although the overall economy has recovered and it is suggested that "these losses have been recovered" - while this may be true on average, a lot of people still see the system as failing them. The Post goes on to talk about legislation as well as other changes to global banking regulations that were subsequently made but point out that these regulatory frameworks, established to protect the consumer, are beginning to be "watered down" as politicians once again seek to reduce regulations. The public believe it is now more protected but in reality, the frameworks may still not be adequate.

The period 2011 - 2020 showed almost no sign of change; business scandals were still taking place and accounting scandals remained in the public eye. The problems remained broad based in Canada, the USA. Iran, China, Japan, Spain,

Brazil, and Malaysia; the firms involved included KPMG, E&Y, Deloitte, BDO, and PwC. Further non-financial scandals also occurred that reinforced a negative public opinion on trusting "the corporate world." However, this type of behaviour would have a significant financial impact - but not on accounting value. This would hurt a key intangible, long ignored by accounting but both key to value and ultimately critical for organizational sustainability - their brand.

5.5 The Bug in the Bug

The Volkswagen emissions scandal, (also known as Dieselgate) began in 2015, when the United States Environmental Protection Agency (EPA) issued a notice of violation of the Clean Air Act to German automaker Volkswagen.

How VW tried to cover up the emissions scandal

By Theo Leggett
Business correspondent, BBC News

5 May 2018

The agency had found that Volkswagen had intentionally programmed turbocharged direct injection (TDI) diesel engines to activate their emissions controls only during laboratory emissions testing which caused the vehicles output to appear to meet US standards during, but they did in fact, emit up to 40 times more nitrous oxide. Volkswagen had already deployed this software in about 11 million cars worldwide, including 500,000 in the United States, in model years 2009 through 2015.

People do things like "working around regulations" - often as conscious decisions. Often, they are told by leadership, but often, in a competitive world where authority for decision making has been delegated to meet the needs of speed and agility in the marketplace, these decisions are made by individuals in what they believe to be the best interests of the company. Brand values take time to build and are based on an organization "track record." The loss of $10 billon in brand value is "material." Not only would this intangible loss be important to the company - but the impact on lost trust between regulators and the company would be significant; there would also be significant "recovery costs" built into the company financials - such as the discounting of the cars that remained, the recall and repair costs, the re-design costs.

What was the total cost to the shareholder of this failure? Brand Finance is a company that tracks on and reports brand values on an annual basis. Brand value can be one of the key intangible assets that an organization builds over time.

> *"At Brand Finance's last calculation VW's brand value stood at just over US$31 billion, making it the world's 3rd most valuable auto brand. It appeared to be motoring ahead, brand value having increased from just over US$27 billion in 2014. The developments of the last few days will undoubtedly send this trend into reverse, **resulting in $10 billion in lost brand value.** The apparent ease with which the company's activities were uncovered makes it all the more astonishing that VW was willing to endanger its most valuable asset. Rather than 'Das Auto', VW's motto might be more appropriate if changed to 'Crass Auto'*
>
> *Extract from Brand Finance website at* http://brandfinance.com

Unethical behaviour puts an organization brand at risk, but it also places risk in other areas. Nick Leeson at Barings Bank probably thought he was doing the right thing. Kenneth Lay at ENRON probably thought he was doing what was best for the company (and himself probably?). The executive team at Carillion probably thought they were doing what was best for the company? The engineers at Volkswagen also probably felt their action were the right thing to do. Every one of these situations involved human decisions. What do these actions create in "tone from the top?" What impact do they have on the integrity of ethics and controls within the organization?

5.6 Ethical Conduct

Another key side effect from global trade, international business operations and increased competition, is the complexity that different cultures and ethics, and legal and taxation systems have on decision making and through this, risk, and control. Investigations by the U.S. Securities and Exchange Commission in the mid-1970s revealed that over 400 U.S. companies admitted making questionable or illegal payments in excess of $300 million to foreign government officials, politicians, and political parties - remember, accountants would have been aware of and involved in all of these transactions. With the Lockheed scandal in 1976 it became apparent that companies were paying bribes which were, in many cases considered "the normal way of doing business" in certain jurisdictions but illegal in the organizations base location - in this case the USA.

The challenge of the bribery of government officials and others who were supposed to act in the interests and benefits of their country had also been identified by the UN during this period and in October 2003, the "United Nations Convention against Corruption" was adopted, that covers bribery, trading in influence, abuse of functions, and various acts of corruption in the private sector. In the 17 years between adoption and 2020, the convention been ratified by 187 countries with very few remaining - however many countries are still in the process of bringing their legal frameworks fully into line.

Behavioural change takes time and when practices like bribery have been built into a countries commercial system for many years - in some cases several thousand years, it is not reasonable to expect full compliance within a generation. This is why, despite "the world" shifting to a commercially level playing field, the reality is that there remain many situations where an organization may act illegally as seen from its home country yet be acting in a normal way of doing business where it is operating. This is a core reason why "the tone at the top" and an organizations code of conduct, especially as it relates to ethical conduct poses such a challenge. This can create challenges for the individuals, including accountants who work in these organizations.

The issue of corporate self interest has always existed but became more apparent after the 1970's when the impact of de-regulation and increased competition started to be seen in daily life. How was it seen? Not just public scandals but also increasingly actions that were perceived to be harming society. Some of the most visible were downsizing and closing plants to move to lower cost environments; ignoring local suppliers to go with the cheapest wherever they may be; eliminating employee benefits including pensions;

replacing full time workers with temporary and part time and efforts to avoid paying taxation. It was believed that the "invisible hand" of the marketplace, where individuals and corporations acted in their own interest was best for society "as a whole."

Up until recently in many states in the USA it was illegal for officers and directors to take any action that could be proven to not be in the best interests of the corporation. This growing level of discontent was demonstrated by the creation and release in 2003 of a documentary entitled "The Corporation". A whole book can be written on opinions of this movie which premièred at the Toronto Film Festival to critical acclaim - however it is used here to both illustrate a point and to demonstrate the growing concern around "corporate behaviour" of which, intrinsically, like it or not accountants form a part of.

The key point of the documentary is that a person who exercises too much self interest can become dangerous to themselves and others through their behaviour; this condition is termed being a psychopath. The documentary asked the question *"can we look at corporations and use a checklist to determine whether in fact their behaviour has gone beyond a reasonable level of self interest within society?"* Here is the checklist identified in the documentary (based on World Health Organization ICD-10, Manual of Mental Disorders DSM-IV) against which corporate behaviour might be assessed:

- Callous unconcern for the feelings of others.
- Incapacity to maintain enduring relationships.
- Reckless disregard for the safety of others.
- Deceitfulness: repeated lying and conning others for profit.
- Incapacity to experience guilt.

It is for the reader to consider the answers to these questions but certainly a case might be made, based on situations such as ENRON, that those leading the organizations and creating the culture / "tone at the top" might possibly exhibit one or more of these attributes. Again - this is not a direct issue for accountants but if it can be argued that the profession acted in a support role for these actions then one can decide whether the reputation of the profession was impacted? For the individual accountants, either acting internally or externally as an auditor or advisor there can be considerable impact.

When one is an employee of a multi-national then one's loyalty is expected to be to the employer. As a senior officer one is expected to fall in line with what is best for the business in priority over most other stakeholders. This is the reality of life in business; some organizations have long held more balanced views and act based on consideration of all stakeholders and many more are moving in this direction. But the competitive world of free enterprise does create conflicts of values and ethics where decisions have to be made. Whose interest should one be acting in? Self, employer, client, profession, national / country? If not measured by a visible push back by accountants, it can be measured by the stress on people involved in these roles.

Two other issues have brought the ethics discussion forward; first, as organizations expand their operations into non-traditional areas with different histories and cultures, they are often faced with local "values" as a basis for decision making; sometimes these decisions may not be appropriate for the parent company which makes the need for corporate values and ethics training and leadership all the more critical. This can be a major area of concern when considering internal controls where individual action will be based on both delegated authority and also "cultural norms."

Secondly, global communications mean that the public at large is increasingly aware of any actions taken by anyone in most countries around the world soon after they occur. This again means that "control failures" become apparent and more visible to a much greater extent than in the past.

In this chapter we have looked at how the business world has developed over the last 50 years and how the last 30 years have been a period of significant change. This has brought many challenges to the accounting and accountants that were never envisaged and which the profession has done its' best to adapt to. It is hard for those within a profession to "step outside" and look at it through the eyes of others. Reflection on who we are and how we are doing has never been more important as the world within which we operate, continues to evolve.

Accounting is intrinsically bound up in the world of business - not just in auditing but in financial accounting, management accounting and all sorts of specialities such as management consulting, tax planning and many others.

Accounting is a unique profession as it is the ONLY functional area in the business that permeates every single other area because they ALL involve the use of financial resources. Accountants have a perspective that few others share about the way organizations work and the impact of decision making; we can therefore be an active player in ensuring that the organizations within which we operate and the governance structures within which these organizations operate, evolve, and develop in a way that sustains and adds value - especially to the society within which they operate. We can be a bystander or a leader. We can help re-arrange the deck chairs on the Titanic or we can help re-build the ship for the conditions it is now sailing in.

5.7 Internal Control and Risk of Failure

Traditional approaches to controls have focused heavily on process - although the impact of human behavior has been recognized and addressed to some degree; however, the once accepted "rationality" of human behavior is now being increasingly questioned; this could also have a significant impact on risk management and controls. The field of economics once based on rationality of behavior has already developed new understandings under the umbrella of behavioral economics and more recently the American Accounting Association has been publishing articles outlining the impact of behavior in the field of accounting. These new theories and approaches recognize that the understanding of human behavior has a significant impact in organizational planning, operations, risk management and controls.

It seems that errant human behaviour, which has always been a risk, has become a much more critical issue in the asset light organization. However good control systems are, management cannot be "on top" of everything all the time. The essence of a good control system is that it balances the need to for a light touch on human behaviour to allow flexibility, innovation, and creativity, (critical factors for business success) with approaches that allow it to be "just in control" so that unplanned actions can be highlighted quickly, and any negative impact minimized.

> *"Now, more than ever, management is a balancing act — the juggling of contradictions to try to get the best of attractive but opposing alternatives. <u>Order is a temporary illusion</u>, strategy a moving target. Leaders cannot impose authority on a world of constant motion; they can only hope to steer some of that action toward productive ends."*
>
> Rosabeth Moss Kanter, Harvard Business School professor, consultant, and author

It is for this reason that the failure of accounting to lead investments in human management systems involved with establishing desired behaviours, effective hiring including pre-employment testing, constant evaluation of leadership behaviour, independent assessments of employee behaviour and other approaches, might be a contributing factor to organizational "failure through surprises." Using metrics like the number of training hours to report on "the people aspects" means almost nothing in an environment where human behaviour is at the core of effective control and value stabilization.

After the big scandals in the early 2000's which were followed by rapid changes in corporate guidance and legislation such as the implementation of SOX (Sarbanes-Oxley) in the USA, one would expect things to settle down a bit and the number of scandals to decline. As we can see that was not the case. Not only did corporate problems occur, but the whole system also came close to collapse.

If there was ever a siren call for change this was it. The events of the first 20 years of the 21st century turned out to be challenging and reinforced the belief in many quarters that "the whole system" was flawed and that capitalism should be thrown out and replaced by something new.

The era had started out with problems. The tech boom had bust; ENRON was followed by WorldCom and Tyco and these led to an economic downturn. However new regulatory bodies were in place - the FCA in the UK and PCAOB in the USA as examples both of whose mandates were to oversee the work of auditors of public companies; accountants had already come under increased scrutiny where it was felt that their work needed oversight. In effect we now had "checkers to check the checkers." Whatever one's beliefs, this all adds cost and bureaucracy to the "free enterprise system." But as the world was to discover this was to make minimal difference from the public's perspective.

There are a number of key events that occurred over the next 20 years; each of these had an impact on either the overall financial system, the accounting profession and, most importantly the general public's belief in the system of economic management that provided employment for so many accountants. To avoid too much detail, we can break these events into significant milestones that furthered the need for change:

The continued growth of the "intangible based, asset light" economy where intangibles continued to grow into the majority of corporate "assets" and consumed an increasing portion of annual corporate resources or cash flows; this impacted the profession through:

- Understanding financial implications of resources being allocated to developing intangibles by management.
- Understanding the growing level of "value" from these investments, and
- Focusing attention on the financial implications of M&A's - particularly those involving "asset light organizations like technology firms, banks and financial services and others.
- Failure of traditional audits to assess going concern of business enterprise.
- Inability of the newly developed regulatory bodies to have a major positive impact on corporate financial problems.
- The 2008 - 2010 financial crisis that further illustrated the complexity of inter-connected financial markets and the risks being taken to remain competitive.
- The growing awareness among the public, that tax planning and minimization often developed and implemented by accounting firms, while good for individuals and corporations was not serving the interests of society nor did them seem "fair and ethical" to the public.

These issues impacted both the technical underpinnings of accounting for both financial and management accountants and also placed auditors in the position of often "having failed" in their audit responsibilities. The historic "assurance" that the public and regulators perceived to be the "sign of good health" proved inadequate in an economy where many of the underpinnings of a successful business model were no longer part of an audit mandate.

5.8 Internal Control and Human Behaviour

Hidden behind the efforts to improve ethical behaviour, especially within the intents behind Sarbanes-Oxley enacted after the ENRON failure, was the importance of "the tone at the top" in developing an audit approach to the risk that would need to be addressed as part of an organizations internal control system. However, it falls under the responsibility of the accountants internally to ensure that an adequate system of controls in in place to protect the organizations assets (and through this what used to be its value) - by definition including both tangible and intangible aspects. The shift to an asset-light framework substantially changes where risk exists and how it might affect an organizations financial position. After all, loss of intangible capability will result in increased operating costs to replace such capability - thus it is a risk issue.

The goal of internal control systems is to have in place "checks and balances" that minimize potential losses to the organization while allowing it to operate effectively. Internal control systems form a core part of an organizations approach to governance and risk management. Deciding upon tolerance for risk rests with owners, investors and shareholders and is a central responsibility of a board and its approach to governance. For the accountant internal controls should be the result of a clear understanding of organizational risk, supported by a policy towards control approaches to eliminate, mitigate, minimize, share, or accept the defined risks.

As new approaches to understanding non-financial aspects of an organizations business model have developed, it raises the question about risk assessment and controls. Organizational risk extends to these other non-financial areas that are known to contribute to the gap between market value and book value. However, although the intangible "assets" that comprise a large proportion of this assigned value they do not appear on the balance sheet. However, there are significant financial risks associated with any depletion or loss of such intangible capabilities and while not causing the operation to have a balance sheet write -off it would cause operational cost impacts.

Specialists in risk management have recognized this and have promoted the concept of enterprise risk management; the intent is to ensure that ALL areas of risk are assessed risk and controls are evaluated on a "total enterprise" impact. However, there are two issues; first many organizations do not have sophisticated risk management systems nor have they carried out a recent risk assessment using an enterprise wide approach. Second, accountants have often not been involved in addressing the reasons behind, and the potential either non-financial controls or financial impacts. The challenges to the accountant include knowing what these risks are and ensuring that they are being addressed where necessary, as a loss will in fact deplete value and at worst render the organization incapable of operating as a going concern.

5.9 International Taxation and the Panama Papers

In the early 2000's tax planning continued to grow as a way to minimize corporate expense and thus create competitive advantage. For most of the public this was a "grey, almost invisible" area. Every so often stories would appear in the media about tax avoidance, many of these citing organizations that had grown during the high tech era and operated globally. Amazon, Apple, and Google were often mentioned[23];

In 2016, Google was accused of using two regulatory loopholes, nicknamed the 'double Irish' and 'Dutch sandwich', allowing it to pay just six percent corporation tax rather than the required 19.3 percent. The same year, Apple was ordered to pay $15.4bn in back taxes to Ireland after it was revealed that the company paid just one percent tax on its European profits in 2003, down to 0.005 percent in 2014.

UK politicians also called for a boycott of Amazon in 2014 when it was revealed the company had paid just £4.2m ($5.6m) in tax on sales of £4.3bn ($5.7bn). It was able to do this by funnelling payments made in the EU through a subsidiary based in Luxembourg.

---

[23] "Top 5 tax scandals," Sophie Perryer, Oct 16th 2018, World Finance Magazine

How Accountants Lost their Balance

The e-commerce giant claims it has since cleaned up its act, but in 2018 it paid just £4.6m ($6.1m) in tax, despite profits hitting a £72.3m ($95.5m) high.

Accountants were "just doing their job" and focusing their attention on what was best for the client, but to the public this was an increasing area of frustration with the system. There had also been stories in the press for many years about high net worth individuals also moving money to off-shore tax havens, but many people felt that it was "just the way things were." However, one could say "the lid blew off" the depth and breadth of the global taxation issue with the release of the "Panama Papers." 11.5 million leaked documents that detailed financial and attorney–client information for more than 214,488 offshore entities were leaked beginning on 3 April 2016.

These documents, some dating back to the 1970s, were created by, and taken from, Panamanian law firm and corporate service provider Mossack Fonseca. This added to the public scepticism around the fairness of the financial system. As people in many western countries were being downsized or their wages frozen it appeared that not just corporations, but the ultra-wealthy, and people that were part of public life were all enjoying the benefits of tax evasion.

"…the leaked documents contain identity information about the shareholders and directors of 214,000 shell companies set up by Mossack Fonseca, as well as some of their financial transactions. It is generally not against the law (in and of itself) to own an offshore shell company, although offshore shell companies may sometimes be used for illegal purposes.

The journalists on the investigative team found business transactions by many important figures in world politics, sports, and art. While many of the transactions were legal, since the data is incomplete, questions remain in many other cases; still others seem to clearly indicate ethical if not legal impropriety. Some disclosures – tax avoidance in poor countries by very wealthy entities and individuals for example – lead to questions on moral grounds[24]".

For "moral grounds" substitute "ethical behaviour." It was not just the revelations about the scope and depth of tax avoidance, but the information that led to the realization that organizations were utilizing these approaches to

---

[24] Extracted from Wikipedia re the Panama Papers

cover illegal activities such as avoiding UN or other national sanctions that would have applied in the home domicile of a company; to transfer monies for bribes and other illegal activities; to hide funds that had been obtained by fraud, bribery, or other illegal sources (an issue that legislation like the FCPA and the UN agreement were supposed to have started to eliminate).

The result was that the role of the accounting profession in tax avoidance was confirmed but also that the public's perception about the business community having the size and capability to avoid the law for their own benefit was reinforced. In several situations, based on information revealed as part of the Panama Papers, investigators were able to investigate broader illegal issues which resulted in prosecutions.

One of the challenges the profession faces in adaptability is that there are many other interests that the profession sees as more important than the underlying issue of human behaviour and the shift in the underlying role and accountability of the profession. A 2018 article in a UK publication[25], had the following headline:

The profession's biggest challenges

The article initially focused on several issues that were seen to be "top of mind" in the profession at the time (2018) that included *"…Staffing, succession planning, tax reform, cybersecurity, merger mania, commoditization of core services, the demand for more CPAs, and the search for relevance — as important as all these issues are to accountants, they pale in comparison to two overarching concerns in the minds of the profession's leaders: the impact of new technologies, and accounting's ability to adapt to the rapid pace of change."* However, there was a key observation later in the article that began to address the underlying challenges".

Despite widespread belief that advancements in technology represent a major challenge for accountants, there was an almost equally widespread belief that they could also offer solutions to many of the profession's problems, and opportunities for significant growth.

---

[25] "Accounting Today," Daniel Hood, October 01, 2018

That raised a red flag, however, for CPA Trendlines CEO (and former Accounting Today editor-in-chief) Rick Telberg, who warned against an over-reliance on non-human solutions.

"Too many firms are looking for solutions from new technology, software and apps, to the detriment of skills-building and process improvements that would better serve clients with broader and deeper services," he said. "In short, firms are primarily using technology to reduce costs and increase productivity, instead of leveraging technology to get better at doing what clients want most — providing proactive insight, analysis and guidance. Technology can replace people, and it is you can see it in hiring trends and in per-partner incomes. But technology cannot replace the judgment and wisdom that clients really want from their accountants. This techno-centric behavior is pushing aside the client-centric habits that have made accounting the great profession it remains today. The profession does so at its peril."

This statement seems to underline both the role of human "intellectual capital" in observing and "connecting the dots" when involved in an audit of an organization, but also suggests that the profession is overly focused on cost reduction rather than the concept of adding value. Given the todays reality that the auditors face a conflict in trying to deliver both audits and fee based consultative services, maybe the issue of adding value should come through a different scope relative to the role of audit?

This "trust gap" is not limited to the US, UK and a few other countries but is global, reflecting the pervasive reality of the profession. A 2019 article in a key publication of the profession in Australia[26]

"The business community generally, and the financial services sector especially, is in the grip of a worldwide trust crisis. But while accountants remain relatively unscathed — at least compared with lawyers, bankers, and politicians — that is no excuse for complacency.

Wholeheartedly embracing the commitment to standards and ethics that underpin being a chartered accountant will be critical if the profession is to successfully bridge the trust gap. That is one of the key findings in The Future of Trust: New Technology Meets Old Values report by Chartered Accountants Australia and New Zealand, released in March 2019.

---

[26] "How accountants can survive the public trust crisis,: Sally Rose and Nina Hendy, 9th April 2019, Acuity Magazine

How Accountants Lost their Balance

In a 2018 article, Steven Mintz presented a well balanced, yet concerning assessment of the challenges of auditors being able to serve the public interest. In his opening brief he summarizes:

The commitment to serve the public interest in accounting has eroded, as personal and business relationships with clients and client management increasingly create conflicts of interest. Many such relationships have created barriers to objective and impartial decision making and threatened the independence of the audit function.

The 2014 recodification of the AICPA Code of Professional Conduct attempts to deal with a conflict of interests when providing attest services through a threats-and-safeguards approach. The problem with this approach is that conflicts may still be permissible as long as they can be sufficiently mitigated by safeguards—creating a situational ethic rather than an outright prohibition when such conflicts exist[27].

The article identifies the challenges that public accountants have in serving the public; he shows this in both an historical context as well as in the evolving evidence that suggest maintaining the balance is all but impossible. Although the AICPA codes have been updated since he provides examples of how all the major global audit forms had run "afoul" of the SEC for apparent conflicts of interest in 2013 (as an example). His article reinforces the "journey of decline" that forms the base of this book.

It seems that the "Big 4" accounting firms, in spite of their best efforts to appear ethical and to "rise above" the criticism, continue to face challenges in the media about their capability of protecting the public. More challenging is that it might appear from the media that when people come forward to try and identify ethical issues and challenges "the system seem to want to fight it." The problem from seeing these things in the media is that they are usually one-sided, however with all the scandals that HAVE been proven and all of the failures that HAVE occurred after audits, maybe it is time for a reflective look by the profession on its own role as being "fit for purpose" in the reality of the business world today?

---

[27] "Accounting in the Public Interest. An Historical Perspective on Professional Ethics," Steven Mintz, PhD., March 2018 Issue. The CPA Journal

Accounting firm EY fights fires on three audit cases that threaten its global reputation

Accountant's role with Dubai gold company, NMC Health and Wirecard put its controls under scrutiny

FT Financial Times
Tabby Kinder and Dan McCrum

This was the headline from the Financial Times November 12th, 2020; it was followed by these revelations"

"Amjad Rihan was …one of the few people to ever take on a prominent accounting firm in court, Rihan had sued EY for forcing him out after he exposed a string of alleged illegal activities by a Dubai gold company and a subsequent cover-up by its auditors.

"I never set out to be a whistleblower but turning a blind eye was not an option," he said, speaking from the house in Warwick where he eventually landed after fleeing the Middle East. "Most of the wealth in the world is audited by the 'Big Four' accountants. It is not always in the interest of the powerful to point out when something goes wrong."

It is the first time he has reflected publicly on his story since an English High Court judge ordered EY to pay him US$11 million in April. The court accepted claims that EY had participated in accounting misconduct that reached its senior ranks. According to the judgment, the firm colluded with Kaloti Jewellery International to hide illicit exports and helped obscure audit findings that included suspected money laundering.

The accounting firm is attempting to appeal the judge's decision. It claimed Rihan, who became one of EY's youngest partners aged 36, was a "liar and opportunist," according to the judge's summary, and that the allegations were "completely without merit."

What went wrong? E&Y is not the sort of firm that would promote a 36 year old to a partnership position without having done its homework and feeling he was competent to "do the job?" Partners are usually not underpaid and often, because of the firms being partnerships, receive a share of the profits. One might think that Rihan had more to lose by coming forward. The sheer fact that situations like this are occurring suggests that maybe the system needs improvement? Also, in a follow up related article[28] it seems that there was a problem that still remains some 8 years after the Rihan case:

But to retain the trade, the UAE may have to police the sector better, having been the focus of numerous reports about its role in the dirty gold trade, and chastised by the Financial Action Task Force (FATF), the world's standards settings body for anti-money laundering rules, for inadequate oversight of the sector in an evaluation report published in April.

A report by the UK's Home Office and Treasury earlier in December also named the UAE as a jurisdiction vulnerable to money laundering by criminal networks because of the ease with which gold and cash could be moved through the country.

Should Rihan have taken a different approach? What do we know about what happened internally? Should Rihan have been able to make his case on a confidential basis to either his professional association (probably the ICAEW) or to the oversight agency, the FCA? The only thing we really know is that this event, combined with twenty plus years of corporate scandals and failures indicates that accounting is "out of balance?"

---

[28] Dubai, Switzerland, London: How the UAE became a smuggling hub for 'blood gold' Paul Cochrane, 26 December 2020, Middle East Eye

6. Mergers, Acquisitions, Goodwill, and Impairment

This chapter will provide a brief bridge between the changing economic and business structures and the increasing challenges posed by the growing level of intangibles on mergers and acquisitions. For the accounting profession this has always been a challenging area and grew in importance as the gap between book values and market values developed. There are several issues that this era has presented:

- M&A's in the service sector, which traditionally created a large amount of goodwill, continued to grow as the sector grew.
- As the overall economy shifted towards a "knowledge economy" the amount of goodwill in almost every merger increased.
- There is little substantive understanding of what the goodwill acquired is comprised of in terms of intangible value and organizational capability, leading to challenges in managing, sustaining, and maintaining its value.
- If M&A's aimed at achieving "economies of scale" through integration and cost cutting, taking action to achieve this, often significantly depleted the value of intangibles.
- As goodwill has grown it has become for many acquirers the largest asset; without it, they would be negative equity.
- Impairment of goodwill (through "real" loss of value or through loss of identity) has created annual financial write-off's that are in the billions.

Mergers and Acquisitions have a long history but significantly grew after the 1980's. We can look back on the early years and in many cases between about the late 1800's until the depression (1930's) most appear to have been consolidation moves as industries which developed during the industrial revolution needed "scale" to grow. This is probably the reason that the US Anti-Trust laws were enacted during the same time period - scale created monopolies which were bad for competition and the consumer and which needed to be guarded against; many of the early legal cases were against the oil industry, the railroad industry, and the steel industry.

Many of these large scale organizations were capital intensive and saw consolidation as a way to gain economies of scale; they had also been some of the earlier growth industries of the industrial revolution. At this time, many of these M&A's mainly involved the acquisition of tangible assets and so the issue of "goodwill" - the excess of purchase price over book value was not a major consideration. From an accounting perspective, goodwill, in the early years was referred to as a "nothing" and usually written off or amortized in the same way as a tangible asset over its' useful life. However, there were often expectations of significant savings from such consolidations and these were often not fully realized.

After the depression, M&A activity resumed and now many organizations, including those who held a dominant position in an existing industry and probably would not be able to grow further in the core business, looked at acquisitions in other industries as a way of diversification and risk reduction. One great example is US based ITT; started in 1920, it by the 1960's it had grown to be a significant supplier of telephone switching equipment and services. ITT refers to its' next growth phase as the "Conglomerate Years 1960 - 1977" during which it acquired more than 350 companies across a broad range of industries. It grew from a telephone based company with sales of $760 million to a multi focused conglomerate with sales of $17 billion. As it purchased more companies in the service industry such as hotel groups, there would have been a growing portion of intangible assets.

6.1 M&A's in the Knowledge Economy

Mergers and acquisitions started to grow significantly in the early 1980's from an average (worldwide[29]) of about $400 billion to a high point of over $4 trillion per year in the peak year of 2007. By 2019 the M&A growth curve was at an average annual level of about $3.5 trillion per year. Underlying this was an economic shift to a service economy - and even in manufacturing, knowledge capital (intangible) now replaced direct labour as software engineers and designers replaced direct assembly line workers. ***This resulted in the increasing level of M&A's also including a growing level of goodwill.***

It has been my personal opinion for a long time that there has been an inadequate bridge between accounting and the underlying value and operational capability to sustain the goodwill being acquired. The rules on accounting for M&A's and goodwill in particular have changed over the years but there remain significant gaps in an investor understanding of the risks associated with the acquisition of these intangibles and of the oversight required to sustain the value attributed to it. The issue of a test for "impairment" is important but is, in my opinion a bit of a "cop out" on the issue of reporting "where the money went" to owners and others.

The outcome of this increase in M&A activity and the underlying growth of intangibles including goodwill on the balance sheets of organizations created increased challenges for auditors as well as other accountants. In effect there was a growing asset that could not be verified and which, increasingly audits had to depend upon managements assessment as to impairment. As organizations integrated existing and acquired operations in order to achieve "economies of scale" and the planned benefits of the merger or acquisition, it became almost impossible to assess impairment of the goodwill that had been created at time of acquisition.

Whilst goodwill was minimal and considered a "nothing" this was not an issue for owners and investors; however, as an increasingly large portion of an investor's capital was allocated to goodwill and intangibles the question of "where did my money go" and "what is my investment worth" took on greater significance. Where an accountant's verification and opinion of balance sheet

---

[29] Statista.com Value of mergers and acquisitions (M&A) worldwide from 1985 to 2019

values had in the past provided assurance of underlying quality and "worth," the quality of validation became increasingly more challenging. Two events started to occur that further eroded confidence in financial reports.

First, many mergers and acquisitions failed to deliver on the promised benefits; in a study as early as 1999, KPMG[30] assessed 700 cross border M&A deals between 1996 and 1998 where, when initially, 82% of respondents indicated the deal was a success. However, when these deals were analyzed it was revealed that only 17% had added value to the combined organizations shareholders, 30% made no discernable difference and as many as 53% actually destroyed value. As we will see later, these failed M&A's were to become a major issue in the confidence in the way business conducted itself and the ability to rely on financial reporting as an indicator of value. The second underlying change was to have an even greater impact as the foundations of the economy started to shift away from tangible assets. This we will discuss next!

6.2 Period of consolidation and turmoil

Several key factors impacted the start of the new century but only some of these created major changes for the accounting profession. Issues such as the terrorist attacks that took place over the period especially the 7/11 attack of the World Trade Centre impacted confidence in the general population; there were also international impacts as "the west" responded. Competitive pressures on not only the US but many western economies increased as China enjoyed double digit economic growth for the many years, increasing their share of world trade, and causing western manufacturers to further consolidate operations and implement downsizing, outsourcing and the move of operations from higher cost to lower cost countries.

Mergers and acquisitions, continuing to grow the creation of "goodwill" on company's balance sheets were a key part of the response to growing competition. One of the challenges increasingly seen was the failure of some of these transactions; it continued to be apparent that wringing costs savings

---

9

out of mergers was a challenge and that, in many cases trying to put organizations together often failed because of different "cultures."

While the financial impact of M&A's continued to grow, so did the write off's and failures. In the period 2000 - 2009 almost 50% of the "worst mergers ever" in terms of both write-off's and the failures to integrate took place. The total transaction value of these 17 failed "marriages" was $326 billion. The organizations reflect the underlying changes taking place in the economy - probably greatest among these the continued growth and consolidation in technology; they include examples such as

- AOL / Time Warner for $164 billion and
- Alcatel / Lucent $13.4 billion.

These problems followed a spate of failures in the late 1990's including the Daimler / Chrysler merger in 1998 for $36 billion, which Daimler later sold 80% of Chrysler to Cerberus Management for $7 billion (a loss, not accounting for the monies spent in trying to make it work, of $29 billion). The key issue is that the period was one of turmoil and re-structuring as technologies developed, and international trade shifted from west to east.

One of the most important underlying trends for accounting was the shift to intangible assets as organizations moved from "owning" many of the resources that they used in their business model to developing partnerships with suppliers and others. Developing these capabilities required significant shifts in financial resources which, because of accounting standards were all "buried" in operating costs. Organizations that successfully created a business model for the "new economy" would be of greater value in the marketplace than one who had less well developed capabilities; however, investors were often unaware of the financial impact and it became a challenge for senior managers to "tell their story" as they shifted resources where needed. Additionally, there were limited mechanisms for investors to ask the question to address the risk of whether, once created these capabilities were being sustained in order to maintain operational competitiveness and capability. As long as "the bottom line" stayed in the range expected everything appeared well.

6.3 The "Goodwill" issue

One particular event in 2017 proved that these underlying capabilities were indeed critical, and traditional audits would fail to identify the problems - especially in terms of how they impact an organization being a "going concern." At time of the Carillion failure, the company was carrying over £1.57 billion of goodwill on its books as a result of mergers and acquisitions and net assets of $729.9 million. Because of accounting approaches to goodwill there is typically a larger portion of acquisition costs associated with intangibles (and thus goodwill) in "asset light" organizations. This includes Carillion but also includes the significant growth of asset-light, intangible asset based organizations that were developing in the knowledge economy. To obtain some perspective of goodwill value below is a summary based on the largest goodwill balances shown in 2018 reporting of S&P 500 companies:

Company	Goodwill	Total Assets	Goodwill as %
AT&T	$146.4	$531.9	27.5%
Berkshire Hathaway	$81.0	$707.8	11.4%
CVS Health	$78.7	$196.5	40.0%
Bank of America	$69.0	$2,354.5	2.9%
Comcast	$66.2	$251.7	26.3%
General Electric	$59.6	$309.1	19.3%
DuPont	$59.0	$188.0	31.4%
United Health Group	$58.9	$152.2	38.7%
Pfizer	$53.4	$159.4	33.5%
United Technologies	$48.1	$134.2	5.3%
JPMorgan Chase	$47.5	$2,622.5	1.8%
Allergan	$45.9	$101.8	45.1%
Procter & Gamble	$45.2	$118.3	38.2%
Cigna	$44.5	$153.2	29.0%
Medtronic	$40.0	$89.7	44.6%

These top fifteen companies are carrying about $1 trillion in goodwill which is about 12% of the asset balances but a much higher percentage of their net book value after liabilities are deducted. As an example, AT&T liabilities at this point were $338.0 billion so the net book value was $193.9 of which goodwill was $146.4 or 76% - i.e., 76% of their book value was goodwill. So, this has become a substantial asset on corporate balance sheets; according to a recent article in the Wall Street Journal[31],

"A brewing battle over how to treat more than $5.5 trillion in assets on company books is pitting investors against businesses, investment advisers against academics and even banks against their own trade association."

"When Amazon.com Inc. bought Whole Foods Market Inc. for $13.7 billion in 2017, the e-commerce giant paid $9 billion more than the value of the supermarket's stores and other net assets. That amount was added to Amazon's books as goodwill."

The recent wave of deal making has created a pile of goodwill. There were $7.4 trillion in U.S. deals the five years through 2019, the highest five-year tally for at least two decades, according to Dealogic.

S&P 500 companies had $3.5 trillion worth of goodwill on their books at the end of September, according to data provider Calcbench. This was up 67% from 2013 and represented 9% of total S&P 500 assets and 42% of total equity, the Calcbench data show.

Clearly goodwill and the accounting for the premium related to intangibles is a big issue. These numbers probably only represent the "tip of the iceberg." If this is what is visible on M&A's when the difference between book and market is crystallized during a merger and acquisition, how much larger is the amount of cash flow impacting operations, within those organizations who are creating internal "goodwill" that is being written off against expenses?

Duff & Phelps produce an annual report on goodwill trends in the US and in their 2018 report[32] they show that M&A activity generated an additional goodwill amount which was added to corporate balance sheets of $319 billion and a write-off for impairment of $35.1 billion. From this we can see that the overall goodwill balance continues to climb yet a portion of the growing balance is being written off against earnings. So, the balance is an issue, representing an increasing amount of corporate assets and impairment is an

---

[31] "Goodwill Sparks Deep Division, at Least on Balance Sheets" John Eaglesham, Jan. 21, 2020

[32] Duff & Phelps 2018 US Impairment study for year ended December 2017

issue in that what was "purchased for value" i.e., cost investors money, is being written off as now worthless.

This concern is not a new issue as it started to develop during the consolidation of traditional organizations and the growth of high technology in the 1990's. A paper which looked at 1994 goodwill showed the following top 5 organizations in the US:

Company	Goodwill $M	Total Assets $M	Ratio
WorldCom Inc.	$2,071	$3,430	60%
First Financial Management Corp.	$1,741	$3,136	56%
Dow Jones & Co. Inc.	$1,305	$2,446	53%
FHP International Corp.	$1,074	$2,169	50%
American Home Products Corp.	$9,181	$21,675	42%

Yes, the first on the list is the same WorldCom that was a scandal in 2002, when they tried to inflate earnings to sustain the stock price; an internal auditor discovered $3.8 billion in fraudulent entries and its assets were overstated by $11 billion by that point.

Some impairments have arisen because the original intent of the merger failed; recent examples are a $22.6 billion hit to 2018 earnings at GE (one of the largest ever); a $15.9 billion write off at Heinz in 2018; an $8.4 billion write off at Proctor & Gamble in 2019; Allergan with a $5.7 billion write off in 2018 after a $3.9 billion hit in 2017.

The impact that intangibles was having on the economy was clear and it has continued to be a challenge for regulators and accountants. It appears that finally FASB are going to take another look at goodwill - but the challenges are significant.

Early indications are that the main issue to be addressed, is the "impairment testing." The CPA article stated *"Many businesses however deem this method, which was introduced in 2001, as costly and subjective. Some investors have criticized the process because goodwill impairments often occur years after an acquisition, lagging behind market moves. The FASB is now considering changing the process to help reduce companies' costs, even though it doesn't have a formal proposal yet."*

One idea is to go back to the old "straight line amortization" approach. However, the article goes on to say *"Even though some investors support amortization, others, alongside analysts and academics, have criticized it because they think it doesn't provide useful information. "Amortization is a very arbitrary annual number to put on the financial statements," said Ray Pfeiffer, an associate accounting professor at Simmons University in Boston. "It doesn't reflect at all the actual change in the value of goodwill."*

The greatest challenge is that once again the profession is looking at goodwill "after the fact." The problem is that goodwill is "not just a number" but a representation of the inherent value that organizations being acquired have created as they built their intangible capacity to generate earnings. Costs which when incurred were already written off as expenses. Goodwill puts them back on the balance sheet. This is a bigger problem that amortization? In this issue, the profession is "way out of balance" with the reality of what is going on "behind the numbers."

7. Change and the Management Accountant

All of the challenges discussed in the previous chapters affect all accountants - however management accounting itself developed to support the evolution of the industrial revolution. Its' foundations are built in the factories and workshops of the age of mass production - as its' original name, Cost and Works Accountants (ACWA), represents in the UK. Management accounting built on the development of scientific management that sought to establish standards processes for labour and materials consumed by each unit of production. The early work of Frederik Taylor (1856 - 1915) who led the industrial efficiency movement formed a foundation for standard costing and the allocation of overheads, with much of the pioneering work in developing costing systems taking place in organizations such as Du Pont and General Motors.

During this period, the aligning of financial costs with organizational investment decisions through the use of more evaluative techniques such as ROI (Return on Investment) also developed as did more detailed financial planning and modeling. By the middle of the 20th century the base for management accounting had been laid and as industry expanded the demand for and importance of management accounting continued to grow. As business became more competitive in the latter part of the 20th century understanding costs played an increasingly important role in effective decision making.

7.1 Supporting management

Management accountants worked side-by-side with operational managers and in most mature manufacturing organizations few decisions were made without the input from the accountants. While ROI techniques helped with decision making around capital equipment managers also depended on cost reporting and feedback to address opportunities for cost improvement. In the 1970's standard cost accounting, often combined with variance analysis was a critical building block in managing and controlling costs. Budgets and spending controls were prominent tools in managing financial performance and providing assurance that earnings targets were "on track."

Responsibility accounting - the practise of having all costs assigned to either a product or a responsible manager through a system of cost centres was woven into a manager's responsibility and often spending controls formed a part of compensation packages. Senior executives in large corporations used management accounting as a critical aspect of managing their business. Harold Geneen who was CEO of ITT from 1959 - 1977 (International Telephone and Telegraph Corp) - which was discussed in the segment on mergers and acquisitions, grew the business from $765 million in sales to over $17 billion and was a proponent of running the business by the numbers. Jack Welch who joined General Electric in 1960 and became the famed CEO from 1981 - 2001 was also a great believer in financial management and controls; many management accountants received their training at GE and once qualified were in great demand elsewhere.

However, Jack Welch was also known as a harsh critic of the budgetary process if not managed effectively. He says in his book [33] "…*(budgeting) sucks the time, energy, fun and big dreams out of an organization.*" This problem with "execution rather than intent" was a problem in the deployment of many management accounting approaches and Jack Welch identified a key failure with business support systems that easily occurs. The budget process can also be costly - one estimate from Ford was they spent over $1.2 billion annually on the process.

Many of the traditional approaches to cost management were built on a "command and control" approach to management. Goals and targets would be set by senior managers and lower levels of management and supervision would then be required to comply and implement. There was little room for innovation and creativity. This worked reasonably well in a stable business environment but as competition increased so did the speed of change and the

---

[33] "Winning," Jack Welch, 2005, Harper Collins

need for innovation and creativity. Management accountants found themselves constantly creating updated forecasts as budgets became increasingly outdated as a fiscal year went on. To make matters worse, especially in large organizations, budgets were often not "signed off and approved" until several months into a fiscal year so the process of using budgets as control systems started to seem less effective.

Additionally, many budgeting processes started off with the involvement of the operational staff who were in control of the spending and who understood the link between the financial resources needed and the operational tasks to be performed. Sadly, as these budgets were consolidated to show the fiscal plan for the budget time period, they often failed to meet the earnings expectations of senior managers or boards of directors and were often sent back to be updated and improved. As planning time frames shrank and the new year rolled around the time for discussion eroded and budgets became directive to be adhered to - often incorporating major disconnects between what was supposed to be achieved operationally and the funding available.

There is a school of thought that believes that limiting budgets and cutting back on staff is the only way to force operational improvement, so in many organizations this approach was not seen as a problem. However, when it came to "human aspects" of employee engagement, commitment and motivation, managers who had budgets forced on them often failed to see the positive opportunity impact; this became especially important when their incentive pay was linked to budgets that had not been agreed to. Budgets became more and more onerous and of less value. Budgets also became less valuable as managers began to believe they were not worth the effort or that the process was flawed. Often managers, believing that budgets would be cut anyway, would submit overstated expectations believing that they would be reduced, and the final number would be what they wanted anyway.

In other cases, managers saw limited value in putting a lot of effort into budgeting and would take the current "run rate" of spending and increment it for the next year without much thought on content or the link to operational processes, plans and programs. This was sometimes true of sales budgets where, again, sales managers would increment the last years actual sales without developing specific targets by area or product or salesperson. Through all of these managers were essentially responding to a belief system that saw some of these approaches to financial control as being flawed. It might be remembered that this was the attitude and culture towards budgets when new tools, such as Hoshin-Kanri were being developed in the 1980's - not a receptive audience!

While budgets formed a key tool for effective management so did product costing systems. Standard costing together with variance analysis was probably the favourite and most universally used but other approaches such as process costing for chemicals and other process industries, project costing for supporting projects such as construction and others. Standard costing, like budgeting tended to work well in a stable environment. Costs were established for the upcoming fiscal year and then each month they were checked against actual results (often using the tool of variance analysis) in order to identify what action was needed. Labour rates were often pre-determined and controlled by job position (often within a union contract) while materials costs were negotiated under annual contract agreements with suppliers.

Usually, operations or production managers were responsible for their direct product costs while all indirect and overhead costs were controlled by each manager through their own cost centre. In order to obtain total product costs overheads were usually allocated to each product on some pre-determined basis. Many managers, especially at the more senior levels were often responsible for a divisional, regional or some other "sub-level" of profitability statements, and in order to apportion shared overhead costs to each business unit, again these were allocated to the manager. It was not unusual for a manager's incentive compensation to also be linked to profitability and the issue of allocated costs often came up as an area of disagreement as the manager often had little control over what these costs were. Financial managers employed in industry often heard the phrase "…but it just doesn't make sense" when looking at statements especially those that included allocations. It is not clear that management accountants were continuing to be seen as adding value.

Two operational changes were having a massive impact on the traditional approach to costing. Allocations and the management of indirect overhead costs were becoming a growing problem; in the early days of standard costs, the direct costs portion (labour and materials) of product costs were usually more than 50% of total costs and more often reached 60 or 70%. Although allocating these costs to products on some relevant basis carried with it some level of inaccuracy it was less of a problem. As gross margins shrank in an increasingly competitive market, and indirect costs became a growing component of total product costs, any implicit errors in the allocation of overheads became magnified. The impact is shown on the following chart which was created to demonstrate the difference between applying the "old" standard cost and allocations approach and the newer ABC or Activity Based Costing approach that attributed all costs based on consumption of resources[34]:

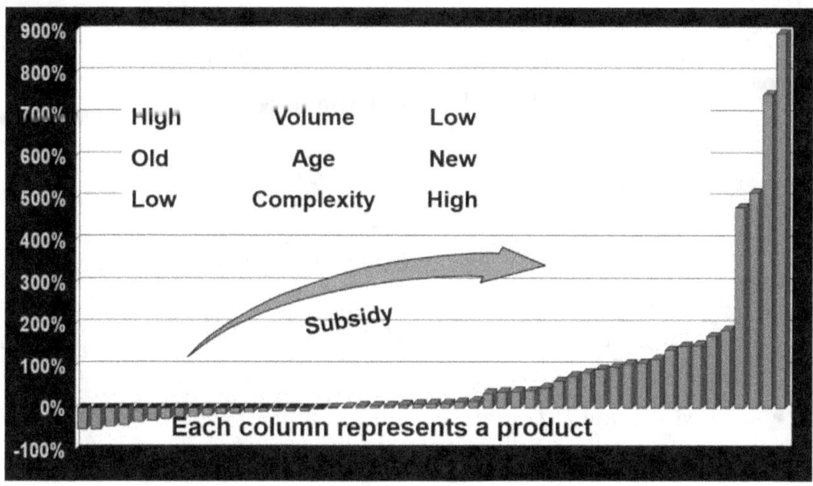

The scale on the left is the change on cost between using allocations and a more accurate approach (ABC) to distributing overheads to product cost; while the costs of about 30% of older, high volume, low complexity products actually decreased in price, and about and 20% showed limited change, almost 50% of products were actually costing significantly more than traditional approaches to costing were telling management.

This was a MAJOR failing in how management accounting approaches ere impacting decision making. It eventually reached a point where managers were focusing their attention on the 30% of sales that appeared to carry the highest margins when, in fact, if overheads were attributed correctly it would be

---

[34] Example from FMI Inc.

revealed that these 50% of sales were actually ALL depleting profits that were being earned by products that had previously appeared less profitable. This problem drove the wrong decision making and caused managers to focus on product decisions that, after being made delivered a totally different result.

The second major issue was the operational shift to what, at the time, were often referred to as Japanese management techniques. Efforts to improve quality, that were discussed earlier, started to lead mangers to research different operational approaches to manufacturing. Several concepts that have been discussed, were introduced during this period and included:

- Hoshin Kanri (planning and improvement)
- KANBAN and JIT - Just in Time inventory
- Kaizen and continual improvement
- Operational techniques like SMED (Single Minute Exchange of Dies)
- Employee engagement, work groups, teams, labour mobility, and cross training
- 5S (Clean up the shop floor: Sort, Set-in-Order, Shine, Standardize, Sustain)
- TPM - Total Productive Maintenance
- SPC, Statistical Process Control (followed by 6 SIGMA)
- Poka Yoke or mistake proofing (work and processes)

Almost all of these techniques became the building blocks to a revolution in manufacturing; historically, mass production techniques had been adopted which were characterized by long production runs and minimized downtime, designed to optimize the recovery of expensive fixed investment created by the use of capital intensive organizations. These approaches had reduced flexibility, "dumbed down" the work to make it repetitive and tedious for employees, and generally created a culture that "stopping for anything" was seen as a problem to be avoided. If equipment problems were reported, employees were expected to work around it; if quality problems were detected then they should be investigated by the inspectors and quality management and "the line should be kept running."

How Accountants Lost their Balance

By studying approaches used in countries like Japan it became apparent that they were in many cases the opposite of the approaches which characterized "the west" and were a carry over from the industrial revolution. The unfortunate problem was that almost ALL approaches to manufacturing costing approaches were founded on the same historical frameworks. As operations shifted to what became called "lean manufacturing," "agile operations" and many other structures based on focusing on quality at the product and process design level, old accounting approaches to costing became a problem.

There was a major disconnect; leaders and managers who understood the operational problems and saw the value in a different approach found that financial reporting - and often financial managers who were still using old approaches, were strongly against their proposed actions - and often the financial reporting even seemed to suggest that their operational decisions were wrong. That is until quality improved, customer satisfaction and loyalty increased, reputations improved and ultimately "the bottom line" got better. The conflict showed up in several ways:

- Overhead cost "recovery" was based on optimizing throughput and any action to reduce throughput would drive up unit costs; as managers introduced down time for employee meetings or "town halls" or allowed work to be suspended to fix a quality problem or even delayed start-up of the line until the process was working properly or faulty equipment was fixed, the accountants would report "excess non-productive" time that appeared to create an overhead recovery variance, negatively impacting profits.
- "Just in Time" inventory would reduce balance sheet costs (good) but would often initially cause production to shut down because a vendor delivered sub-standard product. There was no longer any "insurance" for poor vendor products.

To combat the above, progressive actions to "partner" with suppliers to enhance quality might sometimes result in purchasing costs not being "the cheapest" in the market. While quality improvements would show up in the production area there was no link with the apparent increase in purchase costs - the accounting systems were unable to correlate the two.

There were many ways that a gap opened out between the work of the management accountant and the value that this provided to support the right decision making. There was one other major evolving shift that left management accounting "out in the cold." This was the shift towards the service and knowledge based economy.

As discussed earlier, costing systems, principally standard costing had been developed in parallel to the manufacturing economy and there were no equivalent "robust" costing tools for non-manufacturing. Even in manufacturing, costs that were not considered direct costs were usually controlled by a combination of budgets and departmental costs. The linkage between costs and products or services at the "micro level" in non-manufacturing was not well established.

A greater part of the problem was that because of this lack of a robust costing approach, the task of understanding and matching costs and revenues in service organizations was a challenge for decision makers and worse still, the embedded in efficiencies due to issues such as low productivity and poor quality were not apparent. This created a major gap in management accounting. Tools such as quality costing were occasionally implemented but the use was not widespread. Management accountants were "missing in action" when it came to help management identify and address many issues facing their organizations including problem in:

- Costing of computer systems in particular ROI on capital investments.
- Understanding the financial Impact of good or poor software applications on the productivity of employees who interfaced with the system.
- Understanding costs associated with internal processes that were over or under designed and not "fit for purpose."
- Recognizing costs associated with poor processes and services associated with support areas such as customer returns, repairs, replacements, and call centres.

- Seeing the effectiveness and impact on productivity of internal networks and systems both on user productivity and on client service
- Recognizing costs and productivity impacts related to hiring and turnover of staff and associated costs such as the ROI on training and development.
- Understanding financial impact associated with quality of leadership both in productivity, health costs and stress.
- Recognizing the "cost of complexity" and impact of internal communications on areas such as innovation and creativity
- Understanding the costs and benefits associated with the creation, use and payback of knowledge management systems (i.e., cost of creating databases, updating and payback from access and use)
- Seeing the linkage between financial resources spent on the creation and sustaining of intangible capabilities e.g., supply chain relationships and others.
- Understanding of value of brand and reputation and the costs associated with creating, sustaining, and managing, this corporate "asset."

The result of not being able to link financial resources to operational activities in a non-manufacturing business (and also the nonmanufacturing support operations of a manufacturing business) resulted in "macro decision making" such as across the board cuts to the workforce and the replacement of permanent full time employees with outsourced and part time employees. These decisions often appeared to save money, but depleted other knowledge based capabilities. Management accounting, like financial accounting was not keeping pace with the major sea-changes taking place in the underlying economy.

7.2 Efforts to reduce the drift away from reality.

Change was needed in many areas; in an effort to change budgeting a concept called ZBB or zero-based budgeting was introduced in the early 1970's. The goal of this approach was to start every year's budget from zero - managers would essentially be told that they had no money and would have to develop "work packages" built around the core tasks and activities that they were responsible for and request funding for each individual package. The goal was twofold; first every activity taking place would be scrutinized for its necessity and its resource requirements. Instead of just cutting or increasing overall budgets, ZBB would allow decisions to be made on a more targeted basis. Secondly, if there was a limitation of funding available, instead of making cost cuts across the board - all areas of expense, i.e., the work-packages, would be prioritized and if funds were limited, certain non-critical or non-essential tasks could be dropped completely. Conceptually it was a good idea but in practise it became enormously time consuming and hard to execute.

Standard product costing had been advantageous to accountants as it allowed a solid base for direct cost control and a pre-determined way to value inventories; if there were manufacturing cost variances a portion of these could be taken as an adjustment to inventory costs at the end of the fiscal year. The overheads could be apportioned based on any increases or decreases in inventory and added to inventory as "period costs." However, this also began to show signs of age, when the energy crisis and inflation occurred in the 1970's. Materials were escalating in price more frequently and labour costs were becoming an issue, and in certain cases labour disruptions restricted the use of certain employees on jobs that their contract did not allow them to perform (part of what is often referred to as "work to rule").

In the early 1970's the US was becoming increasingly concerned about the growing competitive pressures from manufactured products from Japan. In the 1950's and 1960's as the Japanese re-built after WW2 their products were typically poor copies of North American and other nations products; products were unreliable, and quality was poor. However, this began to change in the 1970's when Japanese small cars started to take an increasing share of the North American automotive market. Also, at this time the US had a dominant position in the design and manufacture of microchips and other key components for the rapidly growing computer industry, but the Japanese had started to put effort into this area as well. In order to revitalize their approach to manufacturing the US Department of Commerce facilitated the creation of a non-profit organization called CAM-I - originally the Center for Advanced Manufacturing and Innovation, but now called the Consortium for Advanced Manufacturing - International.

CAM-I is a not-for-profit, cooperative membership organization established in 1972 to support research and development in areas of strategic importance to industries; however, it originally involved government, academic and industry representation across the key areas of competitive concerns. In its early year's CAM-I acted as a catalyst in looking at the ways in which American organizations operated and sought areas of "leading practise" improvement. This included approaches to the technical aspects of their activities but also management; thus, they were early leaders in areas such as quality management, computer aided design and manufacturing, performance management systems and costing approaches.

In 1987 a wake up call appeared. A book from Harvard University Press titled *"Relevance Lost: The decline and Fall of Management Accounting"*[35] suggested that approaches used by management accounting were entirely out of touch with the realities of the organizations within which they were being applied. In their opening pages the author's state:

"Today's management accountant information, driven by the procedures and cycle of the organisation's financial reporting system, is too late, too aggregated, and too distorted to be relevant for managers' planning and control decisions."

After publication, their book received many reviews - both critical and supportive as some of its comments were radical; after all, neither of the authors were professional accountants. This was part of the value of the book in that it viewed management accounting through the eyes of users. A good summary was written by Stephen A. Zeff, Editor of Accounting Review[36] in 2014 as an opening comment on another book:

"In their book, Relevance Lost: The Rise and Fall of Management Accounting, Johnson, and Kaplan (1987) suggest an important apparent life cycle in the effectiveness of accounting techniques. They argue that the first phase of the development of cost accounting techniques up to about 1925 was determined by the emergence of more complex multi-product businesses. There was then a second subsequent phase of stagnation, or irrelevance for managerial decision

---

[35] "Relevance Lost: The Rise and Fall of Management Accounting" H. Thomas Johnson, Robert S. Kaplan, Harvard Business School Press, 1987

[36] "The Accounting Review," American Accounting Association, Book Review report by Stephen A. Zeff of "A History of Management Accounting: The British Experience"

making, arising from the emphasis given to financial accounting an accurate valuation of inventories. Their hypothesis has attracted considerable and ongoing debate for a profession that needs relevance, and needs its place in the corporate boardroom, particularly when boards might, post-Enron and post-financial crisis, be viewed as hotspots of sub-optimal decision making."

It is interesting although Stephen Zeff is making this comment in 2014 about a book published over 20 years previously (that is still available and being used by academics and students of accounting), yet his comments demonstrate that the issues raised remain valid.

7.3 New tools and approaches

Management accountants had already started the journey to update and renew the toolkit being applied to financial information for better decision making. By the time Johnson and Kaplan's book as published in 1987

- Budgeting as traditionally applied had been found to be slow, bureaucratic, rigid, and easily rendered out of date by fast moving events.
- Standard costing, while still valid for some was not only less useful in fast moving, flexible production environments but was also in danger of giving the wrong information.
- Direct costs have declined and indirect costs, historically allocated to products on some hopefully relevant basis had been proven to create incorrect and misleading financial decision making.

The economy was becoming less tangible asset / manufacturing based and more knowledge / service based.

Zero based budgeting had been one effort but was proving an administrative headache and was usually opposed by managers who had a significant added workload to justify work that was, in fact going to continue as before. Lots of authors wrote books on the subject, and lots of consultants developed programs to help organizations implement ZBB but, while the concept was a step forward, for many, the burden imposed was greater than the benefit. Some organizations still use the concept of ZBB and do realize savings, but it is usually a modified and more practical approach.

Another approach, that CAM-I became involved with through an entity called the "Beyond Budgeting Round Table" (BBRT, which still exists today) took a different approach. They asked "why budget anyway" if organizations are a) always seeking lower costs and b) always looking at ways to shift, move and re-organize and set better priorities in order to adapt to a rapidly changing marketplace? Conceptually this was a hard "bridge to cross." There was a clear belief, maybe held over from the "command and control" days that employees at the "execution" work level had to be closely watched and supervised and would just start "spending money like drunken sailors" if there were no ground rules for them to be measured against. So, for many this was psychologically a tough suggestion.

Developed originally around 1997 the concept tended to be adopted by progressive leaders who saw "trust and empowerment" as core approaches to a high performance management. There are several core principles around the concept that are foundational to create a climate within which it works. These include:

Leadership attributes	Process attributes
Clarity of purpose	Continuity
Solid foundation of corporate values	Clear targets
Transparency of information	Continual plans and forecasts
Organizational engagement	Responsible stewardship of resources
Autonomy of action	Effective evaluation and feedback
Customer focus	Shared rewards

The reader can research more information around the concept however it is important to consider that budgeting has historically been seen as a core aspect of an effective internal control system and if it is replaced or eliminated there must be adequate safeguards to replace the type of oversight and control that it previously provided.

How Accountants Lost their Balance

This approach was adopted by a number of organizations and has been dropped by some but continues in use by others. However, many others continue to use the traditional approach; some who have adopted the "beyond budgeting" approach in good times, have dropped it in favour of the traditional approach when times "get tough." The problem is that in todays rapidly moving market reverting back to centralized systems for control is often the opposite of what is needed to empower and engage staff to be problem solvers.

Standard costing has remained a favorite tool for many organizations; the US based IMA (Institute of Management Accountants) did a survey in the last 10 years and identified that over 80% of organizations still used this approach - in many cases because of the benefits it offers to inventory valuation. However different approaches might be more aligned with the operational reality of organizations. Direct costs - labour and materials are either "designed in" by the initial product design or managed by purchasing (through external vendors) and by the people controlling the work. For direct cost management, organizations have moved towards "vendor partnering" in order to jointly work on reducing materials costs and on "self managed work groups" to focus on improvements to processes. Two approaches would seem to align better with this reality:

Process costing, where each work cell is considered a self contained part of the process and is given autonomy to manage and control their own costs, and
Target costing, where goals are established for these work cells to identify and work on process improvements through which costs can be reduced.

The alignment of direct costs with processes can start to build financial information for both the direct operators who are engaged in the process but also for the support areas whose work impacts the process. This might include designers, process engineers and equipment suppliers as well as maintenance and support functions. However, management accountants have not yet developed any real "new" alternative to standard costing, the closest comparable approach being process costing.

The same is not true for managing indirect or overhead costs. What was needed was an approach that eliminated the need for wholesale allocations of overhead costs and an alternative approach to linking these significant and growing aspects of resource consumption to an organization's products and services. Robert Kaplan, who had co-authored "Relevance Lost" wrote a number of books in the 1980's related to problems with and new approaches towards costing. He is considered by many, as the founder of an approach called ABC or Activity Based Costing. This approach fundamentally changes the management of indirect or overhead costs.

It looks at costs as being incurred for a reason - usually an event which "turns on" a process which then consumes resources; this event might cause expenses to be incurred in several departments under different managers.

ABC reduces the reliance of traditional "responsibility accounting" where management accountants reported cost by department (what manager is responsible) and by type of expenses (typically the classification of expense type by GL or general ledger cost code), and replaced it by asking "why is this expense being incurred?" (this is referred to as the "driver"). Using this approach, many managers were able to understand cost that they actually incurred but which were caused by another department.

ABC then looked at each of these cross functional or departmental processes and asks, "why is this process taking place and who or what benefits?"

This approach to managing the ever increasing level of overhead costs made conceptual sense to operational managers because it linked their use of resources to the operational activities that they were responsible for. Managers do not actually control costs per se, they manage processes and tasks (or projects) which cause them to consume resources. Additionally, allocations now became much less important, as those who created the demand for the process, were those who paid for it. If you wanted to reduce allocations the best way was to look at how you could eliminate the activity that caused the cost or find a better way to do it. The approach had the potential to revolutionize the whole management of indirect costs.

There was one bright spot, and this was the application of Activity Based Costing to non-manufacturing operations that delivered significant enhancements in understanding cost drivers and the costs of services for organizations such as banks, insurance companies, railroads, government departments and others. However once again its application was not widespread and was often burdensome and labour intensive. This technique was the first new approach to be implemented in many years and helped both the traditional manufacturing economy as well as the growing service and knowledge based organizations.

The challenges of doing the right thing for the business - the growing gap between what the financials suggest, and the operational reality fell to leaders. As an example of the "mind-set challenges involved, Donald E. Petersen, President and then later also Chairman of the Ford Motor Company in the 1980s, oversaw the most radical transformation in the history of that company. By turning Ford's pyramid upside down, giving power back to the employees and capturing the power of teams, he led Ford to the biggest comeback ever in the auto industry. After his retirement Peterson wrote a book[37] about his experiences; one of his key points was that when he decided that regular "town hall" meetings would be held to update employees, the biggest opposition came from the accountants. They told Peterson that it as a really bad idea "look at the amount of fixed overhead recovery we will be losing - this will reduce our quarterly profits."

7.4 Starting to measure the right things.

Internally, operational and business managers were starting to realize that focusing on financial information alone was not enough. Many organizations were already looking at internal performance measures that, in addition to financial performance looked at aspects such as customer satisfaction, market share, accident and safety information, employee turnover and many others relative to their own business.

Robert Kaplan, who had co-authored "Relevance Lost" and also been one of the key proponents of Activity Based Costing, co-authored a book called "The Balanced Scorecard" published by Harvard Business Press in 1996. Whilst Kaplan's work on management accounting had driven change in that area, he was now expanding his thought process to establish that achieving

---

[37] "A Better Way: Redefining the Way America Works," Donald Peterson, Houghton Mifflin Harcourt, 1991

business goals could not be managed by looking at one set of metrics, financials, alone. As the book states in its introduction: *"Imagine entering the cockpit of a modern jet airplane and seeing only a single instrument there."*

While financial performance was one core aspect of the balanced scorecard, the three other dimensions were customer, internal process and learning and growth. Measures within each dimension were not prescriptive and were intended to be populated by each organization based on the KPI's or key performance indicators that would be needed to manage the process of converting strategy to execution. This work led to both a proliferation of books on the concepts of multi-dimensional performance measurement systems or scorecards as well as a number that dealt with the underlying management aspects of effective implementation of strategy using a scorecard. Looking at each dimension the guidance given suggested:

- Financial dimension: typically, this might include both traditional top level financials (revenues, profit, EBIT) as well as specific, key business margins, strategic cost targets and projects. (The concept also worked at not-for-profits as the dimension could be customized and avoid profit).

- Customer dimension: given that customers generate revenues, what customer metrics are relevant? Market share, satisfaction, reputation, new product launches and others.

- The process dimension: this dimension really brought in the ABC thinking in that it reinforced "the process" as the building block of execution; metrics would focus on key core processes and might include cycle time, quality, costs of process, capacity utilization, improvements, and others.

- Learning and growth dimension: this one was more "intellectual" as it requires embracing the intangible aspects of human performance and might include aspects of individual learning; knowledge management systems, leadership, employee engagement and others.

Management accountants were the "operational performance reporting" people in many organizations and often took the lead in encouraging and adopting the concepts of the balanced scorecard. This appears to have set the strategic direction for management accounting; while ABC continued to be the foundation of costing in the emerging economic reality, management accountants appear to have believed their role in the marketplace was to shift towards strategy and the alignment between financial management and effective execution. Management accountants began to adopt a "systems based approach" towards organizational strategy and implementation.

However, while this created some interesting shifts in the profession that we ill discuss shortly, it appears that limited work focused on the crystallization of the concept of "integrated management."

As an example, the four dimensions of the scorecard are all integrated and to be effective all the dimensions must be complementary. For management accountants the largest challenge would be that traditional financial management approached cost collection on a "by responsibility (cost centre) and by type of expense" reporting, whereas the scorecard called for process performance. This created an ideal opportunity to align ABC within the scorecard so that the costs of processes required for execution would be aligned with the non-financial aspects of process - i.e., the process dimension would include cost (based on ABC), quality, cycle time, and quantity metrics. Financials would therefore be aggregated performance, process would be cost and consumption of resources, client would be "end of process" and learning and growth would be the underlying and enabling intangibles - human, intellectual, and relationship. In many cases this was not to be the outcome.

Certainly, at this point the management accounting profession had moved a long way from its roots of focusing on financial resource management through understanding "costs." This seemed to leave a bit of a gap in financial support to management. Financial resources remain the key enabler of the acquisition and sustaining of both tangible and intangible assets necessary to operate a business; the challenge today is that most financial resources are not channeled into tangible assets but into intangibles and operating costs. However there remains an absence of both understanding, measuring, and reporting the application of resources into these areas in a way that helps managers and others understand cost behaviour and profitability.

In the 1980's when this shift was starting to take place there were many writers who were identifying the need for understanding and performance. From a "value" perspective many writers identified that a major shift was taking place away from tangible "balance sheet" assets to intangibles. Skandia and the Danish industry Department developed one of the earliest depictions of this which was discussed earlier. Translating this more to a financial view it has further been developed below:

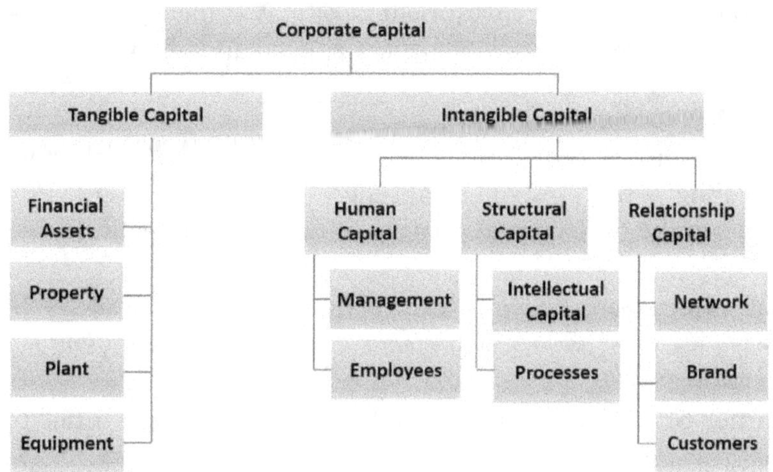

Management accountants appeared to have a good grasp of the left hand side of intangibles but there was limited new ideas towards understanding the resource (i.e., cash) issues related to the management of intangibles. A greater challenge appeared to be in developing cost information for intangibles. Many commentators, in the early years were calling for improvements in disclosure of expenses - i.e., items charged against current earnings that were not relevant to the generation of current revenues but reflected resources being applied to either creating or sustaining intangible "assets." Items such as brand building, relationship building, process development and others. Given that GAAP and accounting standards did not allow for the statutory recognition of these items, it offered an opportunity for management accountants to step in and explain how management was using its financial resources for these purposes.

How Accountants Lost their Balance

One can look at the graphic and the common factor appears to be "staring you in the eye." The common denominator is cash which is required to "fund" the acquisition of, and the ongoing sustaining of all the items listed. Human capital and leadership is not free - how much is being spent? More importantly what is the reason it is being spent? To fund todays revenue creation of tomorrow's capability? How about processes? These used to be tacit knowledge in people's "heads" but as organizations modernized it became an investment both in creating documentation, training materials, staff training and supporting systems. How much was this costing? How much had been invested? How much was the investment worth? Was management sustaining this intangible investment or was it being depleted and allowed to get out of date?

Some well positioned economists and other "big-picture" thinkers were also concerned about the growing absence of information. Prominent commentators at the time were also trying to raise awareness of the issue:

- Alan Greenspan, Federal Reserve Board Chairman stated, *"There are going to be a lot of problems in the future as accounting is not tracking investments in knowledge assets."*
- Former SEC Chairman, Arthur Levitt, extended this principle - *"as intangible assets grow in size and scope, more and more people are questioning whether the true value - and the drivers of that value - are being reflected in a timely manner in publicly available disclosure."*
- Peter Wallison, a resident fellow of the American Enterprise Institute concurred, *"today substantially all of a company's profitability depends on intangible assets, so the accounting problems associated with intangibles become quite serious."*

While those using financial statements appeared aware of the issue, few management accountants seemed to be at the "leading edge" of new approaches. However, others outside accounting were starting to ask questions and develop models that incorporated financial data. Mary Adams of Smarter Companies has been a leader in developing models to better understand the investment that organizations have in intangibles. Her ideas were included in a

2014 IMA publication[38] that sought to cast light on the expanding issue of the financial aspects of intangibles.

In a book[39] that addressed the value that organizations held through intangibles, there was an illustration of how a company might re-cast its financial to demonstrate how items previously expenses were identified as resources being applied to building intangibles for the future. Two leaders in the field of intellectual capital identified that there was *"…a huge opportunity for the accounting industry to get back in the middle of the action[40]."* For years Ken Stanfield in Australia has been developing standards around the understanding and treatment of intangibles. He provides suggestions of how to do this in practise in his book "Intangible Management: Tools for solving the accounting and management crisis" - yet in spite of all this attention and interest It appears that little material progress has been made in understanding costs and values related to intangibles by management accountants.

7.5 The Growth of Invisible Assets

The two core drivers of a shift to heavily technology dependant organizations and the responses to global competitiveness resulted in a gradual building of corporate capabilities that were needed but which failed to "fit" traditional accounting definitions. Cash was increasingly being diverted to fund these efforts, yet both the expenditure and the resulting "capability" or intangible asset was not visible. Financial justification was challenging, because an ROI or return on investment calculation was almost impossible - it was just "the right thing to do" and progressive CEO's went ahead and made the decisions. What they increasingly were juggling was the allocation of funds to build intangible capability, which were being charged as operating expenses and the limiting of these expenses within an acceptable envelope that allowed the organization to meet at least minimal profitability targets. It was hard for

---

[38] "Unrecognized Intangible Assets: Identification, Management and Reporting" Shepherd, N and Adams, M. 2014 Institute of Management Accountants, Montvale NJ

[39] "Intellectual Capital: The New Wealth of organizations," Stewart, T. 1997, P 232-233, Doubleday

[40] "Intellectual Capital," Edvinsson, L., and Malone. M. S., 1997, P 168-169, Harper Business

CEO's to "tell their story" as there was almost no financial or accounting support.

Reflecting on the sorts of operational changes and activities that were taking place we can start to identify the types of invisible assets that were being created. These invisible capabilities always existed but had either never been specifically created through identifiable investment or had been created by lacked a disciplined, structured, and controlled approach. Historically, most investment in employees had been in technical skills training; suppliers were handled "arms length" with price being the major determinant of choice. Process management was developed to some level but mostly in manufacturing areas, and in many cases still focused on efficiency as the prime goal, following the approaches of good, solid industrial engineering. Everything changed.

The last 25 years of the 20th century reflected a rush towards focusing on quality and service satisfaction; initially management thinking was that the people needed re-training and that both quality problems and other issues that were impacting organizational effectiveness were caused by poor attitudes or training. However this was soon changed by the realizations that it was "the process not the people" as discussed earlier. Processes were improved and then the whole issue of organizational strategy started to change towards seeing the work force as a key aspect of competitive advantage and the "creators of value."

One of the largest developing intangible assets is in the area of knowledge or intellectual capital. This is a challenging category as there are several areas where this knowledge can be captured and capitalized when it results in something like a patent, trademark, or copyright. As Investopedia defines it:

"Intellectual property is the value of a company or organization's employee knowledge, skills, business training or any proprietary information that may provide the company with a competitive advantage. Intellectual capital is considered an asset and can broadly be defined as the collection of all informational resources a company has at its disposal that can be used to drive profits, gain new customers, create new products, or otherwise improve the business. It is the sum of employee expertise, organizational processes, and other intangibles that contribute to a company's bottom line.

This definition is a challenge. The company or organization does not own its people, however when the people are paid by the company, to create either something or to develop a capability, it can be considered as being owned by the company as they funded it - even though it is not an asset in accounting terms. Once again, the organization is directing financial resources into the development of this capability. Organizations that have used their employee's skills to develop documented systems and processes have "codified" the knowledge; in many cases this "codification" has been part of the process development and improvement activity. This is often referred to as explicit" knowledge and it is often easier to prove ownership; however, "tacit" knowledge - which is what has not yet been codified is much harder to defined in terms of ownership.

Tacit knowledge might be considered passive as it is only "optimized" when the individual or group of individuals holding it, is motivated to apply it for the benefit of the organization. One can illustrate it this way:

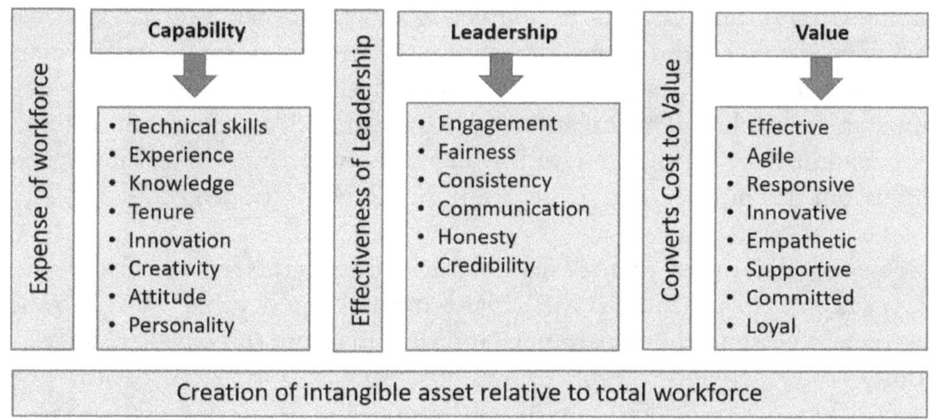

Significant cash flow usually reflected as an expense (i.e., reducing profitability and equity) is spent on paying the workforce. This expense "buys" the potential capability of the people who work for the organization but in the knowledge economy the competitive advantage comes from creating value from this expense. This is the role of leadership who creates an environment within which this potential can be converted to organizational capabilities that add value. Much of the expense paid for the development of both the workforce and those involved in leadership positions is directed at activities related to value creation. It is not the skills of the workforce alone that creates value but the ability of the organization to create an environment within which these skills are optimized.

These intended outcomes, of effectiveness (productivity), agility, responsiveness, innovativeness, empathy, support, commitment, loyalty and probably others are what creates competitive advantage. This is the intangible capability that is an intangible asset; an organization that has developed this operational capability is of more value to an investor; unfortunately, there is little transparency of this whole portion of intangible value to either management or investors based on current accounting or reporting. Yet this is a core driver of organizational value (i.e., what was on a traditional balance sheet) in the 21st century.

The danger is that without the financial link to both the value that has been built and the level of sustaining investment to ensure the capability is maintained, the financial risk of "depleting" this asset will only be seen when capability declines and starts to show up in deteriorating performance. Organizational cash flow is going towards funding these areas - yet there is almost no visibility. The creation of ABC offered to opportunity to start understanding the "application of resources" between current and non-current activity but has not become mainstream thinking or reporting.

One of the other intangibles that has been created has already been discussed and this relates to the organizations "brand value." Organizations that remain close to their customers and remain aware of societal changes will modify their operating approaches to remain "in step" with public expectations. Creating and sustaining brand value is a continual process of understanding what the market values and responding to it in a positive way. Brand value is a major aspect of intangible value that was demonstrated by the earlier chart; if one looks at the FAANG stocks (Facebook, Amazon, Apple, Netflix, and Google) we can see that the intangible asset value at the end of 2019 of $750 billion - making up 15% of their total market value (compared to collective book values of less than 10% - so what might be considered "material?")

The period between the 1970's and the early 21st century was a period of rapid change requiring adaptation by most organizations; those who succeeded in staying aware of these changes and responding saw their brand values protected; those who failed to keep pace saw their brand value decline. In the chapter on social change, we will further discuss the underlying public perceptions that organizations needed to address.

Responding to, and aligning spending with sustaining the brand, and the market benefits that it brings has become a mainstream activity within strategy and. This ensures an organization is market focused and more important it drives decision making around the allocation of financial resources to sustaining a high priority "asset." Yet once again little is financially visible.

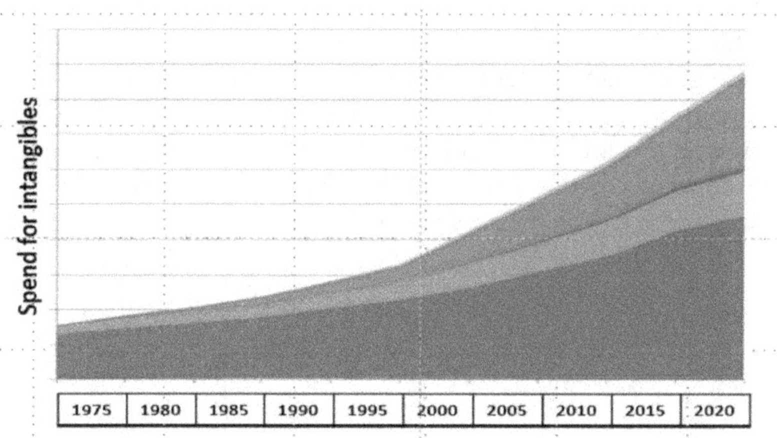

We know that the spend exists because intangibles of different types have been growing, but there is little financial analysis to determine what the percentage of spend is or how one might group and report the spending. Significant cash flow was invested by organizations as they adapted to change and built their operational capabilities; these underlying investments contributed to the growth of organizational value however accounting has not reflected this.

What exactly are the categories of intangibles and how might we group them? How much was spent creating these intangibles? What level of natural depletion exists annually? What should be spent to sustain and maintain the intangibles once created? How would an organization know if the competitive advantage created by these intangibles was being depleted? How do the levels of spend relate to non-financial performance indicators? What is the link between the increasing level of spend and the measures already being used in a corporate "scorecard?" While "managing the spend" is a strategic decision that a CEO may make, the challenge is to balance the spend in such a way that the benefits of all aspects are optimized while at the same time sustaining the level of required financial performance.

So, we know the intangible "assets" are there and we know that the expenses to create them is flowing through the earnings statement; thus, we have a "balance sheet" or value impact as well as an earnings impact. The problem is that neither is being collected or reported as an aid to management decision making. Is management accounting, once again losing its relevance? Is accounting, in the development of its standards, getting better and better at measuring what is less and less important? What might be needed is a paradigm shift in the scope of what accountants codify and report? In the next chapter we will look at some of the barriers to change.

8.   Hurdles to progress

I use "hurdles" rather than barriers because whilst barriers are often immovable, hurdles can be jumped if there is the desire to do so. The reality is that the profession of accounting needs to be renewed and refreshed to fit the world that we live in today (and to be ready to be flexible and adaptable for the world of tomorrow). We are living in a paradigm driven by the reality of the past and what the profession must have is a vision of what could be for the future. Sure, there are challenges and issues in moving forward - but, as is often said "the definition of idiocy is wanting change but continuing to do the same things." If the profession wants to remain relevant it needs to change and adapt - and for that to happen there needs to be a willingness to do something different.

I fear two old fashioned situations may be at work here that is limiting the ability to change. First is the "boiled frog syndrome." The premise is that if a frog is put suddenly into boiling water, it will jump out, but if the frog is put in lukewarm water, which is then brought to a boil slowly, it will not perceive the danger and will be cooked to death. Sometimes I think that events have conspired that we are already in the pan, and the water is heating up, but everything seems to be the same. The other is "the emperor has no clothes." After one chooses a career in a given field it becomes harder and harder, the longer one is in the profession to step outside it and look at it with another set of eyes. I fear that those who are not in the accounting profession believe that it needs to change but few people internally want to "rock the boat." Many are probably concerned about upsetting their boss or being brought up before a board for "conduct unbecoming a professional." (We do not criticize our own profession). But healthy questioning is good for both retaining what is working and putting what needs to be changed under the microscope.

Accounting remains high in the list of trusted professions so that is a great achievement and one to be built upon. What we need to be sure about is that we retain and if possible, GROW that reputational rating but that we also provide services that are both relevant and are seen as adding value to potential clients. It is nice to be in a profession where services are mandated by law (such as audits) but that should be only one of a wide range of services we can offer. Economists, who have traditionally focused on the concept of value have limited presence in the world of corporate finance; accounting is already there and, if value is the field of the future, then accounting must embrace methods and approaches that position ourselves as the leaders in this field of corporate activities. But to do that means not being bound and restricted by only working within our traditional boundaries.

8.1 Bound by tradition.

As outlined earlier, accounting has a strong and increasingly valued role in society; this was enhanced by the elevation first to be a self-governing profession and then by being appointed to certify, through objective analysis the reporting of corporations. This is the tradition, but should the profession be limited or bound by this? No. The profession has already moved away from financial accounting into other fields of specialization - in particular, the creation of a parallel profession of management accounting.

There have also been massive shifts in the way in which accounting is undertaken. We all remember Scrooge and Bob Cratchit bent over their tall desks entering number into the ledgers by candlelight in their "counting house":

It seems that a counting-house is a function or department that exists within a larger establishment — basically the bookkeeping or accounting department. Although this is not the case with Scrooge & Marley, it seems likely that the firm at least offered accounting and bookkeeping services[41].

---

[41] "More About the Business of Scrooge and Marley: an Ethnographic Approach," December 19, 2019 by Stephen Winick who uses this quote from the blog of Ellen Terrell - blog post at Inside Adams

How Accountants Lost their Balance

To place this in the context of our history of accounting, Dickens wrote "A Christmas Carol" in 1843 and their office was located in the City of London - the "city" being about a square mile in the centre which housed the core of trading and finance activities; this was probably the area where the early "deals" were being done in the coffee houses that were discussed earlier. So, Dickens portrayal provides some level of context to where the profession started. Almost all accounting activities were manual (quill pens and green eye shades?) up until the development of the mechanical devices in the early 20th century - the first of which was the Burroughs adding machine in the late 1880's. Following this there was the gradual development and application of mechanical automation especially applied to transaction posting. However, for many organizations the actual "general ledger" continued to be handwritten; almost all of the records were "paper based."

The first revolution was the creation of the computer which, over a period of about 30 years took over much of the record keeping. By the 1960's, with increased computing power and storage, mainframe computers were used by most large companies for their accounting processing and records. With the advent of the PC in the 1970's and with its software tools like spreadsheets and "integrated" accounting systems, almost every business was able to automate most accounting processes. This era significantly changed accounting from the era of accountants as "bookkeepers" and allowed accounting to move into a more advisory role. Approaches to auditing also changed very significantly as the need for internal controls changed in the computer age.

The next revolution was probably in communications where instead of paper based transactions an increasing volume of internal and then external paperwork was eliminated and replaced by computer to computer data transfer. These changes demonstrate that the profession is capable of change; accounting roles profoundly shifted, and the training and skill sets changed completely. However, probably most comforting was the underlying reality was that the "process" of accounting based on double entry bookkeeping still formed the foundation. Accounting standards also continued to be based on the traditional concepts of bookkeeping, underpinned by prudence and conservatism.

As "pure accounting" work became automated and bookkeepers were no longer needed, employment in the profession shifted to other areas such as financial support and advisory services. As technology increased many accountants became specialists in the accounting aspects of business systems, ensuring that the integrity of the accounting process remained even though it was now almost invisible - few accountants have actually seen a handwritten general ledger today and most "postings" of transactions into the general ledger are automated.

The auditing area remained a key focus of the profession where many accountants received their initial training; audits increased in complexity as organizations automated, grew larger domestically and internationally, dealt in multiple currencies, employed creative approaches to financing and tax planning and had to deal with the continual demand of both accounting standards and regulatory compliance. So, the mix of employment roles changed significantly with many accountants not actually "doing" accounting.

These shifts show that the profession can change and adapt; however, while the role of understanding the source and application of financial resources remains a foundational and continuing element of accounting, the development of financial statements to show where the money went is providing less value to those who are interested in the risk of business continuity. A balance sheet that contains only financial assets represents a small proportion of an investors "capital at risk." An earnings statement provides a minimal amount of information to users on how management is using its resources, between earning current income and investing in capability and capacity for the future.

The hurdle here, is our apparent professional desire to limit our activities to traditional reporting of organizational health and sustainability by focusing on financial capital which fails to address the financial impact of the creation, sustaining and, where it occurs the depletion of intangibles that now consume a significant portion of corporate cash / financial resources. The money invested in, and being generated by organizations today is being utilized in quite different ways than in the past and a reader of financial reports receives little insight into that shifting reality from traditional financial statements to assure them that the money is being used wisely, that all material aspects important to business activities has been addressed and that the organization is truly a going concern.

8.2 Maintaining standards

Another area where significant change has occurred as accounting has evolved is in the development of standards - sometimes called "the bible" for accountants as they form the foundational rules upon which accounting transactions are understood and recorded. As discussed in earlier chapters, accounting standards evolved, as the business world changed.

Initially, In the US, the original American Institute of Accountants (now known as the American Institute of Certified Public Accountants) together with the New York Stock Exchange attempted to launch the first accounting standards in the 1930s. The American Institute of Certified Public Accountants developed, managed and enacted the first set of accounting standards in 1939 through the Committee on Accounting Procedures (CAP); in the 1950's the Accounting Principles Board (APB) replaced CAP. Finally, in 1973, these responsibilities were given to the newly created Financial Accounting Standards Board (FASB).

The Securities and Exchange Commission requires all listed companies to adhere to U.S. GAAP accounting standards, (a combination of FASB standards, Government Accounting standards and AICPA directives) in the preparation of their financial statements to be listed on a U.S. securities exchange. FASB is an independent non-profit organization, which has the authority to establish and interpret generally accepted accounting principles (GAAP) in the United States for public and private companies and non-profit organizations. GAAP refers to a set of standards for how companies, non-profits, and governments should prepare and present their financial statements.

In the UK history goes back further. In 1844, business incorporation was made possible by the Joint Stock Companies Act; "books of account" had to be kept, a "full and fair" balance sheet was to be prepared and presented to the meeting of shareholders, and also filed with the Registrar of joint stock companies. At that time, there was no requirement for the preparation of a profit and loss account, nor was the form or content of the balance sheet laid down. Auditors had to be appointed with full access to the books of account and a report was to be prepared for the annual general meeting of shareholders. There was minimal change for the next 100 years with a fairly laisse-faire attitude by government until the enacting of the 1948 Companies Act which extended audit to include a profit and loss account. In 1942 the ICAEW (Institute of Chartered Accountants in England and Wales) created the Taxation and Financial Relations Committee that had a mandate to *"...consider and make recommendations ...on certain aspects of the accounts of companies' and to publish 'approved recommendations for the information of members."* After discussions and review of the issue of accounting practices in 1969, the ICAEW established the Accounting Standards Steering Committee in January 1970 with *"the object of developing definitive standards for financial reporting."*

The development of accounting standards (or the absence of them) occurred in other countries dependant upon the level of commercial maturity and economic activity. After the second world war it had become increasingly apparent that commercial activity was "going global" and that issues of standardization would also have to reflect this - however it was not accounting that was "first out of the gate" but the International Organization for Standardization - known today as ISO which was established in in London in 1947. While global growth and development was making clear the need for some level coordination, collaboration and cooperation, ISO was not involved in any financial standards though, and initially dealt more with developing issues like communications standards, as well as currency symbols, date standards and other items.

The accounting problems of the 1970's and 1980's brought the need for a higher level of accounting "control" and standardization into focus. Additionally, corporations, regulators, investors, and accountants were beginning to become frustrated with having to prepare and interpret multiple versions of financial reports. If a company operated in several jurisdictions' accounts might be prepared using different standards; if a company owned and registered in the UK, but whose securities were also traded in the US it would have to create two or more sets of financial statements to meet US GAAP and securities listing requirements as well as those of the UK and possible other jurisdictions.

Preparing accounts, auditing accounts, and evaluating financial reports was becoming more expensive and more complex. Accountants, as well as users of information such as investors, began to recognize the emerging need for global collaboration and cooperation, and in 1973 the first step towards trying to resolve this challenge was taken. The International Accounting Standards Committee (IASC) was founded in London at the initiative of Sir Henry Benson, former president of the Institute of Chartered Accountants in England and Wales. The IASC was created by national accountancy bodies from a number of countries with a view to harmonizing the international diversity of company reporting practices. Between its founding in 1973 and its dissolution in 2001, it developed a set of International Accounting Standards (IAS) that gradually acquired a degree of acceptance in countries around the world.

On 1 April 2001, it was replaced by the International Accounting Standards Board (IASB), an independent standard-setting body. The IASB adopted, continued, and expanded the work of the IAS as International Financial Reporting Standards (IFRS). Since that date efforts have continued to harmonize these standards across all countries; while some, who had few standards already adopted IFRS in totality. Other countries, like the US which has FASB has taken longer. Part of the challenge has been that, while FASB is essentially a "rules based approach," IFRS are much more a principle based framework.

Another collaborative approach to improve the consistency and quality of accounting was the creation of the International Federation of Accountants (IFAC) in 1977; this is a global organization for the accountancy profession. with about 175 members and associates in more than 130 countries and jurisdictions, representing more than 3 million accountants employed across the profession. The organization supports the development, adoption, and implementation of international standards for accounting education, ethics, and the public sector as well as audit and assurance. It has evolved and now supports four independent standard-setting boards, which establish international standards on ethics, auditing and assurance, accounting education, and public sector accounting. It also issues guidance to encourage high-quality performance by professional accountants in business and small and medium accounting practices. Its' focus on a framework for international ethics increased in importance after the ENRON scandal, and its "model code" now provides a foundation "minimum standard" for every accounting organization that wishes to be a member of IFAC.

So, at the turn of the century two important global organizations for accounting development, consistency, and standardization, were in place. IFAC for the professional training and development of accountants through national member bodies, and IFRS for the move toward consistent standards. These moves were a good sign of the profession adapting to the growth of international trade, the complexities of modern business and the challenges in areas like ethics that had been heightened by deregulation and increased competition.

However, accounting standards continued to focus on traditional approaches on what could and could not be included in financial reporting. IFRS and other standards bodies had recognized the issue of market value relative to tangible assets as well as intangibles such as financial "instruments" and has developed a number of standards in these emerging areas. "Fair Value" representation is now a recognized aspect of a number of accounting standards and the definition and application of how fair value might be accounted for and reported in IFRS #13 Fair Value Measurement. While addressing the challenge of underlying asset depreciation and appreciation the standard offers alternatives that organizations might adopt and has come under some criticism in terms of creating some lack of comparability between organizations involved in similar industries e.g., property management and development.

There are also standards that address the challenge of intangibles, but here unfortunately accounting remains constrained by its historic, conservative views. The challenges to changing the role of accountants and having the profession more heavily engaged in alternative measures of value have been identified by these standard setting bodies themselves[42]. Such as this speech:

---

[42] Speech by Hans Hoogervorst, Amsterdam, June 2012: 'The imprecise world of accounting'

One of the biggest measurement dilemmas relates to intangible assets. We know that they are there. While the value of Facebook's tangible assets is relatively limited, its business concept is immensely valuable (although 25% less immense than a month ago).

Likewise, the money-making potential of pharmaceutical patents is often quite substantial. However, both types of intangible assets go unrecorded (or under-recorded) on the balance sheet. Under strict conditions, IAS 38 Intangible Assets allows for limited capitalisation of development expenditures, but we know the standard is rudimentary because it is based on historical cost, which may not reflect the true value of the intangible asset.

The fact is that it is simply difficult to identify or measure intangible assets. High market-to-book ratios may provide indications of their existence and value. However, after the excesses of the dot.com bubble, there is understandable reluctance to record them on the balance sheet.

What is the reason for all this ambiguity and lack of precision in accounting? Well, to a great extent it is simply the nature of the beast. Valuation is as much of an art as a science and we are fully aware of that. Our Conceptual Framework says: "General purpose financial reports are not designed to show the value of a reporting entity; but they provide information to help users to estimate the value of the reporting entity." Value is ultimately in the eye of the beholder. There is often not a clear cut answer to the question as to which measurement technique is most appropriate to capture it.

Faced with this, is the profession headed for a place where it applies well thought through standards to a smaller and smaller portion of an organizations value for the investor? The reality is that on average, looking at the S&P 500, intangibles now represent between 90% and 95% of investor value. There are two main areas that accounting standards address this. First, in recognizing that intangibles do exist, they provide a set of conditions where they can be added to a balance sheet as an asset. This is outlined in IAS 38 originally issued in 2004. However, the foundations for the accounting recognition of an intangible result in most items failing to meet the requirements to be considered an asset i.e., allowed to be added to the balance sheet. The standard establishes its' definition a follow:

Intangible asset: an identifiable non-monetary asset without physical substance. An asset is a resource that is controlled by the entity as a result of past events (for example, purchase or self-creation) and from which future economic benefits (inflows of cash or other assets) are expected. [IAS 38.8] Thus, the critical attributes of an intangible asset include:

Identifiability. *Separable (capable of being separated and sold, transferred, licensed, rented, or exchanged, either individually or together with a related contract) or arises from contractual or other legal rights, regardless of whether those rights are transferable or separable from the entity or from other rights and obligations.*

Control. *The power to obtain benefits from the asset.*

Future economic benefit. *it is probable that the future economic benefits that are attributable to the asset will flow to the entity;* **and the cost of the asset can be measured reliably.**

Indefinite life: no foreseeable limit to the period over which the asset is expected to generate net cash inflows for the entity.

Finite life: a limited period of benefit to the entity.

If one looks at what attributes create the intangible value that fills the gap between market and book it would be hard to see how most would fit the above criteria, thus under accounting standards they are not revealed. Although many of these attributes that are created as part of a business model are critical to operability and that is what an investor is willing to pay for, accounting cannot recognize them as assets as they fail to meet the above standards criteria.

What is important for accounting is that buried in the daily, weekly, monthly, and annual operating costs are significant cash flows directed by management to create and sustain such capabilities and also have a significant impact on the income statement - yet almost nothing is disclosed. Financial statements cannot disclose the existence of the asset nor are they required to identify the expenses involved in creating and sustaining them - even though they have a significant impact on performance and profitability. Are current financial statements, under existing accounting standards "fit for purpose?" How much has been spent on creating these intangibles that has impacted cash flows and earnings? Is management nurturing the continued contribution of this past spending as an investment or is the value being depleted in efforts to enhance profitability?

The other key area that standards do address is when a market transaction takes place and goodwill is created which represents the difference between book value and the price paid by the buyer. This is, in effect the monetization of the value of the intangibles that exist based on the buyers due diligence; they are either considered i) a key "asset" as part of the cost of the business model being acquired and are considered realistic in "value" to justify "buying " the future earnings stream of the business - or ii) they represent an investment the buyer is willing to make for capabilities that when combined with the own existing organization, will deliver enhanced combined earnings. Accounting HAS to recognize goodwill otherwise the books do not balance! So, there are rules both about certain aspects of the acquired intangibles that CAN be capitalized on acquisition and also rules about the annual review of the "goodwill" on the buyer's books and an assessment of whether the amount has been impaired - Is it still worth the value that was added to the books. These standards satisfy the requirements to recognize reality in a merger or acquisition, *but they leave a lot to be desired in terms of understanding how the organization is being managed.*

If intangibles really do exist, and they impact both cash flows and financial performance, and adherence to accounting standards do not allow the complete picture to be shown, should the profession be looking at an alternative way to address the challenge? The hurdle here is two fold; first the focus on inability to capitalize and report the creation and continued existence of intangibles, and second the absence of any linkage between cash flows and expenses relative to the creation, benefits and sustaining of these intangibles.

8.3 Materiality

Materiality is a concept that underlies the preparation and audit of financial statements (a GOOGLE search will reveal that when asked about "materiality" the majority of definition pertain to accounting). It is a foundational concept although its' history is not clear, yet many writers have discoursed on the subject. One author[43] wrote in a 1984 paper:

---

[43] "The Origins and Development of Materiality as an Auditing Concept"; David C. Selley, 1984, The Canadian Institute of Chartered Accountants

How Accountants Lost their Balance

"Being asked to write a paper on materiality is rather like being asked to write a love poem. If one were to research all love poems previously written one would wonder how it was possible to come up with anything new or different. The materiality situation is similar. There is an immense quantity of material on the subject from standard-setting bodies and commissions, task forces and study groups commissioned by such bodies, practising firms, authors of textbooks and researchers in academe and elsewhere."

It appears from the research in this paper that materiality became an accounting and auditing concept around 1900 and was codified in its current for in 1949. As identified there has been much debate about what materiality REALLY means. For auditors, the IASB defines it as follows[44]:

Information is material if omitting, misstating, or obscuring it could reasonably be expected to influence the decisions that the primary users of general purpose financial statements make on the basis of those financial statements, which provide financial information about a specific reporting entity.

It is clear that the focus is on financial materiality, relative to the "general purpose financial statements." In recent years, these bodies have taken pains to ensure that, given the growing gap between market value between book value and market value, financial statements are not seen as, in any way, representing the value of an organization. Financial reporting and compliance are but one aspect of information about an organization that an investor should be expected to use.

"Moreover, financial reporting does not need to be mathematically exact to be useful. It is a tool to help investors on their way. Warren Buffett is known to use financial reports as a rough-and-ready checklist: more than five or six questions marks are enough for him to decide against making an investment[45]."

Financial reports, financial standards and reporting regulations are by definition historic and based on past transactions. They represent nothing more than a statement of the financial affairs of the company. As an example,

---

[44] Updated amendment to IAS 1, updated 2018, applicable 2020.

[45] "The imprecise world of accounting," speech by Hans Hoogervorst, Chair IASB, Amsterdam, June 2012:

part of the auditors (standard) statement when it issued a "clean" audit report on Alphabet (Google) for the year ended December 31st, 2018:

These financial statements are the responsibility of the Company's management. Our responsibility is to express an opinion on the Company's financial statements based on our audits. We are a public accounting firm registered with the PCAOB and are required to be independent with respect to the Company in accordance with the U.S. federal securities laws and the applicable rules and regulations of the Securities and Exchange Commission and the PCAOB.

We conducted our audits in accordance with the standards of the PCAOB. Those standards require that we plan and perform the audit to obtain reasonable assurance about whether the financial statements are free of material misstatement, whether due to error or fraud. Our audits included performing procedures to assess the risks of material misstatement of the financial statements, whether due to error or fraud, and performing procedures that respond to those risks. Such procedures included examining, on a test basis, evidence regarding the amounts and disclosures in the financial statements. Our audits also included evaluating the accounting principles used and significant estimates made by management, as well as evaluating the overall presentation of the financial statements. We believe that our audits provide a reasonable basis for our opinion.

Remember - that in the case of Google, this audit opinion pertains to about 20% of the investors "value" (see the brand information shown earlier). Materiality as defined and applied in auditing is effective at targeting areas of the audit which must be assessed in order to arrive at reasonably accurate results. But materiality in terms of an annual report containing only financial information tells little of the material aspects of an organizations value or viability. The standards setting bodies are aware of this and while looking to greater guidance for the "management commentary" does not see it in their role to address the wider area. The following comments from a recent speech[46] give some idea of the thinking:

"The IASB has always been aware that financial reporting in the narrow sense has its limitations. In our Conceptual Framework we acknowledge that general purpose financial

---

[46] "The times, they are a-changin,'" speech by Hans Hoogervorst, 18 September 2017, Accountancy Europe, Brussels, Belgium

reports are not designed to show the value of a company and that users also need other sources of information to make their estimations."

"Our awareness of the limitations of financial reporting in the narrow sense is one of the reasons that the IASB issued its non-mandatory Management Commentary Practice Statement (MCPS) in 2010.

This Practice Statement encourages management to provide context to the financial statements. It encourages management to report on the nature of the business, on its objectives and strategies, critical financial and non-financial resources, principal strategic, commercial, operational, and financial risks, performance indicators and information about the company's prospects."

"…Nevertheless, I do not think the IASB is equipped to enter the field of sustainability reporting directly. Our focus on financial reporting for capital market participants is deeply embedded in our DNA; widening the audience and scope of our work would most likely lead to loss of focus and identity. Moreover, our main area of competence is economics. ESG reporting to wider stakeholder groups requires expertise that we simply do not have.

If we want to create more clarity in the somewhat chaotic world of wider corporate reporting, we all need to define clearly what our responsibilities and competences are. If we all try to do everything, the most likely outcome is that nothing gets done properly."

Materiality has a wider concept if it is to be applied to the management commentary that forms a key part of future audited financials within corporate reporting. Is payroll, probably the largest expense a company incurs, material? Yes, but when identified as such the impact is on internal control and the detection of financial resources through errors, misappropriation, or fraud. There is no materiality aspect on "organization culture or commitment" which significantly impact future viability. Is customer revenue important? Yes - but again the focus is on the financial processes underpinning the cash flows involved - not on validating client satisfaction. It is only when revenue starts to decline, and questions are asked under the "going concern" clause that this "asset" starts to be viewed as potentially impaired.

However overall, the major hurdle in materiality is that there is a bridge that needs to be built between what is rightly within the financial reporting -

specifically the analysis of expenditures in a way the enhances the understanding of cash flow relative to intangibles, the management commentary, and other supporting aspects of corporate reporting that deal with nonfinancial aspects. Materiality as currently applied, external to the context of a meaningful bridge between financial and non-financial reporting, lacks the required depth and breadth to connect the financials to other aspects of risk and investor knowledge of future performance.

8.4 Going concern

This phrase seems very self-explanatory. It is often used as an opinion on a successful organization "…it's a going concern." To the lay person this phrase might mean that "all is well?" However, "going concern" is also an important aspect of current approaches to financial reporting, once again a GOOGLE search for a definition of the terminology will reflect primarily accounting definitions. What does the phrase _really_ mean, and could its' use again be a hurdle to understanding information presented in traditional corporate reporting?

The international accounting standards define what auditing is expected to ensure as part of its financial audit; this is defined in the first standard - IAS 1:

IAS 1 requires management to make an assessment of an entity's ability to continue as a going concern. If management has significant concerns about the entity's ability to continue as a going concern, the uncertainties must be disclosed. If management concludes that the entity is not a going concern, the financial statements should not be prepared on a going concern basis, in which case IAS 1 requires a series of disclosures[47].

Auditors do not blindly rely on management to affirm that an entity is a going concern but also perform several tests and look at other information, however, as the importance of intangibles grow in an organizations business model, so it becomes harder to assess the "quality" of the value that these underlying capabilities or assets are providing. In accounting language many definitions of "going concern" deal with a traditional, financial bias. An example of a widely presented definition of "going concern "would include: _"…a business that is assumed will meet its financial obligations when they fall due. It_

---

[47] Deloitte, IAS Plus, https://www.iasplus.com/en/standards/ias/ias1

functions without the threat of liquidation for the foreseeable future, which is usually regarded as at least the next 12 months or the specified accounting period".

Investors, relying on financial reports also seem to be guided by a traditional definition of "assets" when considering "going concern." This example from Investopedia is typical:

A company remains a going concern when the sale of assets does not impair its ability to continue operation, such as the closure of a small branch office that reassigns the employees to other departments within the company.

Accountants who view a company as a going concern generally believe a firm uses its assets wisely and does not have to liquidate anything. Accountants may also employ going concern principles to determine how a company should proceed with any sales of assets, reduction of expenses, or shifts to other products.

"…use its assets wisely." One would assume ALL assets. As discussed, accountants abide by standards that are unable to recognize the intangibles that fill a large portion of the gap between balance sheet values and market values, so the word "assets" in this situation is limited to balance sheet assets. The reason that the marketplace values these items is that they form a core aspect of an organization's business model. Even though the resources which went into creating them have passed through the income statement as an annual expense, they are invisible financially after creation. Even when the expense was incurred, it was invisible, being buried within operating costs.

So, the creation of intangibles which support operational capability are invisible as they are incurred (in fact they deplete earnings) and once created, they no longer form any structured part of an organizations balance sheet. The only place "value" is attributed to them by accounting, is when they are "re-created" as a result of a merger and acquisition and called goodwill. Yet management is directing significant cash resources to both creating these capabilities as well as sustaining them, in most cases through the effective use of human resources.

One example of the significance of resource applied to creating intangibles that form an essential and critical part of an organizations value was demonstrated by a court case involving AOL (America Online) with the following facts (with some added comments underlined), reported by an SEC press release:

At July 1, 1994, the beginning of AOL's 1995 fiscal year, June 30, 1995, and June 30, 1996, the DMAC (Deferred Marketing and Advertising Costs) on AOL's balance sheets were $26 million, $77 million, and $314 million, respectively, or 17%, 19% and 33% of total assets, and 26%, 35% and 61% of shareholders' equity. Had these costs been properly expensed as incurred, AOL's 1995 reported pre-tax loss would have been increased from $21 million to $98 million (including the write-off of DMAC that existed as of the end of fiscal year 1994), and AOL's 1996 reported pre-tax income of $62 million would have been decreased to a pre-tax loss of $175 million.

So, AOL had spent in excess of $417 million (almost $3/4 billion in 2020 value) to develop the subscriber base that it depended upon and had made the decision to add this to its balance sheet as an asset. The problem was that it was in a "new venture" and really had no substantive knowledge of the potential future revenue stream for this cost. Based on this, the IRS disallowed the expenses deduction and the SEC required re-statement of the financial reports. The reality was that without spending this money to create the "asset" of a subscriber base there would be no business.

The $¾ billion expenditure was funded by investors but then became a depletion of earnings and equity, because, if it was not allowed as a recognized asset then the costs were expensed against income. This investment was CRITICAL to AOL in order for it be a going concern and "sustaining" this subscriber base would also have been critical. However, unless addressed in the management discussion and analysis or equivalent report in the statements the magnitude of the impact would not be seen.

These investments, treated as expenses, continue today and the "assets" that are created are a key aspect of an entity remaining a going concern. Airbnb depends on its network of service providers and renters; Uber and Lyft depend upon the creation of its network of clients and drivers as well as its computer systems and capability (in this case the costs of "the app" might be treated as an asset but not the input and output aspects required to create an ROI). Clearly, Carillion was dependant on many aspects of intangibles as a going concern that were obviously not addressed as part of its last annual audit in a way that revealed the level of risk and the depletion of the underlying intangibles assets that investors thought represented value. What is clear is that a "going concern" opinion without some level of linkage between the use of financial resources and the creation, existence, and continual investment in intangibles is not showing a complete picture.

The hurdle to change in this case, is mainly in semantics and in the ability for financial information to be linked to non-financial indicators. Two things are needed; visibility into what exists as intangibles that are critical to operational sustainability and some level of linkage to the financial expenditures directed at creating and maintaining such assets. And of course, a review of impairment!

8.5 When is it ethical to unethical?

The ethics dilemma relative to tax planning and management, is a major hurdle for the profession. How is it that a significant portion of the profession earns fees from undertaking activities that, while (mostly) legal, are considered by society to be unethical? Ethical behaviour and the need to be seen to be "above reproach" and acting in the best interests of society was a founding aspect of the profession; it was a key reason why accountants were placed in a position of trust and asked to present "objective and independent" opinions on the financial records and reporting of others.

Before the growth in international business activity (trade might have been international but financing and ownership were national) there was not an issue or opportunity relative to taxation. Historically - starting in the "feudal" days and even going back to the Roman Empire, tax either did not exist or was targeted at individuals. As an example, the wealthy landowners who were also typically both "the upper class" as well as members of "the establishment" were expected to both provide resources in the way of men for armies to the crown when needed and also paid levies on their property.

It was similar in the US where early income tax focused on the wealthy and was then extended to "the middle class" and then applied across the board.

How Accountants Lost their Balance

Corporate income tax started in the US in 1909 and was at that time quite low; as with many other areas of taxation, the rates went up and down, but the trend was up. For the first 10 years in the US the rate was below 10% (starting at 1%) but it has never again been that low. In the UK Corporations tax was introduced in 1965; although prior to that date corporations had been taxed at the same rate as individuals. This dated back to the early 1800's where taxation arose from different sources; one category was "Schedule D" taxation that applied to "income from trades and professions" which remained the underlying corporate tax until 1965. Most countries developed some type of system for taxation however approaches, frameworks, scope, and rates of tax varied widely.

By the 1970's there was a growing trend by corporations, to both establish "subsidiary companies" in countries around the world where they operated and to move goods and services between these operations. Resultingly many organizations were subject to taxation in different countries at different rates and the call grew for some sort of agreement whereby "double taxation" could be avoided - if a company paid earnings on its income in one country, then that income should not re counted again and be taxed - or if it were included in income (such as the US worldwide approach) than at least there would be credits granted for the taxes already paid. This development in business brought with it a host of challenges for accountants and lawyers. What became quickly clear was that it could be beneficial to have higher incomes in low or zero tax locations and minimal or zero income in higher tax environments.

This started to create a whole new business in the area of transfer pricing of different goods and services that went backward and forward between company operations. Obviously, organizations sought to increase charges to high tax regimes to minimize expenses and reduce taxes, however the countries wanted to minimize these charges so that they could get "their fair share" of tax revenues. Accountants and lawyers developed a whole new business around providing advice on these types of situations to help organizations benefit; the goal would be the lowest possible overall tax paid and therefore the maximum benefit to "parent company" shareholders.

Taxation authorities realized the growing problem and set up national and international working groups to collaborate and cooperate on sharing information on how organizations were interpreting the various laws and how "loopholes" might be closed. It also became an area of attention for international bodies such as the OECD (Organization for Economic Cooperation and Development) which took an early lead:

Since 1979, the OECD has taken the global lead in developing international standards on transfer pricing, the tax rules relevant to determining the appropriate pricing for transactions between associated enterprises and the resulting profit allocation between jurisdictions. The OECD Transfer Pricing Guidelines for Multinational Enterprises and Tax Administrations (the Transfer Pricing Guidelines) originally published in 1979, and updated in 1995 and 2010, provide detailed guidance to tax authorities and multinational enterprises on the application of the arm's length principle, which is the principle that forms the core of the internationally accepted standard on transfer pricing[48].

Several factors conspired to increase the complexity of this international growth. Transfers of tangible products grew and often moved backward and forward between countries; transfers also grew to include services including intellectual property making valuation more challenging. Currency exchange rates around the world also moved up and down affected not just by domestic issues but also by changes in global commodity prices (e.g., oil, gold etc.) and also by the impact of currencies becoming, in themselves a "traded commodity."

In financial markets; interest rates, although influenced by global changes also changed significantly due again to both domestic economic priorities and issues (e.g. type of government and stability of government financial management and levels of national debt) as well as global issues impacted by global financial markets. Trade agreements between countries also developed changing the "terms of trade" between different economies. All of this led to corporations investing large amounts on legal and financial advice to minimize the negative impacts of all these changes.

---

[48] "Transfer Pricing in the New Global Landscape: the OECD's Engagement beyond its Borders" Masatsugu Asakawa, Deputy Vice-Minister of Finance for International Affairs, Japanese Ministry of Finance and Chairman, OECD Committee on Fiscal Affairs.

How Accountants Lost their Balance

What also developed, was a realization that the interests of the corporation were global in nature while the economic environments within which they operated were national. In several cases the financial impact of large corporations in terms in flows between different countries exceeded the total economic activity of smaller nations. The goal of a corporation was to maximize its profits while abiding by the laws of the countries within which they operated. The "level playing field" for corporate activity was the law not some arbitrary code of ethics.

If an organization chose to ignore a potential loophole in either the law or taxation approaches, then it risked being at a competitive disadvantage. This thrust the accounting profession into the middle of a major ethical conundrum. If accountants were to act for the benefit of the society within which they operated, was it then ethical for them to offer advice which exploited potential loopholes, albeit legal, which would benefit the corporation but disadvantage the country being impacted? Where did accountant's loyalty lie? The result is that while accountants position themselves as "being held to a higher standard" where "going beyond the law for the ethical benefit of society" is expected their first loyalty must be to those who pay its' bills - the clients.

Taxation authorities had for many years viewed the accounting profession as partners in upholding the "spirit of the law." Taxation, in fact many areas of law, can never be created and written in a way that foresees all potential events that might be impacted by it. This has been some of the arguments relative to a "rules based system" versus a "principles based approach." While the latter depends upon interpretations with a "spirit of the law" bias, the former suggests that "if the law does not forbid it, then you can do it / try it."

One might argue that this is why some of the most creative financial arrangements seem to emanate from the USA, famous for its innovation and creativity? Now accountants were working "for the other side" - and in many cases facing the legal forces of national taxation organizations in both appeals and court actions related to questionable interpretations of tax law.

The OECD, who were early movers in the challenges of transfer pricing are also key participants in the whole area of avoiding taxation by "gaming the system."

Base erosion and profit shifting (BEPS) refers to tax planning strategies used by multinational enterprises that exploit gaps and mismatches in tax rules to avoid paying tax. Developing countries' higher reliance on corporate income tax means they suffer from BEPS disproportionately. BEPS practices cost countries USD 100-240 billion in lost revenue annually. Working together within OECD/G20 Inclusive Framework on BEPS, over 135 countries and jurisdictions are collaborating on the implementation of 15 measures to tackle tax avoidance, improve the coherence of international tax rules and ensure a more transparent tax environment[49].

To put this loss in context it amounts to about 1.5 times the TOTAL Canadian income tax from individuals and corporations and of course for small countries it would be much greater). Other international bodies are concerned about this issue apart from the OECD - who, as seen from above area already collaborating with the G20 nations. These include The World Economic Forum:

The root of the problem is the way international corporate income is taxed. The current system is based on an approach devised almost a century ago, when large multinationals as we know them today did not exist. Today, individual entities that make up a multinational run separate accounts as if they were independent companies. But the multinational optimises its tax liabilities as a whole.

Instead, we should switch to what's called a unitary model of taxation. The idea is to tax the profit where the economic activity which generates it actually takes place – not where profits are reported. The multinational would report on its overall global profit and also on its activity in each country in which it operates. The governments of these countries would then be allowed to tax the multinational according to the activity in their country[50].

This approach has started to appear in Europe with certain countries looking to levy tax on companies based on revenues. This would be one way to limit the "gaming" - if an organization is getting economic benefit from

---

[49] From OECD website at December 2020, https://www.oecd.org/tax/beps/about/#history

[50] "Countries lose an estimated $125 billion in tax revenue each year. This is why" World Economic Forum

trading in a certain jurisdiction then those benefits should be subject to tax. Understandably, there has been an outcry against this from some areas.

The United Nations also sees a significant role for it to participate in the work of international taxation challenges; as it points out, certain countries are not represented by the OECD or the G20, and their voice also needs to be heard.

There currently exists no single entity with the global legitimacy, resources and expertise to serve as a single coordinating body for international tax cooperation. In the absence of such an entity, organizations active in this area must work together with a view to meeting common tax and development goals in the most efficient, responsive and participatory ways. While each country is responsible for its own tax system, the United Nations universal membership and legitimacy can be a catalyst for increased international cooperation in tax matters to the benefit of developed and developing countries alike. Since the great majority of United Nations Member States are neither members of OECD nor of the Group of 20, the United Nations Committee of Experts in International Cooperation in Tax Matters ("the Committee") has a key role to play, working with these and other relevant forums, such as the Bretton Woods institutions and regional associations of tax administrations, towards ensuring the active participation of developing countries, especially the least developed ones, in relevant activities. Continued effort in terms of its institutional capacity and resources is needed in order for the Committee to effectively pursue its proper role in international tax cooperation.

While the accounting profession is obviously heavily involved in the various committees and structures to address these issues, as long as opportunities exist to act within the law for the benefit of the client, the profession seems to view this as acting ethically. It is an interesting debate - "when is it ethical to act unethically?" The profession itself struggles with this; the 2016 edition of the International Ethics Standards Board for Accountants (IESBA part of IFAC) has no mention of the word "society" and only one mention of "social" (which is a convenient change from the past wording).

At the time of the ENRON scandal in 2001 all accounting bodies who were members of IFAC including those in Canada, USA, UK, and most other nations, had in place "Codes of Professional Conduct." There was much "soul searching" at the time especially given the role that Arthur Anderson, the CPA firm played in document destruction and "creative accounting" as to how this scandal could happen if all members were abiding by their code? I believe that there was only one accounting body worldwide that decided having a code was not enough and implemented mandatory training for both existing and newly graduated members around their code. This was the Certified General Accountants of British Columbia (CGA-BC) who were members of the national CGA Canada. This body has since merged into the newly created CPA Canada. In 2008 the CGA-BC Code had a specific section called "Responsibilities to Society" (and the word "society" was mentioned 12 times in the code. In the new code, developed at the time of the merger, "society" is now mentioned once as a principle:

"Registrants have a fundamental responsibility to safeguard and advance the interests of society. The reliance of the public, generally, and the business community, in particular, on sound and fair financial and management reporting and competent advice on business affairs - and the economic importance of that reporting and advice - impose these special obligations on the profession. They also establish, firmly, the profession's social usefulness."

The hurdle facing the profession is the apparent conflict, especially in the eyes of the general public between acting in the client's best interest and acting in societies best interest. In a world where organizations span the globe and operate as though there were no boundaries, the profession faces the potential of conflicting interests. This is the type of headline the public sees:

"How These Fortune 500 Companies (Legally) Paid $0 In Taxes Last Year" Fortune, April 11, 2019

"An in-depth analysis of Fortune 500 companies' financial filings finds that at least 60 of the nation's biggest corporations didn't pay a dime in federal income taxes in 2018 on a collective $79 billion in profits, the Institute on Taxation and Economic Policy said today. "If these companies paid the statutory 21 percent federal tax rate, they would owe $16.4 billion in federal income taxes. Instead, they collectively received $4.3 billion in rebates". Institute of Taxation and Economic Policy, April 11th, 2019

"Biggest companies pay the least tax, leaving society more vulnerable to pandemic – new research," The Conversation, March 30, 2020

"The CRA says Canadian corporations earned $298 billion in taxable income that year and paid about $40.9 billion in federal taxes. That means if their estimates about tax leakage are correct, the taxman missed out on about a quarter of the corporate tax revenue that could have been recouped." "Our government is committed to cracking down on tax evasion and aggressive tax avoidance, in Canada and offshore," said Diane Lebouthillier, Canada's minister of national revenue.

Until the EU tackles tax avoidance, big companies will keep getting away with it," The Guardian, Aidan Regan July 16th, 2020. This article stated: But the reality is more complicated. Although Apple has a huge presence in Ireland, where it employs some 6,000 people, this was not Irish money – it was profit generated from sales in other countries. The profits that accumulated, tax free, in Apple subsidiary accounts in Ireland ought to have been declared and paid in the US. Apple was simply exploiting a loophole in US and Irish law that allowed it to store its profits without paying tax legitimately, if it signalled it eventually intended to send this money back to the US.

While there the profession is engaged in activities to solve the root cause of the problem, its' reputation is tarnished by its association with what appear to be actions that are clearly not in an individual societies best interest.

8.6 The Boiling Frog Syndrome

If we return to the story of the boiling frog, it will appear that there are all sorts of changes taking place that are going on around the accounting profession, but which are each seen individually but not collectively, so many cannot feel the heat rising. I believe if one steps back and looks at the profession with a dispassionate eye using the approach "I believe what I see, not what you tell me" then these challenges that we have discussed, add up to the beginning of a sea change where the profession is drifting towards the reef rather than setting a new course. There are hurdles to change but if change is needed the response cannot be "we can't do this because" but rather "how can we do this?"

The role of accounting relative to financial management is an important one and, together with standards and foundational principles should continue to form a significant portion of the work that professionals do. However, there are events taking place that have changed the way money is used and what people who "own it" need to understand about how it (their money) is being used. Risk has also changed; while financial risk remains an important aspect - after all many companies still fail because they run out of cash, other risks to being operationally sustainable have increased.

While the world is looking at sustainability in the context of the way in which organizations operate and impact society from an environmental and social perspective (which to some degree is impacted by what we have discussed) there is another whole field of sustainability that is being missed. Traditionally this would have fallen under the "going concern" issue but today finance is but only one aspect of an organization continuing ability to be a going concern. Non-financial aspects and capabilities that organizations have invested in, are now critical to operational sustainability.

These must now be embraced by the accounting profession that is in the best position to understand the challenges. There is a major risk to investors, in the age of intangible capabilities. Is accounting part of the solution? What ideas are we putting forward that will help both update our approach to financial management but also start to shift our own paradigm and take on a new area of professional work involved in trying to explain corporate value. Economists, who are the experts in value, do not have the positioning that the accounting profession has in the world of business. This sounds like and opportunity to start building a new area for the profession.

In the next chapter we will look at the broader social and contextual changes that are, in fact helping set the stage for the direction we might shift towards.

9. Social changes and supplemental reporting

Although accountants have been living through the social changes that have been taking place, most have had their time full of worrying about issues that directly concern them. Most accountants I have known over the years have had little time to deal with things other than their day-to-day work pressures. However, to understand the direction the profession must take, we must look at a wider range of issues - many of which DO have an impact on our own profession.

In parallel to the financial and accounting changes, there have been societal changes taking place. Many of these were initiated by interest groups focusing on issues and agendas that were outside the direct concern of the accounting profession; however, there is a DIRECT link between these changes and the accounting profession.

I refer to this as "the big picture!" and can be thought of like the diagram: We, the humans live within a "system" - some of which we understand, some of which we can control and some which is "beyond us." The natural and animal aspects of the system are impacted by us, but we cannot claim that we created the animals or the planet.

What we do create is the societies or communities within which we live and within these what might be called the "social norms" around how we behave. We also create an economic system which is the "business aspect" of the society and social order that we create.

In the earlier part of the book, we placed a lot of attention on how that

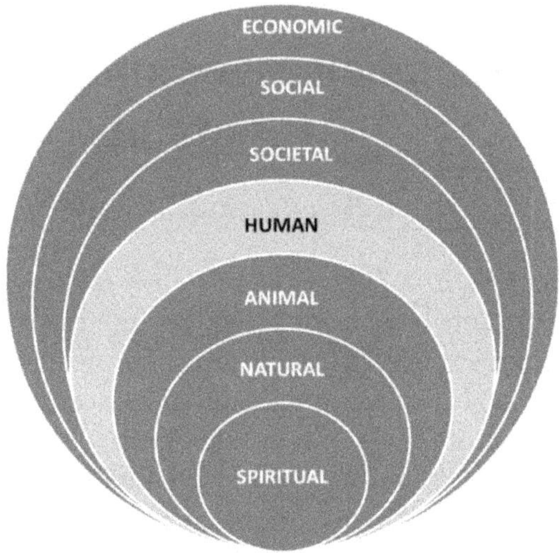

economic part of what we created, supposedly to benefit society, was actually operating. Throughout history there have been discussions and opinions about what sort of approaches to these systems that we create work best. As a social system, many support democracies while others support communism. As an economic system some support capitalism others support the centrally controlled economy that develops as a part of communism. All of these are not "absolutes." Democracy can be right wing or left wing; communism has been seen to be able to adopt aspects of the capitalist economic system.

When the Berlin Wall was brought down in 1989 not only was there exuberance in Germany, but the rest of the world also breathed a sigh of relief that the old divisions had, symbolically, been removed. Even more importantly there were headlines That "Capitalism had Won." It is beyond this book to argue the merits - however clearly there have been incredibly positive benefits from capitalism, yet, as we shall identify in this chapter it might be drifting in a direction where it is not serving society as well as it might. Adam Smith, who is oft quoted as being the proponent of capitalism also suggested that we are naturally interested in "the fortunes of others and render their happiness necessary" despite deriving no reward except "pleasure." This was from his first book, The Theory of Moral Sentiments. It is his second book, The Wealth of Nations, which is often quoted to support the practise of capitalism, that focuses on the role of self-interest in driving markets. For our purposes there seem to be two themes that will impact the future of the profession:

- Public perceptions are changing, both through observing the failures of the economic system, (which many experienced personally) and about the role of corporations within society.
- The professions foundation, based on a tangible and mainly national corporate world, was fast being outdated.

While it will be suggested that change and improvement is needed, this book does not subscribe to the notion that capitalism needs to be replaced. Two quotes of Winston Churchill come to mind, firstly about our social system and then about the economic framework:

> *"Democracy is the worst form of government, except for all the others." (He also said…)*
>
> *The inherent vice of capitalism is the unequal sharing of blessings; the inherent virtue of socialism is the equal sharing of miseries.*

It is all about balance, that "middle of the road" position where excesses are avoided but so is the belief that anyone is owed anything by the state. It is a case of balancing the behaviour of human beings within the system. This was expressed effectively by a prominent US politician:

> *"There is nobody in this country who got rich on their own. Nobody. You built a factory out there - good for you. But I want to be clear. You moved your goods to market on roads the rest of us paid for. You hired workers the rest of us paid to educate. You were safe in your factory because of police forces and fire forces that the rest of us paid for. You didn't have to worry that marauding bands would come and seize everything at your factory... Now look. You built a factory and it turned into something terrific or a great idea - God bless! Keep a hunk of it. But part of the underlying social contract is you take a hunk of that and pay forward for the next kid who comes along."*
> — Elizabeth Warren

The framework that allows this to happen is the application of Adam Smith's writing in "The Theory of Moral Sentiments" that suggest corporations do, in fact have a level of corporate social responsibility as a member of the society within which they operate. They need to operate "in balance" serving the needs of their shareholders in a responsible way.

9.1 Rumblings of a need for balance

While today the term "stakeholder" is recognized and used widely, it only became part of corporate "parlance" in the 1980's; up until that time any conversation about corporate responsibility revolved around the shareholder. The "shareholder theory," posited in the early 20th century by economist Milton Friedman, says that a company is "beholden only to shareholders" - that is, the company must make a profit for its shareholders. Many States in the USA still follow this "shareholder primacy" which makes "strategic investment" in items that cannot be causally linked to generating a "bottom line" impact, or through improving overall "net worth" can be harder to justify. This introduction from an article[51] summarizes the US situation:

---

[51] "The US and Corporate Social Responsibility in International Business Transactions: Has Anything Changed?" May 5, 2018, Samantha Bloch, Denver Journal of International Law and Policy

In the U.S., although corporate law is enacted separately in each individual state, it is possible to say that legislators and courts have largely endorsed the shareholder primacy doctrine. This makes the adoption of integrated and sustainable decision-making processes by CEOs and boards of directors more difficult but not impossible. As stated by the authors of a legal study on CSR relying on the situation in the state of Delaware "… integrated decision-making is not contrary to the duties and mandate of the directors of a Delaware corporation. However, neither is integrated decision-making required or specifically encouraged. Furthermore …to the extent that it is permitted … [it] is contingent on whether it can be ultimately linked to the best interests of the shareholders". The shareholder primacy principle is thus foundational in the analysis of CSR in the American legal system.

The goal of this chapter is to demonstrate how many of the initiatives, often considered under the umbrella of CSR are, in fact beneficial to BOTH shareholders and many other stakeholders. This is a key area, where the engagement and involvement of the accounting profession, to back up, support and financially justify key sustainability initiatives, and the support of intangibles, is so critical. As it currently stands, the law could easily show that items charged to expenses that are building intangibles are reducing profits and therefore having a negative impact on shareholders. However, if accountants embraced a full fledged capability to demonstrate the link between intangible investment, value and organizational sustainability i.e. an ROI from investment in intangibles that are not on the balance sheet, this must be a way forward for the profession.

The strongest initial push is for corporations to address environmental issues. It was also at that time that CSR was beginning to be universally understood, both as an "externalities" issue but also as a corporate behavioural issue. It was increasingly seen that through both tax avoidance and by "not caring for" and / or "not paying for" their impact on the natural world, corporations were getting a free ride. These efforts were initially focused on the recognition that the "externalities" that were absent from corporate accountability, were impacting society and should be addressed. In economics, an externality is the cost or benefit that is imposed by one or several parties (in this case corporations) on a third party (the general public), who did not agree to incur that cost or benefit.

It is an economic issue which is part of the challenge in that accountants and accounting had ignored or neglected the concept; one could argue that it is, in some ways, like intangibles. We know that it exists and that someone, somewhere is ultimately paying for it - but for the company, there is no direct cash flow involved. Like goodwill, it only becomes an accounting issue when cash is involved. Two British economists are credited with having initiated the formal study of externalities, or "spillover effects." Henry Sidgwick (1838–1900) is credited with first articulating the concept, and Arthur C. Pigou (1877–1959) is credited with formalizing it - so, it is not a new concept.

Pigou argued that a tax on negative externalities (e.g., costs incurred by others through actions of a corporation) could be used to reduce their incidence to an efficient level - an example would be a carbon tax. Subsequent thinkers have debated whether it is preferable to tax or to regulate negative externalities. Prior to the imposition of carbon taxes, regulation was the primary approach. During the 1980's there were two elements of externalities that were growing in public concern. The first was the impact of corporations on the environment both through its' consumption of "free" resources as inputs, and the impacts of its outputs, for example emissions that impact the air and water as well as its impact on public services.

Many of these changes started to be discussed under the general umbrella term of the "triple bottom line." This concept was first crystallized when Ben and Jerry's Ice Cream voluntarily published its first CSR (Corporate Social Responsibility) report, in about 1987. As a progressive organization, they believed that while reporting on financial performance remained important, it also added value to report on other aspects of their organization's activities. At that time, the triple bottom line applied to "People, Planet and Profits." This idea was then further developed by John Elkington, the founder of SustainAbility some years later and continued to evolve.

The challenge remained that two parallel approaches to accountability were developing – one the traditional financial reporting against a well established set of GAAP and emerging International Standards, and a second CSR approach that was often "home grown" and at the same had little or no standard reporting - although gradually some countries, in particular in Europe started to require specific reporting of environmental issues as part of their annual reports.

Early studies, in the 1980's, were conducted to try a develop a framework to recognize the growth in "nonfinancial assets;" Skandia, a financial services company in Sweden was an early pioneer to develop one of the early models - at a time when most intangibles were captured in the category of "intellectual capital." At that time there was recognition that intangible assets were a part of this framework that added value to an organization.

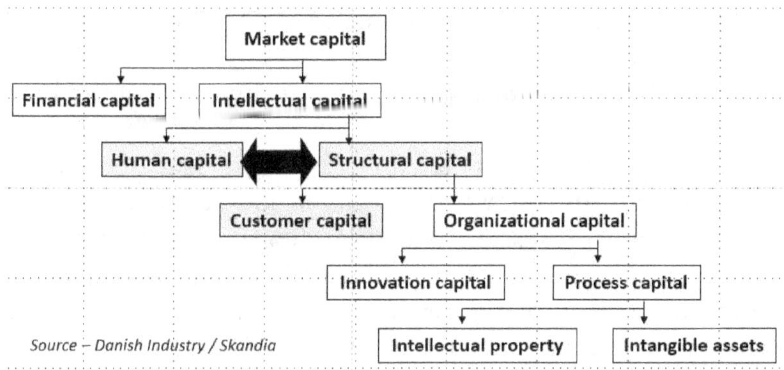

During this period, many books were written around intellectual capital including one by Thomas Stewart[52] who defined it as *"Intellectual capital is something that you cannot touch but it makes you rich."* His book also contained several early approaches to try and "value" this capital such as the use of "market to book" (that remains a key indicator) and Tobins Q as "total system" measures; it also suggested measures for human capital, structural capital, and customer capital.

9.2 Shifting public attitude to corporate behaviour

It is easy to blame the media for the constant reporting of corporate misconduct, but the reality is that stories about "problems" with the economic system have impacted public perceptions of corporate accountability. It is hard to determine whether there are more or less unethical events or accounting

---

[52] "Intellectual Capital: The New Wealth of Nations" 1997, Thomas Stewart, Currency Doubleday

problems than in the past; it is also hard to disassociate the profession of accounting with the reputation and behaviour of corporations because they are "part of the system." Hiding behind "compliance with the standards" is akin to telling an unhappy customer that the company "is following procedures." The response is the same - dissatisfaction. In reality, the public still seem to trust the accounting profession as a whole in spite of the obvious areas of involvement. (Reminding one of a story):

Balloonist:	Can you tell me where I am?
Accountant:	You are in the air in a balloon about 10 metres over the field
Balloonist:	You must be an accountant
Accountant:	How did you know that?
Balloonist:	Because what you told me is technically correct but useless

Accountants rank ahead of lawyers, NGO's, and Government tax authorities in terms of trust[53] however, the actual level of trust is still only 55% of respondents. For a profession that was chosen to report to the public "objectively and independently" and to place "the needs of society" first, this is not a good rating? Part of the problem is not being seen as "leaders of change." The words and efforts have often been there, as well as changes in regulation yet problems involving the profession continue. Almost 20 years ago, after ENRON the AICPA published a clear statement of the need to do better:

This is a difficult time for all of us involved with the financial reporting process. The repercussions of the Enron collapse are being felt on many levels, none more so than within the accounting profession. The AICPA shares the distress of all Americans concerning the tragic breakdowns that contributed to the fall of Enron. We take seriously our public responsibility and are committed to doing everything possible to restore confidence in our profession.

These are not just idle words. Our profession has a more than 100-year history based on public trust and integrity. Each year more than 15,000 audits of publicly traded companies are completed successfully without restatement or allegations of impropriety. Thousands more

---

[53] "Trust is just the beginning" Daniel Hood, March 4th, 2019, Accounting Today. Study from ACCA, IFAC, and CA ANZ

audits of private companies and business enterprises—from hospitals, charities, and youth groups to the newest businesses—are performed successfully by our members. Collectively these audits serve as the bedrock of the U.S. economy[54].

Yet scandals continued as we have discussed. The challenge reminds me of the definition of lunacy when seeking change "expecting different results but doing the same things." There was a growing feeling that organizations were not doing their part as members of society - in fact, they were taking advantage of their position, and accountants did not seem to be helping solve the problem.

The primary role of accountants in many of the scandals that were reported, was as auditors. The public clearly felt that the system of oversight including audits was failing. Even with the introduction of an additional layer of oversight for those auditing publicly traded companies as well as legislation designed to limit collusion between auditors and their clients and to strengthen the role of the board, problems remained. In a critical article on the accountancy profession published in 2018 the author[55] stated:

The demise of sound accounting became a critical cause of the early 21st-century financial crisis. Auditing limited companies, made mandatory in Britain around a hundred years earlier, was intended as a check on the so-called "principal/agent problem" inherent in the corporate form of business. As Adam Smith once pointed out, "managers of other people's money" could not be trusted to be as prudent with it as they were with their own. When late-20th-century bankers began gambling with eye-watering amounts of other people's money, good accounting became more important than ever. But the bean counters now had more commercial priorities and – with limited liability of their own – less fear for the consequences of failure. "Negligence and profusion," as (Adam) Smith foretold, duly ensued.

It was not just the overall picture of scandals, but the underlying failures of the systems of oversight such as the controls necessary to avoid these

---

[54] "Restoring Public Confidence," James G. Castellano, April 1, 2002, AICPA Accountancy Journal,

[55] "The financial scandal no one is talking about," Richard Brooks, 29th May 2018, The Guardian

problems. Many of the major scandals such as Barings Bank and Allied Irish Bank involved internal fraud carried out by employees. A 2014 report titled "Global Economic Crime Survey (GECS), "Economic Crime: A Threat to Business Globally," published by PwC (PricewaterhouseCoopers). stated: "Fraud rates increased from 30% of companies in 2009 to 34% in 2011 and 37% in 2014. According to the survey, the five most common types of fraud consistently reported are asset misappropriation (69%), procurement fraud (29%), bribery and corruption (27%), cybercrime (24%), and accounting fraud (22%). These numbers are significant especially considering the global scope and size of organizations today. The public might feel "how can people get away with this?"

These frauds were tied in with the audit failures and placed auditors once again in the cross-hairs of the public's opinion. It also seemed that those in a position of trust, such as senior executives - even CEO's were part of the problem; these were the individuals who were expected to set "the tone at the top." It is human nature, if one sees one's boss stealing or misappropriating company resources, to start asking "well if he / she can get away with it, why shouldn't I?" These were also the people signing the internal control statements for the auditors. Another quote from the Richard Brooks article suggests the challenge that audits and auditors face:

The chairman of HBOS, arguably Britain's most dubious lender of the boom years, explained to a subsequent parliamentary enquiry: "I met alone with the auditors – the two main partners – at least once a year, and, in our meeting, they could air anything that they found difficult. Although we had interesting discussions – they were very helpful about the business – there were never any issues raised."

HBOS had been caught up in the financial crisis in 2008 and had to be "rescued" by Lloyds Bank and the UK Government, yet KPMG, its auditors, had considered them a "going concern" at their last audit before the crash. The regulatory body, FRC investigated KPMG and eventually cleared them of any wrongdoing as such a problem "…would have been difficult to foresee." In a statement, after being cleared a KPMG spokesperson stated:

"The collapse of HBOS and other examples of corporate failure and fraud in the last decade have highlighted a gap between what society expects of an audit and what an audit

has been designed to do. Since 2008, whilst we recognise that there is more to be done, we have worked hard to contribute positively to this debate and have explored ways to close the expectation gap, for example, by offering extended audit opinions which give a view on corporate risks."

Unfortunately, it is still hard to assess what changes are being made and whether these will significantly improve the audit? There remain other significant issues in the ability of the audit profession to achieve the goal of true objectivity and independence; just four major global firms – Deloitte, PricewaterhouseCoopers (PwC), Ernst & Young (EY) and KPMG – audit 97% of US public companies and all the UK's top 100 corporations, verifying that their accounts present a trustworthy and fair view of their business to investors, customers, and workers. While the appointment of auditors, the review of their report and the approval of their fees is usually a board of directors' role, the reality remains that audit fees are an expense paid for by the company out of its own income.

This problem becomes greater when the CEO is also the Chairman of the Board. This situation was recommended to be changed many years ago, yet many large, publicly traded companies still have the two roles carried by the same person. One might question the independence of the board? There are also the issues created by the close relationships between audit firms and their clients, such as the movement from audit firms into key finance roles in the company's they audit; the fee revenues flowing into the consulting arms of the accounting practices (where still allowed - although many now get around this because of the rotation of auditors), senior finance officials who have no ethical code as they are not members of a recognized professional accounting body and others.

Although in this instance the FRC essentially cleared KPMG, many remain in doubt of its effectiveness to "protect the public." Dame Elizabeth Gloster in her December 2020 report into the UK regulator's handling of the LCF scandal, which was published in December 2020, heavily criticized the FRC for its mis-handling of the LCF (London Capital and Finance) affair. The FCA's poor response, in spite of warnings as early as 2017, meant 11,625 savers had invested £237 million into the toxic minibonds sold by LCF by the time of its administration in January 2019.

The UK Serious Fraud Office also started an investigation into LCF. Andrew Bailey, who ran the FCA for about four years during the time of this problem, (before leaving to become governor of the Bank of England in March 2020), was singled out in the nearly 500-page report and was heavily criticized for the work of the regulator under his leadership. He publicly apologized after the report was issued.

Linked to the above issues of control and fraud, is the issue of executive compensation. It does not help for example, that after the FCA's failure to regulate LCT the following headline was seen *"The Financial Conduct Authority (FCA) has cancelled £205,000 worth of executive bonuses after a damning report found the watchdog had failed to properly regulate a collapsed firm."* These bonuses were to be paid to people in leadership and oversight positions. Other challenges come from issues that have included the manipulation of financial results in a way that benefits the pay of executives - either through the payment of a bonus or the benefits to be gained through receiving and exercising stock options. An article[56] summarizes the perception that the public has of executive pay - especially in terms of "fairness and reasonableness:"

CEO pay has been controversial in the United States for more than a century—for as long as corporate management has been a profession separate from ownership. In economic booms, CEO pay skyrockets and, after the inevitable bust, it attracts attention—as the million-dollar paychecks of executives such as W.R. Grace of Bethlehem Steel and Charles Mitchell of National City Bank drew notice in the 1930s. But the most recent debate focuses on the staggering, uninterrupted rise in CEO pay over the past three decades, following a long period of moderation in both executive pay and in overall economic inequality. Between 1940 and 1970, average CEO pay remained below $1 million (in 2000 dollars). According to the Economic Policy Institute (EPI), from 1978 to 2013, CEO pay at American firms rose a stunning 937 percent, compared with a mere 10.2 percent growth in worker compensation over the same period, all adjusted for inflation. In 2013, the average CEO pay at the top 350 U.S. companies was $15.2 million.

The question is not as to whether this is right or wrong it is whether these changes have impacted the public perception about the conduct of

---

[56] "The Overpaid CEO" Susan Holmberg, Fall 2014, Democracy

corporations? When this fact is added to the continuing list of scandals and other issues, the public starts to question the whole system. For accountants, the issue is that the incentive for fraud, manipulation and short term decision making is increased; this in itself increases the challenge of assessing risk and internal control. In a paper published on the relationship between fraud and executive compensation the following conclusions were stated:

The distribution of Financially Related Fraud (FRF) is highly concentrated in specific years and certain industries,

The increase in executives' option incentives raises the likelihood of financial reporting violations,

The effect of (share) option incentives on FRF is moderated by auditor effort (the relationship between option incentives and FRF is weaker or stronger when auditors pay more or less effort,

Another proxy for the measurement of executives' option incentives, namely, the number of vested options by executives, is highly correlated with the CEO's vested stock option sensitivity.

(The) Our results suggest that higher executives' option incentives increase a firm's likelihood of FRF. In addition, the effect executives' option incentives on a firm's likelihood of FRF varies by auditor effort. Hence, auditor effort could help a firm weaken the influence of executives' option incentives on its accounting irregularities.

The issue of rapidly escalating executive pay was identified as early as the 1970's when many Japanese approaches to management systems were being implemented and on problem seemed to be the large gap between executive and average employee compensation.

Accountants are also connected to the development of compensation and executive tax planning approaches. Which brings us to the impact of tax schemes and the revelations caused by revelations such as the Panama Papers. Tax avoidance, although maybe considered unethical is not illegal; however, the Big 4 accounting firms are clearly connected to a large proportion of the multi-national tax planning schemes according to a paper published in 2018:

Our results suggest that the role of the Big 4 accountancy firms is far from insignificant. In aggregate, MNEs that use a Big 4 accountancy firms have a significantly higher tax haven incident rate compared to those firms that do not use a Big 4 auditor. Hence this paper demonstrates clear evidence of a strong correlation between tax haven use and the use of the Big 4[57]

Large accounting firms have also been in the news related to personal tax shelters. An example was the major 2003 - 2005 case involving KPMG who ultimately agreed to an out of court settlement with the US government. *"Under a deferred prosecution agreement, KPMG LLP admitted criminal wrongdoing in creating fraudulent tax shelters to help wealthy clients dodge $2.5 billion in taxes and agreed to pay $456 million in penalties. KPMG LLP will not face criminal prosecution as long as it complies with the terms of its agreement with the government. On January 3, 2007, the criminal conspiracy charges against KPMG were dropped.*

National tax authorities around the world, as outlined in our earlier chapter are facing the challenge of tracking down and acting on tax avoidance; another case in Canada also appeared to involve KPMG:

"The Canada Revenue Agency has once again made a secret out-of-court settlement with wealthy KPMG clients caught using what the CRA itself had alleged was a "grossly negligent" offshore "sham" set up to avoid detection by tax authorities, CBC's The Fifth Estate and Radio-Canada's Enquête have learned."

While the accounting profession is only exploring opportunities to save their clients money, the degree to which practices, deemed by the public to be unethical is having an impact on public perceptions. Articles like the following sum up the growing attention to the issue:

Tax abuse, and particularly tax avoidance by multinational corporations, has received considerable public, media, civil society and government attention in recent years. Coming against a backdrop of financial crisis and struggling economies, a series of leaks and investigations concerning tax and banking practices in countries such as Panama, Luxembourg and Switzerland has brought the issue of tax to the fore[58].

---

[57] Tax haven networks and the role of the Big 4 accountancy firms" Chris Jones, Yama Temouri, Alex Cobham, Feb 2018, Journal of World Business,

[58] "The Elephant in the Room": Corporate Tax Avoidance & Business and Human Rights; Published online by Cambridge University Press: 12 August 2016

Finally, the size and scope of the impact on some governments who are foregoing the results of creative approaches to taxation have been estimated as follows[59]:

Although the estimated amount of the tax gap may vary depending on the definition of aggressive tax planning, a research paper of the European Parliament clearly shows the magnitude of the problem and estimates the loss of tax revenue to the European Union (EU) Member States through aggressive corporate tax planning to be around 160–190 billion euros per year.

In the United States, a study shows that the US Treasury is losing over $381 billion per year because of tax avoidance and evasion.

A study of the Dutch Centre for Research on Multinational Corporations shows that, as a result of Dutch tax treaties, developing countries lose 770 billion euro per year of withholding taxes on interest and dividends

Other research estimates that multinationals relocate about 40% of their profits to tax havens each year. Besides the financial dimension for government budgets, aggressive tax planning also undermines trust, shared understandings and commitments, and organizational integrity

There is no question that tax avoidance is impacting public opinion and that governments are finally trying to move to change this. "Real" change like moving from taxing profits to taxing domestic revenues are already being met with major "push back" - examples being the European approach aimed at organizations like Apple, Google, and Amazon.

There are other behaviours that once again, impact public perceptions - even though accountants are not directly involved they are "implicated". The types of corporate behaviour included unfair and unethical sales practices (Madoff scandal, Wells Fargo accounts and credit cards); eliminating of local suppliers due to outsourcing to lower cost areas and countries - this would include both the North to South movement in the US and the move from the western world to lower cost economies such as Asia and even Mexico. These

---

[59] "A Real Option Approach to Sustainable Corporate Tax Behavior," July 3rd 2020; Anne Van de Vijver, Danny Cassimon, Peter-Jan Engelen; Sustainability Journal (EU)

moves left communities with the loss of small business, local tax revenues and overall employment.

To protect themselves banks and other financial institutions often moved rapidly to foreclose on properties when mortgages went unpaid - both in the 1982 recession as well as after the property bust in the US in 2008 - 2010. In this latter case it later became evident that in many cases, banks were employing contractors and agents to foreclose, and the paperwork was in error or had never been completed at the time the mortgage was granted. Organizations appeared to be protecting themselves no matter what the social and societal costs were. There was other "rumblings of discontent when corporations seemed to get preferential treatment - such as tax cuts, "bail outs" (especially at the same time that people were losing their jobs and their life savings) and political involvement - such as lobbying in the US and examples like the SNC Lavalin affair in Canada. Banking problems also raised their head in Canada as demonstrated from a headline[60]

'We are all doing it': Employees at Canada's 5 big banks speak out about pressure to dupe customers.

All of this "social impact" would occasionally show up in public protest and demonstration. One such movement was the "Occupy" protests (which ultimately missed their opportunity through lack of a clear "cause" to be focusing on). They did demonstrate the breadth of unhappiness with corporate conduct.

"The first Occupy protest to receive widespread attention, Occupy Wall Street in New York City's Zuccotti Park, began on 17 September 2011. By 9 October, Occupy protests had taken place or were ongoing in over 951 cities across 82 countries, and in over 600 communities in the United States[61]"

The also indicated how fast the message could spread using new approaches to communications through social media and how quickly the protests "struck a chord" in many, many countries. Importantly the responses also indicated

---

[60] (Headline from), Erica Johnson April 11, 2017, CBC News
[61] Wikipedia Occupy Movement (see also Occupy Wall Street)

the degree to which those in power understood the changes that were taking place. Mark Carney, who at the time was Governor of the Bank of Canada and went on to become Governor of the Bank of England appeared to understand the issue[62]:

As protesters prepare to bring the Occupy Wall Street movement north of the border, Canada's top banker says he is sympathetic to their frustrations. In an interview with CBC's Peter Mansbridge, Bank of Canada Governor Mark Carney called the demonstrations, which are slated to spread to cities across Canada on Saturday, "entirely constructive."

"I understand the frustration of many people, particularly in the United States," he said. "You've had increase in inequality because of … globalization, because of technology. You've had a big increase in the ratio of CEO earnings to workers on the shop floor. "The financial crisis, he says, has only exacerbated those feelings." There's a frustration with policy, that is understandable, and a frustration that, 'Are things going back to business as usual … in the way the financial system functions?'" he said. "Now if I may say, that is not what's going to happen, but I can understand the frustrations that are there."

Meanwhile, Democratic responses in the US also tended to sympathize while Republican sentiments seemed to reflect the traditional approach to the social responsibility of business; *"House Majority Leader Eric Cantor (R-Va), in a speech to a Values Voter Summit, characterized the movement as "growing mobs"*

Was this one of the signs of the need for a sea-change in corporate accountability such as had happened before? Certainly, the level of growing public discontent can be traced back through a series of events, each one of which hardened attitudes towards business and accounted for the demand for greater transparency and accountability. Accountants are clearly part of the system and are in an important role of "public assurance" that the "system" is working well.

But the continuing failure of audits, the involvement of the big 4 accounting firms in scandals, the creativity of personal and corporate tax planning is all part of the actions that are feeding a demand for change. Accountants do not

---

[62] "Occupy Wall Street Protests' Constructive says Mark Carney, Bank Of Canada Governor: Rachel Mendleson, 14th Oct 2011, The Huffington Post

appear, to the public to be leading these initiatives with progressive new approaches. What they do appear to be is presiding over audits that increasingly fail to disclose audit, frauds, scandals and failures and increasingly involved in anti-social tax avoidance.

9.3 Growing environmental awareness

Although governments responded to many of the "behavioural issues" and audit problems with legislation and greater regulation, a greater level of public attention was being paid to the evolving environment impact of societal activities by corporations (the externalities). This was a growing issue where, for many, awareness started with incidents like The Love Canal (*Love Canal is a neighborhood in Niagara Falls, New York, and the location of a 70-acre landfill that became the site of an enormous environmental disaster in the 1970s. Decades of dumping toxic chemicals harmed the health of hundreds of residents and was eventually cleaned up by government funding*). Awareness was also heightened by major oil spills such as The Torrey Canyon, Exxon Valdiz and others that impacted sea life.

Various public and private bodies such as Greenpeace were started in the late 1960's and into the 1970's; the emergence of the "One World" idea of a shared planet was reinforced by the views of the earth from the Apollo Space Shuttles; The Club of Rome was formed and published "Limits to Growth" which was the widest and largest selling environmental book in history.

One of the key milestones was the Brundtland Commission formed in 1984 which, in 1987 published their report "Our Common Future;" this galvanized attention on the many areas where human behaviour was having a negative impact on the planet. Many individual initiatives were also being undertaken and were focusing on the impact of humanity on the natural environment. In 1985 the hole in the ozone layer over Antarctic was discovered, apparently caused by a combination of emissions such as aerosol propellants being used, freon gas, carbon dioxide emissions and others.

It may be that all the initiatives building since the 1950's were finally crystallized in the Brundtland report and the hole in the ozone layer, which raised international awareness to a level where something needed to be done. The United Nations Framework Convention on Climate Change was published in May 1992, just prior to the first ever UN organized "Earth Summit." From this point forward, environmental issues were on the mind of not just activists and politicians but as a business issue.

There were clearly risk involved in organizational activity that impacted the environment, and this led to the creation of many "business initiatives" and responses. It also started a "patchwork" of legislative compliance requirements which further complicated corporate reporting. Accountants had the challenge of different accounting standards depending upon where their shares were traded and now organizations had an added burden of additional reporting that depended on their national jurisdiction.

In 1992 he first environmental management system standard, BS 7750, was published by the BSI (British Standards Institute) group. In 1996, the International Organization for Standardization (ISO) created the ISO 14000 family of standards at a generally agreed approach to implementing a minimum level of policy, planning and control within organizations. As was the case with the release of the (process) Quality Management Standard, ISO 9000 in 1987, the accounting profession provided little financial analysis and support for implementing such initiatives; however, many organizations that decided to put an environmental management system in place, and to start following a more "earth friendly" approach soon discovered that there were financial savings involved. While there was a cost of implementation and sustaining such systems, these were often offset by savings from reduced and alternative energy use, and replacement of materials being used by others with less environmental impact. Savings also came from the recycling of materials and supplies and the re-use of what had previously been considered waste products. Reputations were also enhanced.

While several UN initiatives were now underway, a key milestone was the creation of the World Business Council on Sustainable Development (WBCSD) that was founded on the eve of the 1992 Rio Earth Summit. WBCSD was founded by a group of CEOs who recognized the world was changing and corporate behaviour also had to change, and it remains active in promoting awareness and operating initiatives. In addition to CEO's who saw the need for a strategic response to growing public and government interest, the financial community also started to become active. This was not new;

anytime that investors see risk there is a need to respond; in fact, the history of "impact investing" goes back several centuries.

On this occasion, investors became concerned about both risk from a broad range of concerns; these include profitability impacts from potential fines, taxes, and other operating costs; loss of revenues from impact on reputation and brands; supplier risk from sourcing of materials; capital risk from the decline or complete failure of their business model and interest cost risk from other lenders, such as banks who might start to add a premium to interest costs should risk be seen as increased.

CDP (Carbon Disclosure Project) was formed in 2000 by a group of institutional investors and investment funds, that focused in on the impact of carbon emissions aspects of environmental issues. CDP encouraged publicly listed companies to voluntarily disclose aspects relative to their carbon related risks in an effort to develop action based on awareness. This group is worldwide and has successfully leveraged its position, which now represents trillions of invested capital, into a significant level of carbon disclosure and from this action plans. The CDP work links in directly with the UN work on climate change.

Some organizations had already started supplemental reporting that included environmental aspects such as Ben and Jerry's ice cream discussed earlier. It was quickly becoming apparent that some level of consistent framework might be needed. Accountants were visible in this developing area of reporting, in particular the ACCA (Association of Chartered Certified Accountants) in the UK, who partnered with CERES (The Coalition for Environmentally Responsible Economies) to create an annual series of awards *"...to contribute to reporting on sustainability, environmental and social issues by corporations and other organizations across the United States"* and to *"...reward best practice and provide guidance to other entities that are publishing or intend to publish sustainability reports, and increase accountability to stakeholders."*

The initial focus on the US expanded globally as the years went by with many other countries being included. The ACCA did establish itself as an early leader in "beyond traditional accounting" and has continued to be involved in innovative and creative thoughts, ideas, and approaches. The challenge in the early years was to even define what a supplemental report might look like and what the definitions would include. What is sustainability? What should be included in environmental? What are the social issues that should be addressed?

An organization called The Corporate Register was established in the early 1990's as a repository where organizations could file their supplemental reports and also access the reports of others so as to develop their own approaches and ideas. Many organizations at the time were

developing their own reports and these had little consistency. This chart from the early years of "sustainability reporting" (from large, usually public organizations), demonstrates the growth in worldwide reports starting in 1992.

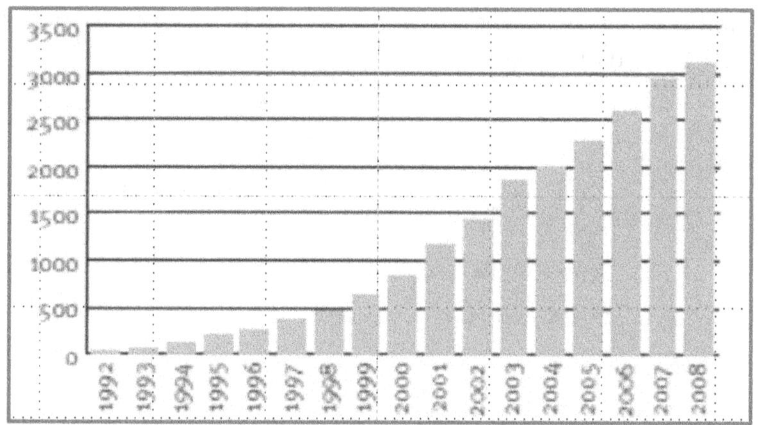

The challenge was that although many organizations were producing reports there was an evolution around what type of the reports they were and what content they included. What is important to note is that almost all the data was non-financial, and the reporting was separate from the "annual financial report." This, in spite of the fact that to have initiatives to report upon, there must have been a growing impact on the allocation of financial resources. This would be especially true about areas such as "brand impact."

By now it was becoming clear that organizations that were failing to address environmental concerns were in danger of depletion of their brand (intangible) value. According to the Reporting Exchange, here is a summary of the types of reports being issued in the period 1992 - 2008 (approximate %):

What can be seen is the early focus on environmental reports and then a shift to sustainability and corporate responsibility together making up about 65% with the integrated concept just starting to emerge.

The first "structured" approach to non-financial reporting was developed by the Global Reporting Initiative (GRI) which was founded in Boston in 1997 (following public outcry over the environmental damage of the Exxon Valdez oil spill). Its roots lie in the non-profit organizations CERES (which was the organization that partnered with the ACCA) and the Tellus Institute (and with involvement of the UN Environment Programme). The aim was to create the first accountability mechanism to ensure companies adhere to responsible environmental conduct principles, which was then broadened to include social, economic and governance issues.

Emerging Trends: Type of report	1992	2008
Social / community reports	8%	4%
Philanthropy		2%
Integrated (Financial + Non-financial)		5%
Sustainability (Environmental+Social+Economic)		33%
Corporate Responsibility (EHS+Community +Social)		32%
Environment, Health & Safety and Community		2%
Environment, Health and Safety	12%	3%
Environment and Social		3%
Environment	80%	14%

The first version of what was then the GRI Guidelines (known as G1) was published in 2000 – providing the first global framework for sustainability reporting. The GRI evolved from initiatives started in the late 1990's in response to a growing awareness that change in accountability and corporate reporting was needed. By now the focus on shareholder had expanded to focus on a broader range of "stakeholder" interests. The GRI guidelines were not prescriptive but provided a framework for both thinking through an approach to non-financial reporting as well as a portfolio of potential performance measures. The original framework included:

Guidelines for defining report content.
Principles for report content, quality and "boundary setting"
Framework for developing an organizational profile.
Framework for explaining managements approach to sustainability.
A range of performance indicators (both core and optional)

While some performance indicators were financial there was little linkage back to traditional financial reporting. The GRI framework also provided a series of "sector guidelines" and included steps to assess stakeholder priorities and issues such as materiality.

METRIC GROUP	CORE	ADDITIONAL
Economic	7	2
Environmental	17	13
Social - Labour Practices	9	5
Social - Human Rights	6	3
Social - Society	6	2
Social - Product Responsibility	4	5

The original framework had metrics around six key areas covering the three topics of Environmental, Economic and Social aspects (as can be seen from the emerging trend chart earlier). By 2008 this was almost one third of total reports and overlapped with the other large group (Corporate Social Responsibility - where most organizations had started supplemental reporting) and the newly emerging concept of "integrated reporting." The original metrics included a total of 49 core indicators, with social and environmental being the largest and 30 additional, supplemental indicators.

While there would have been financial costs related to strategy and execution relative to these performance areas, it was rare to see any bridge between financial data and these non-financial indicators. The economic indicators did have financial data but again were often prepared in isolation. It would be reasonable to say that "accounting was not in the room" nor was there any bridge between financial and non-financial reporting. This was at a time when the investment into intangibles, many related to these areas was growing.

The GRI framework has since developed into a series of recommended standards that can be used for comparison across organizations. GRI and CDP appear to be the more solid of the reporting frameworks, although others such as the Dow Jones Sustainability Indexes (DJSI), the GRESB (formerly known as the "Global Real Estate Sustainability Benchmark") that now covers real assets including infrastructure. SASB (Sustainability Accounting Standards Board) formed in 2012 is also continuing to develop guidance on non-financial reporting in conjunction with US based SEC requirements.

Again, most of the work in these areas has little additive linkage to traditional financial reporting and while accountants are often aware of, and even involved in some areas, there had been no solid approach to linking financial and non-financial reporting. The economic category includes a significant amount of financial information, but most provides little additional information nor is it "contextual."

One key area is the addition of a taxation disclosure standard that closely follows the recommendations of the OECD. While the involvement of the accounting profession is clear, the way in which the data is presented appears to mainly focus on payroll and sales taxes, with limited additional exposure on tax on income - the main area of tax avoidance.

9.4 Missing in action - intangibles

Corporations have been shifting in two strategic directions. First, to respond to the competitive pressures brought about through globalization, technological change, and increased competition. Secondly, progressive organizations were also recognizing the changing societal expectations and were making significant strategic changes to sustain what is often referred to as "their license to operate" from society.

Through this process, organizations were building significant levels of intellectual capital including their brands and reputations, but because this shift involved operating expenditures rather than the purchase of new machines, the majority of costs flowed through the income statement and left no trail. Yet the "tip of the iceberg" shows up in market valuations including the growth of goodwill as shown below[63]:

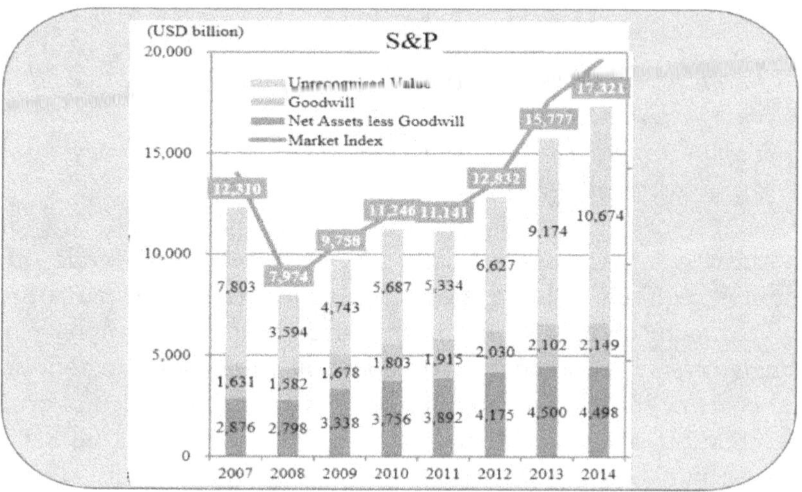

The size of intangibles, in particular the growth in goodwill has not escaped the profession[64] - albeit a bit late in the game!

The Financial Accounting Standards Board has recently elevated goodwill accounting to the top of its agenda, after political pressure stemming from high-profile company failures in

---

[63] "Quantitative study on goodwill and impairment" Staff of the European Financial Reporting Advisory Group (EFRAG) and Staff of the Accounting Standards Board of Japan (ASBJ), July 2016, EFRAG,

[64] "FASB Turns Up the Heat on Goodwill Impairment Testing," Sandra Peters, CFA Institute, February 12, 2020

the U.K., notably Carillion's, pushed the International Accounting Standards Board to address the topic.

In the United States, the significant goodwill write-offs at General Electric and Kraft Heinz have been political fuel for FASB, which was already considering whether to revisit the idea of permitting or requiring public companies to amortize goodwill.

In 2018, U.S. public companies had $5.6 trillion of goodwill on their books. That amounted to 6% of their total assets and 32% of their equity. S&P 500 companies accounted for $3.3 trillion of such goodwill, representing 9% of their total assets and 41% of their equity.

CFA Institute's comment letter to FASB …highlights (that) the S&P 500 companies with the largest goodwill balances and notes that 25% of S&P 500 companies have goodwill in excess of equity. Changing to amortization would be a problem because it would schedule the write-off of this goodwill against equity.

The growth of intangibles is a growing problem; while the actual expenditures required to build these capabilities have been part of operating expenses for many companies for more than 30 years, a portion have now been increasingly crystallized in acquisitions. The dilemma facing accounting is that the total costs of building intangibles has never been revealed over the years, and the creation of goodwill has allowed the problem to be set aside on acquisitions; part of the solution has been the "impairment" strategy but if these assets have been impaired, is that because the acquirer destroyed the original value that existed at the time of acquisition, or have they now been integrated in the acquiring company's activities and, once again disappeared in operating expenses (where the acquiring company's own intangibles went in the first place).

9.5 Efforts towards integrated reporting

With the growing recognition of the importance of ALL stakeholders, not just shareholders, and the proliferation of supplemental reporting frameworks, an initiative was started in 2012. This brought together both financial reporting authorities, users, and regulators, with those involved in the non-financial, supplemental reporting area, in order to investigate whether a single, integrated report could be created. The goal would be to have a single report from organizations that depicted both their financial performance as well as their activities in the other areas of interest such as the environment and social areas.

In 2010 a new body called The International Integrated Reporting Committee (IIRC) was created with the goal "…to develop an internationally accepted integrated reporting framework by 2014 to create the foundations for a new reporting model to enable organisations to provide concise communications of how they create value over time. This initiative brought traditional together financial bodies such as IFAC and the ACCA together with organizations such as GRI (Global Reporting Initiative). The effort was headed by some prestigious names; Mervyn King as Chairman, was a retired Supreme Court judge from South Africa who, in 1993 had been asked by the South African Institute of Directors to chair a commission on corporate governance; their 1994 and subsequent reports are considered major milestones in changes for corporate accountability. Leslie Ferrar was one of two deputy Chairs, who was Treasurer, Household of the Prince of Wales and the Duchess of Cornwall and represented HRH Prince Charles who has long been a "champion" of socially responsible corporate behaviour. Many of the other initial directors were drawn from the accounting profession.

Some accounting bodies have been involved in seeing a need for change and the ACCA, who is represented on the IIRC, partnered in some ground-breaking work in the early 2000's in the SIGMA project, that resulted in an integrated reporting framework for accountability. While the ACCA started with a natural bias towards financial capital as an essential core part of any new system, they also included aspects of other stakeholders.

The SIGMA project established the concepts of other "core capitals" that complemented financial capital, and these included natural capital (environmental aspects), human capital (people aspects), social capital (societal aspects) and manufactured capital (tangible assets). All five capitals were seen to contribute to an organization's business model and the organization should be accountable for performance in each of the 5 areas. The model was good but gained little real traction until the formation of the IIRC, who conducted its own research including progress over the five or so years since SIGMA was created. The six capitals adopted by the IIRC expanded on the SIGMA model and are listed below with a short definition as provided by the IIRC prototype framework in 2013:

Capital	Summary inclusion
Financial	The pool of funds that is available to the organization for use in the production of goods or the provision of services obtained through financing, such as debt, equity, or grants, or generated through operations or investments.
Manufactured	Manufactured physical objects (as distinct from natural physical objects) that are available to the organization for use in the production of goods or the provision of services, including: buildings, equipment, and infrastructure (such as roads, ports, bridges and waste and water treatment plants).
Intellectual	Intangibles that provide competitive advantage, including intellectual property, such as patents, copyrights, software and organizational systems, procedures, and protocols; the intangibles that are associated with the brand and reputation that an organization has developed.
Human	People's skills and experience, and their capacity and motivations to innovate, including their: alignment with and support of the organization's governance framework and ethical values such as its recognition of human rights; ability to understand and implement an organization's strategy; loyalties and motivations for improving processes, goods, and services, including their ability to lead and to collaborate
Social and relationship	The institutions and relationships established within and between each community, group of stakeholders and other networks to enhance individual and collective well-being. Social and relationship capital includes common values and behaviours; key relationships, and the trust and loyalty that an organization has developed and strives to build and protect with customers, suppliers, and business partners; an organization's social licence to operate
Natural	Natural capital is an input to the production of goods or the provision of services. An organization's activities also impact, positively or negatively, on natural capital. It includes water, land, minerals, and forests; biodiversity and eco-system health

This included much of the "learning" that had taken place by organisations working with models such as GRI. After a consultation process, the IIRC published the first version of its 'International Integrated Reporting <IR> Framework, in December 2013. This model went further than SIGMA in that it provided the context of a business model within which all the capitals were involved (to some degree); it looked at each capital in terms of both its input and output aspects. (In early 2021 an updated version of the guidelines was issued by the IIRC).

A review of the list demonstrates that financial capital, that is cash flow is required to" activate" any one of them; thus, there is a definite role for the connection of intangibles with the newly developed reporting framework.

From looking at the reports being produced since the development of the <IR> it seems to be that the "bridge to intangibles" has not been built. Even with the heavy representation of the accounting profession in the activities it looks like an "opportunity lost." Financial reporting does not yet seem to have embraced and integrated with the other five capitals; while CEO's continue to recognize and manage their organizations around balancing all of the resources available to them, considering all stakeholders needs, accounting seems to be content with adhering to accounting standards and going no further. CEO's understand balance but accountants seem to have lost theirs.

The IIRC model termed the <IR> framework was solidly promoted and well received. Key stakeholders were involved in its development and were expected to assist in moving its adoption forward. These efforts have been partly successful, but it appears that two major problems continue to exist.

First, few organizations have adopted a true integrated approach; although the IIRC framework provides a solid basis for adopting and applying the <IR> approach it would appear that there is no true "integration" involved. While the reports may integrate many indicators, the indicators do not integrate between themselves and into the business model. The model is also not prescriptive in nature and has relied on organizations developing their own approaches to adopting the model. Historically financial performance has been considered the best indicator of integration; management has brough together all the disparate resources needed and is judged based on its financial outcomes.

The <IR> framework has not provided any alternative to system wide "integrated performance" and so what is often provided is a broad base of performance measures in the six areas of capital. The metrics used to populate the six capitals still seem to rely heavily on the "silo based" functional management framework. (Recent changes with the IIRC, joining forces with SASB, CDP, GRI and CDSB announced early in 2021 may improve this situation but again seems to indicate a bias towards the ESG aspects and not address the "bridge" to financial capital?)

Secondly the challenge of organizational sustainability as it applies to enterprise continuity seems to have been subsumed by the focus on sustainability of the enterprise from an environmental and social perspective. The <IR> framework for reporting has created a good model that recognizes that a combination of resources is required to achieve organizational purpose, goals, and objectives.

Organizations are investing their financial resources in building these capabilities yet accounting information provides no perspective on the financial impact of these changes. As a result, the goals of improved visibility and transparency has not yet been achieved as it applies to knowing whether the intangibles that have been created, many of which populate these other five capital categories, are being nurtured and sustained to ensure organizational continuity. The framework is there but the bridge to accounting is not built.

10.   The Path Ahead

We are at a point fifty years down the road since the start of a sea change in society. We have seen a series of crises that often reflect that the systems for economic governance having failed; the system that was designed for an industrial economy. We have seen, especially in the last twenty years, leaders of organizations, shift the use of financial resources towards the creation and sustaining of intangible "assets" to provide the capabilities needed for successfully operating in the new economy.

We have seen growing discontent around the real or perceived behaviour of organizations who, in the process of achieving their own goals do not appear to be considering their impact on the societies that they are a member of. We have seen the value placed on many organizations by the marketplace, rise way beyond their traditional accounting or book value. We have witnessed a major increase in corporate goodwill together with major write-downs for impairment. What we have not seen is a sea change in the role of professional accountants.

It almost looks as if the profession has, indeed lost its' balance. Audits, appear to many, to be conducted in collusion with the clients rather than providing an "arms length, independent and objective" overview. Tax support services appear to be aimed at hiding taxpayer wealth, both corporate and individual from the tax authorities; accountants are no longer ethical partners with tax authorities, seeking to implement "the spirit of the legislation" but to exploit its opportunities as adversaries.

There is no longer any reasonable balance between the accounting representation of value and the economic perspective. The representation of a "true and fair view" as a balanced perspective appears to be missing large aspects of significantly material information. The balance of materiality and of a "going concern" seems, based on revelations after audits and opinions, not to be representative of a balanced view of what is important and what might indicate increased risk.

Can the accounting profession make any difference? In an "asset light" intangible asset world will the accountant's role be to follow its traditional standards and ignore the rise of intangibles? Will the balance sheet continue to decline in importance as the true assets of an organization's business model? Will the earnings statement remain a place to bury all expenses incurred in the year even if, in reality, the work being undertaken has little to do with generating current revenues?

Financial reporting remains critical; cash flow is the life blood of any organization and control of the use of cash for any purposes remains a key aspect of risk management, yet accounting might be seen as the "manufacturer of buggy whips in the world of automation." Progress is built around looking beyond "what is" and speculating on what might be. That is where we need to go. Getting creative (after all in many areas of traditional accounting it Is as much an art as a science).

In this last chapter we will look ahead; but, like any good consulting project, we must start with reality - where we are today. That has been our task to date - laying out how we got to where we are. Now we must look at the future. If the profession is to survive and remain as a key part of the economic and business system, it must be seen to add value. This has always been a challenge for the profession as a core part of its role is mandated by statute - the performance of audits. However, the profession has already moved way beyond this and has adapted. The creation of a new line of business - management accounting, in the industrial age.

Individuals have adapted and used their financial training in all areas of business. The profession can and should adapt especially if it wishes to remain vibrant and valued by society. With the knowledge that accountants have on "how the money flows" and how organizations operate, the profession is well positioned to be a leader in the next revolution.

Three clarifications before we go further. First, I do not profess to be an auditor but a supporter of the concept of an independent 3rd party verification approach; my ideas are gained from experience both in business and the accounting profession including observation of the "business of audit." Second, I believe there remains a role for auditing as well as the traditional approaches to accounting - however if the profession is to continue in the future it must adapt and grow - including changing its approach and scope to address the reality of an intangible world.

Finally, I use the term "sustainability" in the wider sense than only environmental and social needs to adapt; I believe that _enterprise sustainability_ is an issue both from an organization's ability to adapt and change in its' response to the world outside but also, and possibly more critically, to address the health of its whole system of resources, tangible and intangible that go to make up its' business model. Organizations must be reflective in this new age and think both internally and externally to remain viable and competitive.

10.1 Improving both Accounting and Capitalism

The result of many of the changes and adjustments that we have witnessed in our journey has been a decline in belief in "the system." There are those who call for the replacement of capitalism and for more oversight (yet again) of the profession. I believe that accounting should continue to lead the world in understanding the traditional approaches to "the numbers" but should change its scope to address the health of the system within which the numbers are generated. I also believe that capitalism is a sound model that balances human behaviour with innovation and creativity and, as a result moves humankind forward. Capitalism will never be perfect; to try and make it so would be to remove the essence of what makes it work. However, the "dark side" of capitalism should be more broadly revealed and those who try and gain excess from the system at the expense of society must be called out and removed from positions of trust.

The foundations of accounting remain valid; money is the currency of transactions, even in a bitcoin or cyber-currency world there will remain a system of exchange. Even if the concept of blockchain replaces traditional "bookkeeping" - again there will be a need to keep track. Accountants ultimately answer the question "where did the money go?" From this information, managers, and decision makers as well as investors and regulators can make decisions and choices.

In a way, accountants use their ability to track and report numbers as a storyteller would; to add value in the future, accountants must expand their scope in a way that helps managers both understand their choices better and also tell their story effectively as to how well they are deploying their resources. As long as the focus remains heavily on performance being evaluated by profitability alone, the story will be incomplete and even misleading. CEO's along with their senior management teams are often in a position of "sacred trust" where their whole life is managing and protecting value that belongs to others. Most do this extremely well; to be "value added" in the future accountants must support and assist the story telling of the "good one's" and have the ability, through reporting, to call out those who abuse their trust.

The concept of auditing also continues to play an important role and should continue - hopefully with added simplicity, that would help the business "system" operate more competitively. However, the scope and approach to audits needs to change. As many situations - such as Carillion show that checking the financials alone sheds little light on operational issues that can quickly turn a going concern into a massive failure. This "scope shift" of audit is increasingly necessary as much of the "process" component has been automated.

A good financial "generalist" might not be the best audit leader; greater complexity of financing arrangements calls for greater skills in the analysis and reporting of traditional financial structures. Great process complexity leads to specialization in IT and systems capabilities. The challenge will be that as the scope of audit shifts and changes and looks at the health of the business on a broad basis, audit teams will need to be composed of business specialists and headed up by operationally biased leaders.

The calls to "get rid" of capitalism reflect the growing concern and a reactive response, but what is needed is both a modification of reporting and oversight and a far greater focus on the leaders who "set the tone' for how operations conduct their affairs. Human behaviour within an organization is what "gives capitalism a bad name." While the system is working effectively for a large percentage of organizations and serving society well, the actions of the few bad players give the impression that the whole system should be replaced. It is beyond the scope of this book to address many of the corporate governance changes, it is fair to say that it has been proven that more control is not necessarily going to solve the issue.

Maybe the time of poor leaders will pass naturally? Many ascended to their roles over a long period of time and have been convinced that their way of doing things still works; as they retire and new blood comes in, maybe the values that drive leadership behaviour might change? However poor leaders who treat their positions as their own private "piggy bank" must be exposed for what they are. Unethical individuals who fail to lead by balancing the success of their own personal life, their organization, and the society within which they operate. Effective leadership is a key corporate resource, and the assessment of its effectiveness should be part of an assessment of a going concern.

10.2 Sustainability, Materiality and "A Going Concern"

For accountants and auditors, the issue of sustainability, materiality, and the assessment of the business as a "going concern" were essentially driven by cash. The accounting definition has traditionally been:

> *For a company to be a going concern, it must be able to continue operating long enough to carry out its commitments, obligations, objectives, and so on. In other words, the company will not have to liquidate or be forced out of business. If there is uncertainty as to a company's ability to meet the going concern assumption, the facts and conditions must be disclosed in its financial statements.*

FASB reinforced this definition with specific points in 2008; the determination of obligations focuses on financial obligations - "…the ability to pay debts as they become due." Auditors might broaden their assessment of what obligations mean, but, if one is to use some of the failed audits as examples it is clear that the application of the traditional test did NOT reveal an inability to continue as a going concern which, renders the organization unsustainable. This is a key factor for those using annual reports. So, this "test" needs to be much broader if post-audit business failures are to be avoided. Which brings us to the underlying questions of materiality - what should be checked to ensure that an audit uncovers issues that are likely to have a material impact on BOTH financial results and the scope of the audit as well as the organizations ability to continue as a going concern and be sustainable?

The definition in the <IR> framework appears to be a good one. It broadens the issue of what is "material" beyond looking at financial records and obligations to looking at the "sustainability of the enterprise as a whole - its' business model. This is the definition used[65]:

> *In Integrated Reporting, a matter is material if it could substantively affect the organization's ability to create value in the short, medium, or long term. The process of determining materiality is entity specific and based on industry and other factors, as well as multi-stakeholder perspectives.*

If an integrated report is to be an integration of the six capitals proposed by the <IR> (although there is no obligation to use them), that create value within the business model, then the bias should be away from purely financial capital towards an assessment of whether all six capitals are being equally optimized and sustained, as a basis for the organizations system of value creation.

Unfortunately, application of the <IR> definition appears both biased towards financial aspects and heavily driven by traditional accounting and financial reporting concepts. The current guidance on "<IR> Materiality" suggests some leading practise reports to view as examples of how this approach should work; a review of these approaches reveals application of the GRI process to determine what is important to strategy (which is a solid approach) but then fails to link each of these to the six capitals.

---

[65] Materiality booklet, IIRC, Extracted from Executive Summary

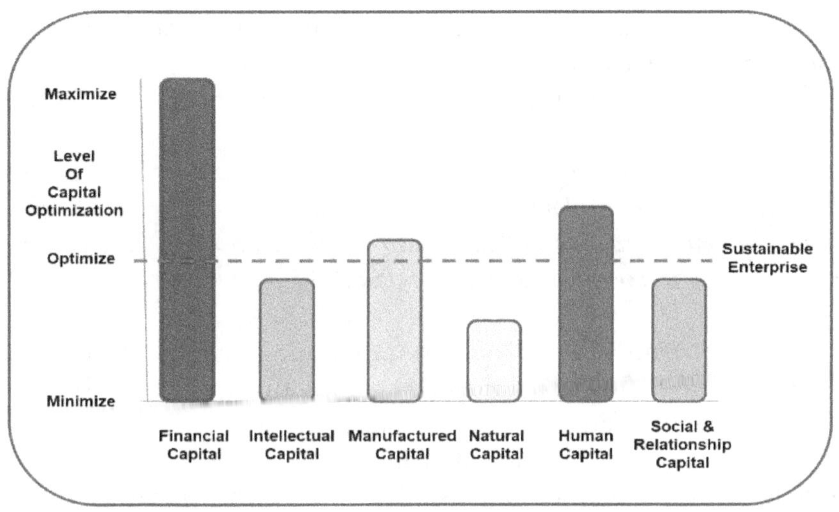

As an example, on Page 49 of the 2014 Gold Fields report (which is recommended by IIRC as a leading practise), there is a list of "material issues" that cut across all capitals but there is no bridge between the financial obligations funded from operational expenses to create and sustain these "areas of concern" nor is there any commentary on the existing "value" of the intangible asset that the company is concerned about. If there was true integration the link between financial performance and these "material issues" would, in some way be addressed. In a more recent example of a "leading report" the company[66] makes the following statement related to its' materiality approach

> *"Materiality contributes to ensuring that the groups strategic choices, their implementation and resulting reporting, take into account both the more significant economic, environmental and social impacts that our activities generate, with the social and environmental factors that might affect the Group in creating value to a greater extent."*

---

[66] Annual Integrated Report and Consolidated Financial Statements 2019, Generali

Once again, the focus in the sustainability report is the "economic, environmental and social impacts." For example, in the Generali report a discussion of these factors as an important issue in its' brand value and the investments necessary to sustain that, would be useful to investors and others. Especially when one looks at the Generali website and reads the following:

Generali Group remains the best Italian brand for strength and value. According to Brand Finance 2016 ranking - leading consulting and valuation company of intangible assets - Generali is the leading brand in the country with a value exceeding € 9.23 billion and A ratings; confirming in this way the result obtained in 2015.

€ 9.23 billion brand value. Is that an important asset? Is this important to investors? Is there a financial bridge that links the company's brand value (asset), actions to sustain the brand value (expenses) and its marketplace behaviour in terms of economic, environmental, or social conduct? I would think this is both material and an issue for both sustainability and financial capital?

There is an opportunity here for the accounting profession to start creating a "thinking model" that connects investments on intangibles and key topics in other areas of the other five capitals. Sustaining "the brand" is clearly "material" from an investor perspective as it contributes the market value. Sustainability reporting has identified other capitals that contribute to the brand that impact operational resource allocation. Why is the financial aspect not material?

A similar discussion could be made around the materiality of customers that drive the revenue stream and employees that drive a major portion of the expense stream. These both involve "material" allocations of resources - to keep customers happy and to pay employees. Almost all sustainability reports cite customers and employees as of "key strategic importance" i.e., material - yet the financial impact of these intangible assets - the customer base and the employees, in terms of "value" and the cost of sustaining such value is not usually linked. Yet the cost of maintaining a motivated workforce, through effective leadership development and behaviour, as well as activities focused on customer orientation and satisfaction is not discussed. It is material and core to going concern sustainability. Plus, it is a core part of sustaining an investors value.

10.3 Risk, Control and Behaviour

The long history of scandals, fraud and other "corporate misconduct" should demonstrate that evaluating risk and the effectiveness of internal controls is not working as well as it might. As the Enron collapse demonstrated, organizations are often saying all the right things, but effective deployment does not mirror what senior executives might think or what they may tell the auditors. Historically, especially in a highly supervised "command and control" management structure, the opportunity for individual misconduct was limited, but with global, decentralized, downsized, multi-ethic, multi-cultural organizations the assurance of the desired behaviour is much less assured.

Much research has been carried out over the last twenty plus years that prove three things; first, people will not always act as one would expect (e.g., the work of behavioural economics). Second, values and beliefs, which drive individual behaviour vary widely around the world; thus, the baseline expectation set by a "parent organization" located in one jurisdiction cannot be natural expected to be the same in other locations (e.g., World Values surveys). Finally, unmotivated, or demotivated people, as well as those how perceive unfairness and injustice will not act in the interests of their employer.

These factors, combined with the growth of a "human based" knowledge economy, mean that the whole approach to building confidence in systems of internal controls cannot be assured unless the risk assessment delves deeply into the _culture of the organization_. Not just what it says but what it does. Accountants who rely on what they are told about "tone at the top" and organizational values and behaviours by senior managers (with whom they may have "peer based cozy relationships") are facing a risk of underlying control issues.

Approaches to human resources or talent management are no longer a separate functional part of an organization, separate from financial controls. The approach to planning, selecting, hiring, compensating, leading, motivating, and communicating with the workforce is an inherent and critical part of an organizations internal control system and the scope of audit must expand to include this. While traditional audit may focus on the total amount of cash flow that is expensed in paying the workforce, a significant portion now goes to the acquisition, nurturing and managing of the human resources through which a major intangible asset is being created. Part of this investment is in ensuring that the behavioural expectations necessary to underpin a "reasonable" level of internal control is being maintained.

Reducing the risk of control system failure due to unplanned and unexpected human action starts with ensuring that a system of sharing expectations has been put in place by management and permeates every single part of management activity. While organizational strategy has historically focused on clarity of task through "strategies, plans and actions" there must be equal focus on behavioural values. This way an organization has clarity of both what is to be done and what behaviours are expected in the execution process. Failure to provide this assurance is both a risk and control problem but it is also an issue for management accounting as it sub-optimize the potential of human capital. In terms of audit scope and risk / control assessment, accounting must ensure that the core elements.

There is a clear role here for accounting to build a bridge between financial expenditures for the workforce and the creation and support of effective internal controls as well as the investments necessary to sustain the intangible value of one of the largest intangible assets. For example, having in place a set of values, that permeate every aspect of human resources management, including on-boarding and annual reviews, and are periodically measured by tools such as 360° assessment on individuals in supervisory and leadership roles, would clearly support whether "people aspects" were a control risk.

10.4 Building on the Balance Sheet and Income Statement concept validity

Accounting already has the ideal framework in place around which to build the bridges necessary between the six capitals identified in the <IR> framework and the growth and nurturing of the intangible assets that underpin the gap that has grown between market value and book value. The underlying commonality between tangible and intangible assets is cash flow. Funds are being expended to buy (or build) tangible assets in the same way that funds are required to create intangible "assets." The problem that currently exists is that accounting standards and GAAP determines that certain expenditures cannot be added to the balance sheet; the cash is flowing but because the resulting asset, required to create operational capacity is not tangible, it cannot be shown as an asset of the existing balance sheet. Therefore, by default, any cash flows assigned to the creation of non-balance sheet assets remain as expenses on the earnings statement. There is in fact a "balance sheet of intangible assets" but it is invisible; it as a phantom balance sheet that only emerges when crystallized through an acquisition and becomes (a lump of) goodwill. It is interesting that some of the early experiments with handling "intellectual capital" suggested that a supplemental set of statements should be created, which did not meet Standards or GAAP, but which demonstrated both the "assets" that had been created and what the impact would have been after adjusting the earnings statement for these expenses.

There is also clearly an underlying or phantom earnings statement; currently, a typical earnings statement can be thought of as a "consolidated statement;" the base statement reflects income and only expenditures specifically incurred to earn each "unit of income;" on the revenue side there would then be any adjustments made to sustain the goodwill of the customer base - price adjustments, initial discounts, credits, and others.

On the expenses side there would then be added expenditures incurred to create "new" intangible assets and costs to sustain the existing assets. If expenses were then understated because some level of intangible asset was being depleted, this would also be reflected. The other side of the entry would be the changes reflected on the "phantom balance sheet."

None of this would meet accounting standards but it would now provide some level of financial bridge between financial capital - and its source and (especially) application and the sustainability of the other five capitals necessary to sustain the business model.

This graphic depicts what a model might look like; on the left is the traditional GAAP based balance sheet and earnings statement, but then the key aspects of intangible capital, although expensed against the income statement could be identified and given some notional value. This approach would go some way towards reconciling or building a bridge between accounting values on the balance sheet and those attributed by the market.

This would in no way be an exact science but it would start to clarify "where the money went" and to identify the financial aspects of areas being reported on using non-financial indicators.

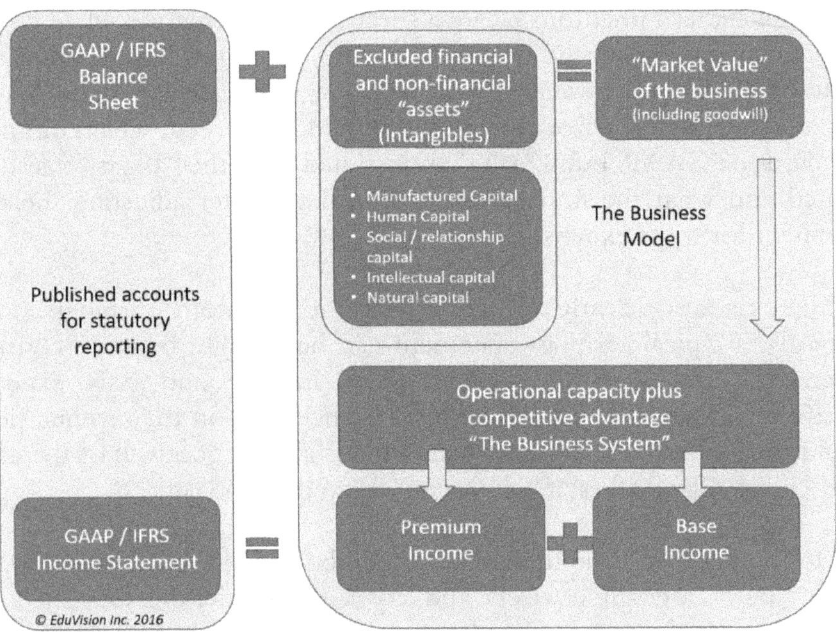

If accounting were able to create such a model it would go a long way towards explaining the gap between market and book values of a business. It would also provide a base for questioning as to why market values may be either higher or lower than the "phantom" balance sheet plus the traditional financial one.

This cannot be achieved by trying to force fit an intangible world into the existing accounting framework of standards. What accountants need to do is to expand their scope so that resources assigned to intangibles are both visible and linked with non-financial performance indicators. "Exactness" is not the goal, but a relative link between accounting tracking of resources and the management on non-financial capitals is what is needed.

This would bring a level of structure to materiality, going concern as well as the choice of non-financial indicators that need to be chosen to demonstrate the importance of non-financial capital in sustaining the business model. If we consider the <IR> "capitals "then we can start to think about the connection to intangibles. What is on each of these balance sheets?

<IR> Capital	Accounting Balance Sheet	Phantom Balance Sheet - definitions from original <IR> framework
Financial	Cash and investments	Credit lines available
Manufactured	Fixed Assets, inventories	Tools, fixtures fittings and non-capitalized assets
Human	Labour costs involved in creating allowable capitalized tangible and intangible assets	Competencies, capabilities, and experience. Alignment with and support for an organization's governance framework, risk management approach, and ethical values. Ability to understand, develop and implement an organization's strategy; loyalties and motivations for improving processes, goods, and services, including their ability to lead, manage and collaborate
Social / Relationship	Receivables and payables and any other assets that support relationships. Customer lists.	The institutions and the relationships within and between communities, groups of stakeholders and other networks, and the ability to share information to enhance individual and collective well-being. Social and relationship capital including shared norms, and common values and behaviours; key stakeholder relationships, and the trust and willingness to engage that an organization has developed and strives to build and protect with external stakeholders; intangibles associated with the brand and reputation that an organization has developed; an organization's social licence to operate
Intellectual	patents, copyrights, software, rights, and licences	Tacit knowledge, systems, procedures, and protocols
Natural		All renewable and non-renewable environmental resources and processes that provide goods or services that support the past, current or future prosperity of an organization. Including air, water, land, minerals, and forests; biodiversity and eco-system health.

This chart is illustrative only, but one can see from the <IR> guideline definitions, that significant financial resources are passing through an organization's earnings statement in the creation of these "capitals." There are also a few areas missing. As an example, intellectual capital includes tacit knowledge however explicit knowledge, that has been codified either through a knowledge base of documented procedures and work instructions, would clearly be part of the <IR> category of manufactured assets. It will also be obvious that these items have increased significantly as the knowledge economy has evolved. Additionally, in an acquisition the acquiring company would be buying these intangibles as part of obtaining ownership of the entity. The loss of these acquired intangibles that become part of the goodwill on acquisition, is the reason behind the impairment requirements.

<IR> Capital	Initiatives flowing through an earnings statement that create the assets suggested by the <IR>
Financial	Building and sustaining investor relationships
Manufactured	Non-capitalized asset expenses; building and sustaining partnerships with equipment suppliers (and amortization of fixed assets); codification of operational processes and sustaining effectiveness including quality systems
Human	Creation, implement and sustain corporate values including ethics programs; selection and hiring of staff; orientation of staff; supervisory training of staff; creation of surveys including 360° assessment of all leaders and supervisors; new skills and behavioural development programs such as establish key team initiatives; build / maintain union / other relationships; creating infrastructure support systems such as health, safety, employee advisory programs
Social / Relationship	Creation of supply chain relationships; joint investments in process and product development; long term community support; brand building promotion and support; non-investor relationships (regulators and other 3rd parties); establishing corporate values and standards in external relationships; building relationships with non-employee workforce and partners;
Intellectual	Provision of libraries including IT systems for knowledge base; costs of building knowledge base; costs of "experimentation;"
Natural	Implementation and sustaining environmental management systems; development of discretionary processes to enhance environmental performance;

While portions of the above initiatives would be considered period costs there are also "asset building" aspects which should be captured. Many of these intangibles are "wasting assets" so certain minimum levels of expenditures would be required to sustain such initiatives. An example of added transparency of interest to investors would be to know how much expense is being retained in times of economic downturn, order to avoid loss and depletion of intangibles such as the workforce. The decision on what to "add" to the intangible capital asset versus expensing it would be similar to the decisions around sustaining the capacity of fixed, tangible assets such as planned maintenance versus upgrades or re-builds.

Significant expenditures are required to both build and sustain these intangible capabilities and management is constantly making "trade off" decisions; cash resources are always scarce, and the challenge is to optimize overall performance without excessive depletion of the intangibles. This is a major, hidden risk. Organizations, under pressure to enhance financial performance may be depleting the reinvestments needed to sustain intangible capability. While short term performance may appear to be acceptable, in time capability will be reduced and areas such as competitive advantage will deteriorate. By the time this shows up in traditional reporting through flat or dropping revenues, it will be too late. In a manner, this approach to short term improvement while depleting intangible assets, is similar to the "asset stripping" in the tangible asset era.

One key change that could be made in statutory reporting is the expansion of labour reporting; currently there is truly little analytical information. Sadly, even developing models like the ISO Human Resources Management Guide to External Reporting (ISO 30414: 2018) is built on HR information using traditional, aggregated financial data. It would be possible, although would require some level of judgement, to track labour costs between those specifically incurred to generate current income and those paid for "other" purposes such as the creation and sustaining of intangibles. If integrated reporting is expected to provide transparency into all capitals, then the financial impact of expenses being incurred to achieve these goals should be identified and integrate with the non-financial information.

How might the intangible balances be presented? The pool concept would probably work best so that amounts flowing through the income statement could be reconciled; each category of intangible, based on the <IR> capitals could be shown and for each an opening balance plus additions - i.e. expenditures added in the year that have longer term benefits (each pool might have sub-categories such as items amortized over 3, 5 or 10 years); pools could also have specific sub-categories such as manufactured capital could include the management systems that have been implemented separate from non-capitalized assets. From this sub-total would then be deducted and amount representing the annual amortization of the pool. There might be specific adjustments (to earnings) to represent unplanned events that significantly impacted the capital - such as when the Volkswagen "Dieselgate" scandal occurred.

Category	Manufactured	Human	Social / Relationship	Intellectual	Natural
Opening balance					
Additions in year					
Sub-total					
Amortization					
Adjustments					
Closing balance					

The additions, amortization and other adjustments could be reconciled to labour and other costs on the income statement with supporting notes in the non-financial commentary areas. Relevant non-financial key performance indicators could then be linked to at least a relative impact of the financial statements. Where there might be either standards to calculate some of these items or 3rd party information, then these could be used as a valid indicator. Let us look a bit more deeply into each of the "capitals."

10.4.1 Human Capital

With recent changes in SEC requirements, which add mandatory reporting of human capital to annual filings, the issue of combining financial and non-financial indicators is more important. Standards Australia is doing some leading edge work on developing life-cycle management for human resources which can provide a solid base for non-financial indicators or metrics but might also provide the foundation for aligning the application of financial resources to certain parts of the process. This life cycle complements the work of the International Standards TC 260 Human Resources Management approach and supports several of the standards and technical guidance documents already issued.

How Accountants Lost their Balance

The distortions being caused by the expensing of "intangible human capital creation" has been a problem since the 1960's and Baruch Lev of New York University has been one of many suggesting that some level of capitalization of HR expenses should be considered. Jane Gleeson-White In her book "Six Capital" points to several organizations internationally who have already developed supplemental reporting of human capital, in particular related to training and development.

One current problem is that one of the typical non-financial indicators being used is "number of hours of training" (and equivalent metrics) but while this cost could be tied to financial investment, as a single figure it means very little; is it "new skills training" for the whole work force or refresher training? Is it orientation training for new recruits? Is it leadership training for all levels of supervision? Is it ethics training required of part of establishing an effective "behavioural based" internal controls program? Is it re-training because of a performance review issue? Is it training that includes external 3rd parties like suppliers as part of relationship building?

Diversity and inclusion	To meet both legal requirements but possibly to reflect other "socially responsible goals" like the UN SDG's
Company values (including ethics)	Creation of broad based training approaches (not refresher training which is an expense item)
Core HR processes	Creation of underlying HR "selection and procurement" processes;
"On boarding" costs	Costs associated with the hiring of each individual (the total hiring cost / person plus initial orientation and training; possible inclusion of minor items that are non-capitalized e.g., office / IT equipment / person.
Health and Safety	Costs to put in place both legal and discretionary requirements of H&S compliance (including meeting standards such as ISO 45001)
Accessibility	Costs associated with creating an accessible workplace that meets legal and discretionary requirements
Leadership development	Costs of designing and establishing a leadership development program including assessment and feedback tools.
Talent management system	Creation of the processes necessary to treat the workforce as an "investment in talent;"

If a notional "capital" valuation is to be created, it can only include costs that are "initial investments" and aimed at the development of a base level of human capital, necessary to provide operational capability. As an example, creating the following systems and processes (i.e., developing policy, procedures, forms, instructions, and the initial training of all staff in the requirement) might be considered an element of human capital; note that some may be to meet statutory needs while others are discretionary as part of the company strategy:

These and many others will consume resources to create and will provide underlying value beyond one year - as such they could be "capitalized" as an intangible (non-balance sheet) asset, and then an amortization schedule could be developed. As in ABC (Activity Based Costing), every time someone goes through any one of these established processes, there will be a cost involved; in this case the individual "per person" cost could become part of the "capitalized value of the workforce."

There could then be a workforce financial database that, for each person contains the cost of hire, cost of orientation, cost of other foundational training, upskilling costs, and other expenses that the organization "invests" in this person. The cost of "the pool" could then be amortized over a period of time relative to either average retention periods, or retention by category. So, as an example, the loss of an experienced, highly qualified scientist in less than, say 10 years, would appear as a higher cost than a less senior individual. This financial metric would then link to non-financial human capital reporting.

Other non-financial indicators such as health and safety statistics could also be linked to the financial information. As an example, an assumed (maybe zero) goal of health and safety might be established and if this starts to change it might raise questions about whether the "health and safety system asset" had been impaired. This is nowhere near an exact science, but it might start the ability to bring the financial cost of human capital into focus. At the macro level, those costs that had previously all been aggregated as an expense on the earnings statement could be analyzed by:

- Creation of intangible human capital (i.e., Creation of the systems and the cost to run the people through the system each year as necessary - not once is an investment, re-training would be an expense). These costs would b notional intangible capital.

- Sustaining the human capital - costs associated with managing human capital on an annual basis, which again would be an annual expense.

- Human capital "cost of production" being those costs paid specifically in operational processes. These again would be expenses.

One of the challenges might become whether the financial investment in the HR "system" would be classified as manufactured capital or HR capital? This is less of an issue - what is important is the visibility of these items being identified.

The challenge for accounting is that it MUST become a key part of developing the metrics for human capital reporting. The current approaches appear heavily related to the HR function and non-financial indicators. For accountants this should not be acceptable as the costs of the workforce are a major consumer of financial resources - no matter what the workforce is doing. It is material in terms of its financial impact on the business, it is of MAJOR interest to the assessment of a going concern (sustainability) and is a major part of corporate value.

10.4.2 Manufactured Capital

Similar to human capital a major part of building operational capacity in the "asset light" economy is the quality, agility, reliability, and consistency of work processes. The investment in initiatives to create this level of performance has been significant; as an example, GE spent over $1 billion in implementing its 6 Sigma initiative that led to major improvements in operational processes and brought about major costs savings. However, while there was an "operational ROI" the process also created an underlying and lasting approach to process management - a system and structure was put in place that should have lasting benefit. GE shareholders funded this effort and had to "forego" income to do it.

With the recent upheavals and changes in GE does any of this investment remain? Or is enough to just justify the expense on the savings already achieved and ignore the reality that an intangible asset was created?

The same is true for other process approaches such as implementing ISO 9001 Quality Management System. Following are some examples of the areas where organizations have made potential investments to create continued operational capacity in the intangible era:

Safety, Health, and safe Workplace	Either customized approaches to meet legislation or broader approaches that include both statutory compliance and standards e.g., ISO 45001
Quality management	Internally developed operational processes based on industry standards frameworks (e.g., auto) required to qualify as a vendor including ISO/TS 16949 (technical specification)
Risk management / control	Internal enterprise risk management (ERM) frameworks and approaches to risk mitigation or application of standards e.g., ISO 31000
General compliance (risk)	Frameworks and structures for general compliance - either by process area of using an overall baseline framework e.g., ISO 19600
Environmental risk and compliance	Either internally generated environmental risk and compliance processes and frameworks to meet legislated and internal commitments or based on standard baseline guides e.g., ISO 14001 and ISO 50001
Administrative management systems	Internally generated support process systems for all support areas whether internally developed or utilizing frameworks like the ISO 9000 family
IT Management systems	Frameworks for effective planning, execution, and control of all aspects of IT management, possible using the structures in the COBIT (Control Objectives for Information and Related Technology) created by the ISACA (Information Systems Audit and Control Association)
Preventative Maintenance Systems	Operating investment into permanent systems to track, monitor, plan, schedule, and report on equipment optimization. Examples CMMS systems and support frameworks.
Privacy systems	Implemented to meet legislated (e.g., PIPEDA in Canada) or internal requirements related to both data and other privacy issues. Possibly using ISO 27000 series for personal and data privacy.

All of these initiatives give an organization the opportunity to create a lasting intangible asset that, if maintained will help reduce process risk and increase operational sustainability. A system that remains in place and is maintained is, in effect as good as, and important as a critical piece of tangible equipment in a manufacturing process. While this is not to be a "ringing endorsement" of ISO standards it points out that over the last thirty plus years these has been a proliferation of tools and frameworks for putting in place management systems for the intangible economy.

There is no question that many organizations treated these expenses as "projects" - one time initiatives that were considered an expense. Sadly, many of these saw the expenditure as a cost to be minimized to gain recognition and certification, rather than seeing an opportunity to create a lasting intangible asset.

Certain components of the above operational processes, especially computer based systems might have been capitalized on the balance sheet as an asset - however in many organizations the costs related to creating these capabilities would have been expensed against earnings as incurred. While investment in tangibles to create value has declined, developing, and implementing intangible operational capability has increased.

Traditional financials would show the investment in these tangibles and the level of accumulated amortization, so an investor would have a clear view as to the potential risk of an organization using old assets. However, there is zero visibility into the investment, accumulated amortization, and residual "value" of intangibles. In effect the financial implication of depleting intangible assets is not important to investors?

10.4.3 Social / Relationship Capital

This category of capital might be considered a "composite" as it reflects the outcome of effective interaction with external 3rd parties; this results in three quite different types of intangible asset; both are important but for different reasons. Depletion on any of these is a problem.

Direct Operational relationships	Operational relationships such as supply chain relationships of both products and services, and outcome relationships with distributors, retailers, agents, and others.
Indirect operational relationships	Relationships with external bodies such as those involved with regulation, monitoring, oversight and governance, community and planning, ratings agencies, investors, and others
License to operate relationships	Impacted by all of the above but includes independent outsiders and the broader aspects of "public opinion."

Firstly, for many organizations their supply chain has become a "competitive advantage." While this may have initially been driven by product costs such as outsourcing to a low labour cost location, it still has a level of shared investment. Organizations have also significantly de-centralized and shed many operational capabilities that they once had "in house." While these are now performed by independent 3rd parties, their performance (quality, time, costs, quantity / schedule) can have a significant impact on the buyer's operational performance. Effective supplier relationships have evolved, for many buyers, to be an extension of their own organization. Also, in many cases this deepening relationship has created a higher level of interdependence. While there remain suppliers and parts of the supply chain that are driven by cost where the product is generic and easily substituted, for many suppliers have become part of their "asset base."

One key strategy over the years has been to reduce overall suppliers and to focus on building relationships with a few, committed, long term partners. This requires investments by both parties - not just on the product or service side, but in areas like design, development, and administration. Like any relationship, to be optimized, these must be viewed as long term and mutually beneficial. If one partner seeks to gain leverage over the other for their own benefit the value of the relationship will decline. GM gained notoriety in the 1990's for its efforts on cost cutting that upset many suppliers - yet a key goal of partnering must be constant improvement. The problem often occurs when a large buyer is negotiating with a smaller supplier and uses excessive leverage. A recent article demonstrates the continuing challenge of supply chain partnering[67]

I encourage you to read "Supplier Feud Threatens GM Plants" in the July 12, 2016, issue of the Wall Street Journal. It's the tale of yet another General Motors supplier gasping for air and declaring bankruptcy in an attempt to crawl out from under the weight of this automotive behemoth. Clark-Cutler-McDermott Co. (CCM), based in Franklin, MA, filed bankruptcy last week, blaming the move "on an unprofitable contract with GM that has drained it of $30,000 a day since 2013."

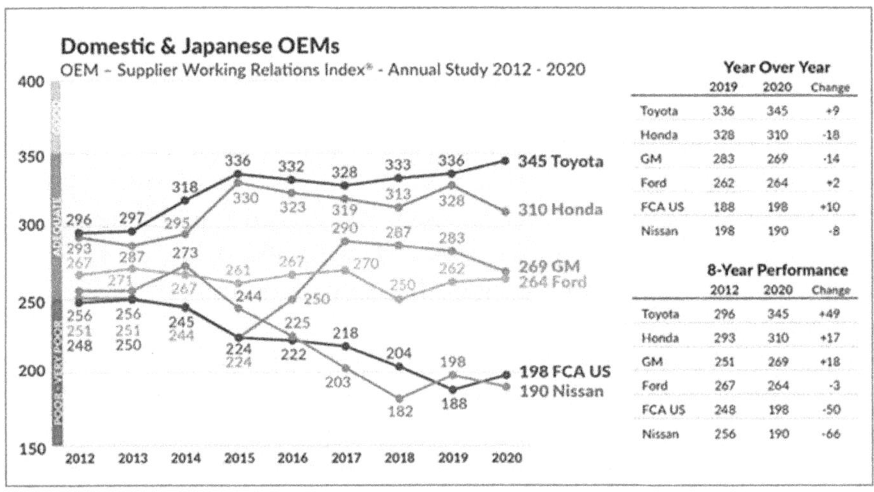

Because of the global nature of the business and the constant competitive challenges, supplier relationships[68] in the auto industry are an example of supply chain "capital" that could link financial investment and supplier satisfaction. The information shown on the chart below, is available in the industry, and could be used by both buyer and seller as a part of supporting and validating financial decisions around the Social / Relationship category;

---

[67] Another automotive supplier victimized by General Motors' purchasing strategies, Jul 13, 2016, Clare Goldsberry, Plastics Today

[68] 20th annual North American Automotive OEM - Supplier Working Relations Index® (WRI®) Study by Plante Moran

the scale scores companies from 100 to 400, based on survey results. Scoring 100 to 200 means relationships are very poor; 200 to 250 is poor; 250 to 350 is adequate; and scores of 350 and higher mean excellent relationships. It is unlikely that poor relationships will lead to mutually beneficial improvements.

Outbound relationships are the same and depend on collaboration and cooperation. Again, these will differ depending upon the type of product or service. Distribution is a rapidly changing marketplace but for sellers whose products require "value added" selling (i.e., non commodity type products), having a committed partner becomes an essential competitive advantage. Investments between manufacturer and distributor will often be required in joint marketing programs, product training, sales training, after-sales support, and other activities. To save costs administrative integration might be implemented - all of which are mutual investments to create an intangible asset. Not only is there an intangible asset here, there is a lasting income statement benefit from having a partner who saves the buyer costs.

One key thing about relationship capital is that there is a "spill over effect." Many years ago, when the world was more focused on improving service quality in non-manufacturing organizations, the CEO of Scandinavian Airlines (SAS), Jan Carlzon talked about "moments of truth" as being *every time anyone has an interaction with someone representing SAS, that is a moment of truth in determining our commitment to service."* Any time a customer comes into contact with a business, however remote, they have an opportunity to form an impression and this is where relationships intersect. It was Carlzon's position that if you managed every interaction to create a positive outcome, the business would be successful. That theory proved right for his airline, which eventually became one of the most admired in the industry.

While an individual person may have a good or bad experience in dealing with another person in a buyer or sellers' organization (or in a regulators office, or a community event or anything else) this will impact both the buyer / seller relationship but will also impact on the organization's reputation and brand value. As an example, how often do accounting people talk with the customers organization - doing things like chasing up unpaid invoices? How well do they contribute to "brand and reputation?"

An organizations brand is a key "value" that it has generated by both the presence of its products or services in the marketplace but also by its wider behaviour - as has been identified, it is a key component in the intangible value of a business. The following chart from Marketing Charts[69] provides the type of drivers that would need to be connected to investment:

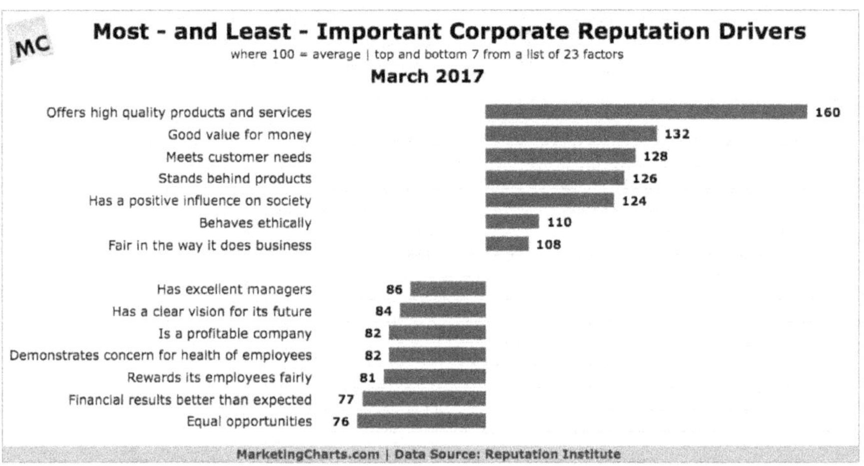

While certain costs relative to brand might be capitalized the majority remain an intangible. In order to further align financial and non-financial integrated reporting, any organization must know the key non-financial indicators relative to bran protection and sustainability; from this strategy would evolve to areas that require investment to sustain the brand. Each organization is unique and the "drivers" of its brand and reputation will be somewhat unique. Incorporating published brand value by organizations such as Brand Finance or Interbrand (or others) as part of the social / relationship aspect of integrated reporting, could provide a solid bridge between a key intangible asset and the areas of financial resource allocation necessary for this asset to be protected. information produced.

---

[69] https://www.marketingcharts.com/brand-related-75550

10.4.4 Intellectual Capital

Several categories of intellectual capital are already allowed to be capitalized and reported as part of an organizations balance sheet. Other areas identified by the <IR> framework might overlap with the discussion on either process management, which were discussed as part of manufactured capital or human capital. Organizations have the flexibility to determine what might be selected within each "non-financial" grouping - however one area that is hard to determine and represent is the implicit knowledge of those either within or connected to the organization.

In many cases intellectual capital that has not been codified remains "tacit" knowledge. While this is valuable, especially among employees who have several years experience as well as others who may have extensive industry or other relevant experience, while it is tacit it is at risk. This issue is a key challenge in the knowledge economy and the more an organization fails to direct resources to converting tacit to explicit knowledge, the greater the risk.

Many organizations have extensive legal approaches to protecting their "intellectual capital" but as long as this has not been codified and remains "in the head" of the employees the more difficult protection and control will be. For tacit knowledge to be of value it must be converted into ideas and applied to competitive advantage. In this way tacit knowledge is like a passive asset, like a machine that an organization has purchased but has not yet turned on. Toyota may be a leader in the field of tacit knowledge in its application of employee suggestions, which has a goal of two suggestions per member (employee) per month.

3M was one organization that developed an effective outcome metric for the effective use of intellectual capital and his was *"...the Thirty Percent Rule, 30% of each division's revenues must come from products introduced in the last four years."* Integrating financial and non-financial measures for intellectual capital must be based on an understanding of what intellectual capital, especially the tacit knowledge of the workforce.

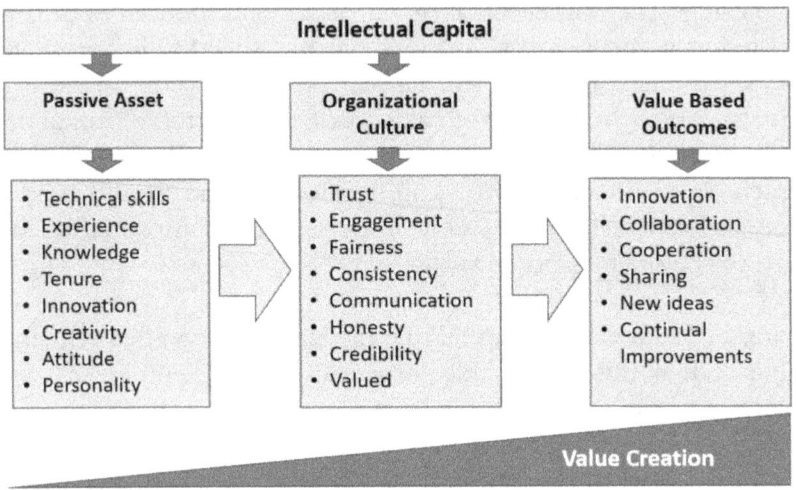

Intellectual capital is essentially a passive asset; if it is to be assigned any value it must be the base value of having the workforce discussed earlier. Having an "inventory of skills (technical, experience, knowledge etc.) is only of value once it is energized to convert potential into reality. Non-financial measures can be used for the passive asset, but the organization must establish the resources needed to create and sustain an organizational culture where the value creation can take place.

Investment in the "corporate culture" is an important aspect of both internal controls as well as to optimizing the financial investments in human capital. Outcomes can be measured both financially, like 3M assigns a revenue goal, or as non-financial indicators. Effective research can establish a "band of operational effectiveness" that must be maintained through investment to optimize the climate for value based outcomes.

Intellectual capital is the "store" of ideas for the organization that drives continual improvement, innovation, and creativity. For many organizations it is the source of organic growth in the development of new revenue streams and updated products and services. Some portion of goodwill can represent the same category of intangible if this "core of ideas and innovation" is purchased in a merger or acquisition. Part of the reason that many mergers and acquisitions fail to meet their expected results is that, while the workforce can be purchased, the stream of ideas can be "turned off" if the culture that energized the potential knowledge base is removed. From a financial standpoint, accounting could create a value of this "potential" through capturing the revenue growth (e.g., 3M) or the savings created (e.g., Toyota) and calculating a future potential value (maybe discounted for a base level of knowledge worker losses).

Cash flow needs to be invested in the constant empowerment of this potential to optimize its benefit to the organization. How much is the right amount, how should it be spent and how should it be controlled? These will all be company dependent and a few specific examples might help:

The profit balance example

One electronics company generated its revenue from a mix of low margin funded R&D programs and more profitable production programs. Executive management and the board wanted to increase margins and began to turn down lower margin (lower risk, cost recovery type) development projects to increase average margins. However operational managers knew that the technology developed using the "learnings" from these development projects went towards the higher profit production programs. To accept too few development contracts, production would eventually become less innovative and creative, and the company would lose competitive advantage; however, to do too much would deplete profitability. What was the right level or mix of business to protect and grow intellectual capital while still optimizing profitability? After extensive market study of competitors and financial modelling an optimum range of development / production mix was agreed upon with the board which drove the business strategy for the next several years, during which revenues grew 10 fold.

MORAL: an organization can optimize non-financial and financial capitals but maximizing one (financial) can risk losing another (intellectual), eventually leading to financial loss.

Using knowledge to be responsive to market changes

A successful business that focusses on professional learning and development was hit by changing technology and needed to re-position its offerings in the marketplace. The Vice Chair of the board would not allow the purchase of PC's (Personal Computers) as he told staff they were a "passing fad." The managers and executive (Vice President) running the business knew what was needed but senior management refused to change strategy and placed pressure on the business to cut costs and eventually sold off the division in a "fire-sale." The VP ended up buying back the business, developed a business plan, attracted an investor, grew the business in both revenues and profitability, and eventually "went pubic."

This can be an especially attractive area where by-products of research and development efforts can be "spun off" as new ventures, or if there are patents held, these can be sold to others who may be able to profit from them.

MORAL: find ways to retain your intellectual capital as a strategic asset and provide a forum for strategy shifts to be led by the marketplace.

Re-assignments: Valuing providers of intellectual capital

This medium sized industrial distributor was implementing significant changes to its' IT systems that impacted its whole operations, especially sales. There were significant (technical) implementation problems and over a two year period 50% of its sales staff left the company because they felt they could no longer serve the customers (a significant loss of human and intellectual capital). Many long serving and experienced managers were also struggling with the changes. The owner felt that some of these managers, many in the 50's with more than 30 years of product and customer experience (having spent their whole career in the business), should be "let go" and replaced with younger people who had much less product and customer experience but were more IT oriented. The replacement salespeople who were being hired, needed to rapidly get up to speed and re-build relationships with the customers; however, while it usually took 2 years to gain about 80% knowledge it took many more years of experience to get the remaining 20%. How could the company speed this up? It spent the resources (in challenging financial times) to reassign some of the most knowledgeable managers, who the owner wanted to fire, as coaches and trainers for the new sales staff. While these added new positions and cost not planned for, it was estimated that the company gained several million in additional annual sales and re-built its' brand and customer capital faster in the process.

MORAL: Reassignments of people with strong tacit knowledge to roles where they can share this and empower others creates a significant ROI.

The Value of story telling.

A new IT system was introduced to automate the scheduling, planning, and reporting of field engineers; while this was a significant investment the payback was also significant in improved productivity and less travel expenses. As a result, they would no longer need to travel to their regional office to receive work assignments and submit reports. The system worked well but it was slowly realized that problem solving effectiveness in the field was declining; it was realized that engineers often swapped stories while at the office about unique problems and fixes they had encountered especially with new equipment and services that were being deployed. The company implemented regular group meetings specifically aimed at story telling and problem solving. This, together with the creation of a knowledge base returned the field problem solving back to its old level and gradually started to improve that performance.

MORAL: Intellectual capital needs a forum for story telling and idea generation, because ideas tend to build when shared.

Flexible working arrangements

As many organizations face an ageing workforce, alternative ways to retain accumulated knowledge needs to be found. Innovative approaches to employment, such as part time retirees, shared work arrangements, early retirement or reduced hours prior to retirement can all allow an organization to retain their linkage to their knowledge workers. In many cases these changes in work approaches will in fact save money and optimize intellectual capital. (However, money saving approaches such as downsizing and forced retirements with reductions in or elimination of pensions does not create a climate where intellectual knowledge will thrive or be shared).

Reassignments can also be a significant approach to empowering intellectual capital' as organizations change and adapt, many "shed their workforce" along with whatever intellectual capital they possess, creating a loss of potential. Organizations that invest in re-assignments and re-training may have slightly higher initial costs but will retain the accumulated intellectual capital within the workforce.

Another financial measure of knowledge capital might be the investment to include a knowledge base for the organization - however the danger in thinking this constitutes the asset is probably flawed because it is again part of the passive knowledge asset.

10.4.5 Natural Capital

This is one area where the financial community has stepped in and become deeply involved. The first major guidance work came from the World Business Council on Sustainable Development (WBCSD) who continue to issue guidance for reporting. The GRI also has strong metrics for natural capital areas. The Sustainability Accounting Standards Board (SASB) also has a history of reporting in this area. The Carbon Disclosure Project (CDP) has also been instrumental in reporting suggestions. Accounting for Sustainability (A4S) is also a leading body, largely from CFO's that is also heavily engaged in reporting for climate change. A4S is funded by the Prince of Wales Charitable Foundation and complements some of the work related to <IR>.

Another key leader at the international finance level has joined the debate of reporting on natural capital. In 1999 an organization called The Financial Stability Forum (FSF) was established to better coordinate the work of the global financial community focused mainly at the national, central bank and financial community level. The Financial Stability Board (FSB) was established in April 2009 as the successor to the Financial Stability Forum (FSF) and charged to *"… strengthen its effectiveness as a mechanism for national authorities, standard-setting bodies and international financial institutions to address vulnerabilities and to develop and implement strong regulatory, supervisory and other policies in the interest of financial stability."* This organization created the Task Force on Climate-related Financial Disclosures (TCFD) in 2015 that has recently come out with recommendations that are now being proposed for risk reporting of climate issues[70]. Recent releases by the CDSB (Climate Disclosure Standards Board)

---

[70] FSB encourages the IFRS Foundation and authorities to use TCFD's recommendations as the basis for climate-related financial risk disclosures, 21 December 2020

have also now established a series of links between IASB standards and the materiality of climate reporting.

Natural capital traditionally fell in the "externalities" category; the use of "free" resources, and the generation of "non-responsible outcomes" in the business model. Much of the change needed to address externalities has to be strategy driven as "environmental responsibility" is a societal shift, supported by a plethora of legislative, guidance and voluntary requirements. With the variety of legal requirements around the world many organizations face the challenge of meeting the minimum standards necessary in whatever jurisdiction they operate in which may be below "leading practise" in a more advanced jurisdiction; because of this, there is a financial story to tell about investments being made at, and above the minimum necessary so as to reinforce an organizations commitment to global goals such as the UN SDG's (Social Development Goals).

Accountants need to understand the connection between addressing natural capital needs and its brand. Changing social expectations are demanding that business no longer treat externalities as "free to use and pollute" and organizations that are seen to not be responding to this are in danger of their reputation being harmed. The phrase "green washing" was coined some years ago to classify those organizations who "tell a good PR story" on their environmental sensitivity and activities but are found to not be making the levels of commitment necessary.

Management accounting has a key role to contribute to understanding an organization "carbon footprint." Many organizations have developed product costings that identify the environmental impact on the products and services they produce; using this information management can assign resources to the greatest impact first and gradually work their way to over improvement and hopefully zero footprint. In many cases focusing on reducing carbon footprint can result in innovation and benefits that bring financial benefit as well as enhancing environmental performance.

In addition to achieving compliance and building a more positive social license, being seen to be environmentally sensitive in the expected behaviour of the organization can bring benefits in being more effective in attracting talent to the organization. Many individuals entering the workforce today, consider corporate behaviour and social responsibility a key issue in deciding where to work; respecting natural capital helps build other capitals such as social, human, and intellectual.

10.4.6 Including audits of non-financial systems

As part of establishing their intangible "asset base" many organizations have looked to operational systems to provide increased structure and discipline. Implementation costs were often incredibly significant for these initiatives (many of which have been discussed), and in many cases were of questionable value; in some cases this occurred because there was little financial involvement is seeking methods to justify the ROI. ISO 9000 was one of the earlier management system standards, released in 1987 driven by both the global desire to increase quality management but also to try and simplify quality certification across national boundaries.

Traditionally processes "evolved" and there was little assurance of system predictability (schedule), cost (resources used), capacity (system capability) or quality (zero defects). While ISO 9001 did not guarantee solving these problems by bringing structure to the processes, ("something wonderful happens in here") ISO at least provided a structure as to what was supposed to happen. ISO was a framework designed to convert tacit knowledge into explicit knowledge, that could then be used for knowledge transfer.

In addition to the significant investment to create the asset (the process), ISO also requires an ongoing audit to verify that the systems are working as desired. Yet few organizations - even those adopting integrated reporting have made the connection between these intangible assets, the importance of predictable processes in sustaining brands and overall operational capability and the financial costs involved. While some financial audits may access ISO 9000 audit records there is little visibility in most integrated reports.

The secretary of TC 176, the committee that developed this standard was quoted as explaining that adopting ISO 9000 would not solve quality problems, but it would provide a foundation from which enhanced understanding and control could be built.

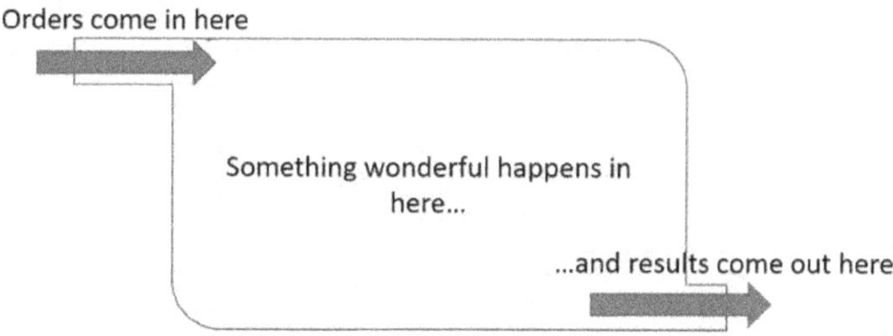

He referred to "process with a framework such as ISO 9000, as being like a house built on shifting sands." He often drew this picture to demonstrate the "power of prayer" in process management (something wonderful happens in here." ISO brings structure to this. The ISO structure a framework allows "codification of implicit knowledge into explicit knowledge" which is now a more visible intangible asset.

The same opportunity exists in ISO 14000 Environmental Management Standards series of standards introduced in 1996. Again, many organizations invested in this system at a significant cost. It also requires annual audits, and this can form a significant element of ensuring environmental (natural capital) compliance. Many of these ISO (and other) standards reflect conscious management decisions to go "over and above" the minimum legal requirements of compliance (although in some cases buyers may have required their suppliers to show evidence of certification to the standard, as part of system risk mitigation).

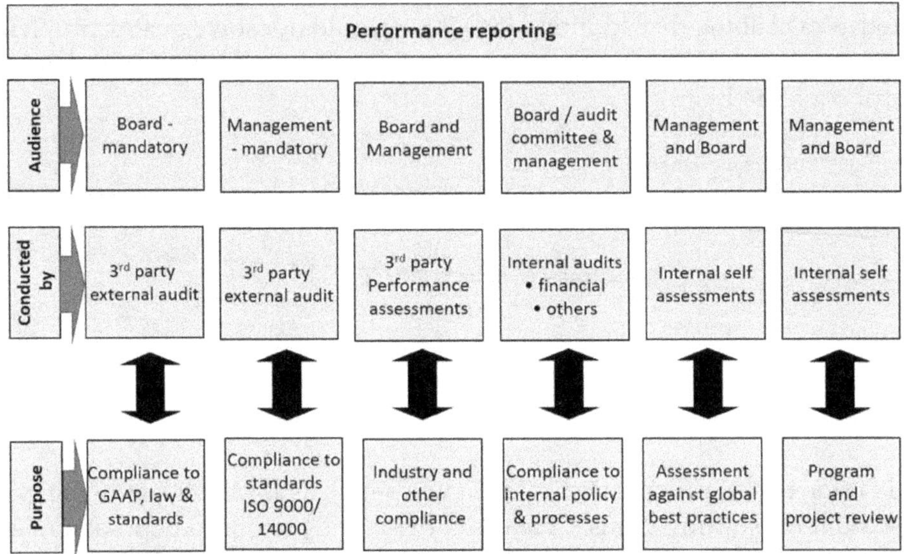

What provides an opportunity is that as part of these management standards (and possible other management systems), an annual systems audit is required to maintain the certification or recognition. These existing internal and external non-financial "audits" can be valuable in assessing the risk and sustainability of the intangible investment that was original expended. Financial audits can use these again, as a bridge to non-financial reporting.

Many organizations declined to adopt ISO 45001 Occupational Health and Safety because they were already required to meet an existing legal health and safety requirement - but saw this as duplication; however, some adopted it, once again to go "over and above." ISO 26000 Social Responsibility is one of the more recent guidance documents and again its implementation involved "over an above" the minimum legal requirements; it is compatible with the GRI framework in that it includes human rights, labour practices, the environment, fair operating practices, consumer issues and involvement and development.

Given that the initial investment by an organization to implement these frameworks for intangible capability - i.e., making tacit into explicit, then that knowledge becomes part of manufactured capital. It is the "asset" that makes operational capability auditable.

10.5 Auditing from a system concept

Ever since the balanced scorecard of multi-dimensional performance measures approaches started to gain traction in the 1990's it has increasingly become clear that basing an assessment of only financial information fails to present the whole picture. Financial assets remain important and cash remains necessary to finance the acquisition or "renting" of intangibles and assets not owned by the organization. However, expenses on an earnings statement are no longer restricted to those incurred "to earn income in the current period."

Because of the rules of capitalization (what can be placed on the balance sheet) cash flow expended to create intangible assets is buried in the current expenses; there is also no depiction on the balance sheet that these assets exist and no representation to users of the reports as to whether management is building or depleting these intangibles. These issues were identified in my 2005 book[71] that discussed the need for change in governance approaches and identified the balanced scorecard as an early indicator of the need for broad based performance measurement. This book also contained many checklist and frameworks for assessing intangible quality and sustainability.

While the <IR> framework establishes the existence and importance of six capitals and talks about integration, suggesting a "system concept," there is almost no guidance of any "total integrated system" performance measurement other than the traditional financial approach. What is needed is some sort of holistic measurement system that provides assurance that the integrated system of ALL capitals is working effectively.

Accountants, who have been heavily represented in the development of the <IR> might have a bias towards believing that financial performance remains an effective whole system measurement. This appears to be a missed opportunity for accounting, probably because it requires moving away from the definitive approach of financial accounting to an approach that requires a

---

[71] "Governance, Accountability and Sustainable Development: An agenda for the 21st century," 2005, Nick A Shepherd, Thomson Carswell Canada

more subjective assessment of the system as a whole. While financial reports are important part - they are just that, a part.

What is surprising is that the finance and accounting industry already makes significant use of subjective measures, specifically the work of the financial rating agencies who assess organizational risk. These agencies are not restricted to just accounting figures but look beyond these numbers to the operation of the whole business as a "going concern." (Readers may feel that the ratings agencies subjective approach was what caused their inability to warn against the credit risks associated with the 2007 financial crash, but the issues were somewhat broader).

If the accounting profession can accept that a "going concern" and enterprise sustainability extends beyond purely financial numbers, then the journey can be started by bringing together traditional financial reporting and non-financial information to develop an "opinion rating" that is comprehensive and represents the whole system of six capitals? When the "Six Capitals" (book) was released, Jane Gleeson-White asked the question[72] "Can accountants Save the Planet?" Several years down the road it is not yet apparent that the profession has fully embraced the concept. Some concepts have already surfaced. Tobins Q that was identified earlier is a whole system measure; also, in the early days of intellectual capital there was a suggestion that the "book to market" approach could be used to identify organizations that appeared to be making better use of their intangibles. The concept suggested that organizations be grouped by their industry (SIC) code (or by their market grouping) and then an average market to book value could be calculated. It was suggested that those organizations in the group that demonstrated a higher market to book were making better use of their intangible capital and thus were of less risk.

One organization that has spent several years trying to develop a broad based, composite measurement is the UK based Maturity Institute. Through their research they developed a series of questions that looked across all key aspects of organizational performance, each of which could be awarded a

---

[72] "Six Capitals," 2014. Jane Gleeson-White, Allen & Unwin

score. These scores were then weighted, and an overall "maturity" rating could be calculated.

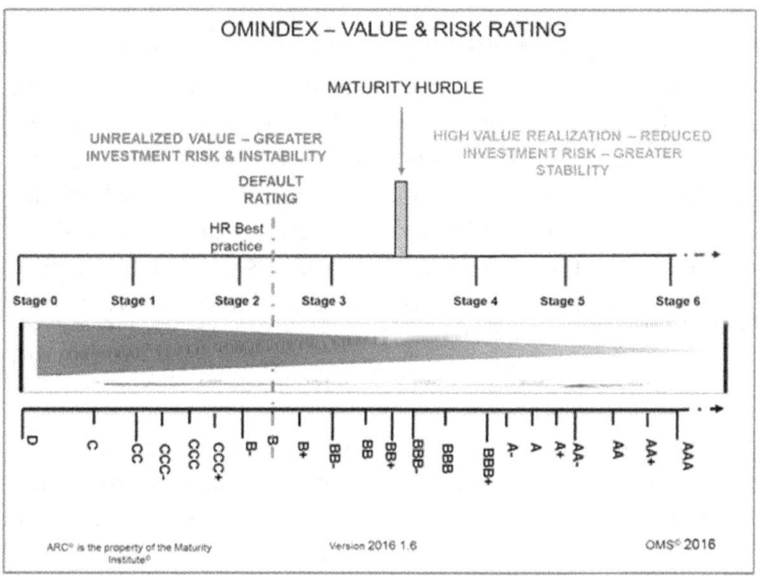

The assessment is called OMINDEX, and the rating system (shown on the horizontal scale) adopted by the Institute is the same scale as that used by the financial ratings agencies so that some level of comparison can be created. Once all the questions in the assessment have been answered the company rating can be placed on a chart; the left hand side suggests a less mature, greater risk organization while the right hand side suggests that management has a more holistic view of managing "the system" (equating to the <IR> business model.

The Institute has been tracking a number of organizations for some years and, although it will take several years to definitively link the maturity score to long term organizational performance, the work has already generated significant interest. As an example, one of the highest scoring organization under the Maturity rating is the Swedish financial institute, Handelsbanken. This company has also been an adopter of progressive approaches to most areas of "intangible assets" such as its' human resources and was one of the earliest organizations to embrace "beyond budgeting" and decentralized management approaches. The overall scale is illustrated below:

The "default rating" and the "maturity hurdle" have both been developed as part of the initial analysis of organizations; "default" demonstrates where the average performance is placed, and the hurdle is the point at which an organization approach to HR is seen to start becoming an integrated, strategic level. Handelsbanken achieved a score of A+ In 2018 when the Maturity Institute assessed a range of banks for comparison purposes. (It also conducted a correlation between CEO compensation levels and "system performance" and it was quite clear that there was little correlation between the "maturity level" and the compensation - suggesting once again a failure in long term thinking).

The Maturity Institute went one step further and combined the OMINDEX rating with the market to book value of each organization to create a TSV or Total Stakeholder Value; this assumed that the combined rating would provide a composite between what the marketplace felt about the value of an organization and what the OMINDEX analysis demonstrated. While the OMINDEX has garnered interest from almost all areas from academics, researchers, regulators, organizations, investors and investment advisors and senior management individuals, it has not yet reached mainstream application. This may be because there is no "champion" of integrated performance reporting approaches. No one has yet emerged from the traditional functional silos to embrace an integrated measure. It may also be that once enough time has elapsed the predictive value of an integrated performance indicator will become more evident. There are signs that this may be happening.

In 2016, The Maturity Institute, and OMS LLP, in conjunction with Harvard Law School's Pension and Capital Stewardship project, conducted an evaluation of AT&T, as an example of how the whole system approach could use information generally available to assess an organization. The results showed:

AT&T's OMR rating of B+ indicates a relatively low level of maturity with incipient signs of organizational instability and unnecessary levels of risk. Minimal recognition of the potential value opportunity available from its own 280,000 employees, or those employed within its supply chain, is evidenced, or exhibited. No clear Human Capital strategy is outlined, and its management policies and practices reveal no prior, underlying hypothesis to justify their use in business value terms. It appears to view its people primarily as a cost, not a source of value, and manages them accordingly. The efficacy of its people management practices is limited, partly by incoherence and partly by operational managers having no operational imperative to connect them to measurable value. From an investment perspective, a B+ offers a significant value opportunity once the maturity level is understood and leadership recognises the need to improve it. Immediate risks are not particularly high but without specific and careful attention to recognise and understand the nature of human risk they could become more significant over the medium term in the face of the combined threat of technological change and increasing competition. B+ organizations have inadequate human systems to enable adaptability and agility in their chosen marketplace and are prone to poor assimilation of acquisitions. In the case of AT&T the risk will potentially increase as the company strives to implement its strategic shift to a higher, value added, product and service delivery.

This report was produced just after AT&T had acquired Direct TV - a move that added significantly to the company's debt *and which included $34.6 billion in goodwill*. Based on the period since and how the acquisition has worked out it appears that the OMINDEX rating gave some evidence of risk? Here are two observations:

(Forbes): We believe it's safe to say that the acquisition of DirecTV hasn't really lived up to expectations, as the business has under-performed the broader pay TV market and appears to have failed to improve loyalty for AT&T's other core offerings[73].

(LA Times) But the change in ownership also led to a culture clash. "When it was DirecTV, if you had a good idea, you could run it through the channels," said a former executive who was not authorized to comment and requested anonymity. "But with AT&T, they expected you to stay in your place." Frequent reorganizations have left workers on edge. "They treat people like they are widgets that can be replaced," the former executive said, noting that the company calls laid-off workers "surplussed[74]."

---

[73] Was AT&T's Acquisition of DirecTV A Mistake? Aug 9, 2019, Great Speculations Trefis Team Contributors, Forbes

[74] Nearly 3 million subscribers ditched DirecTV last year. Will AT&T do the same? Jan. 31, 2020, Meg James, LA Times

(Multichannel News) AT&T Told to Sell DirecTV by Hedge Fund Investor," By Daniel Frankel September 09, 2019

The comments about people, or human capital (…treat people like widgets…") seem solidly "in line" with the results of the earlier assessment and suggested that this would be an area of risk. Using an integrated performance measure, because it is not based on absolute numbers, can only be a judgement decision. However, using an approach like OMINDEX provides an approach which is based on a consistent set of questions. Over time, the responses to these questions and the ratings produced, especially when benchmarked against competitors in the industry can provide investors and others with greater insight into possible risk.

While the S&P or Moody ratings indicate the level of financial risk as a going concern maybe the use of OMINDEX or an equivalent could provide an assessment of risk at the six capitals enterprise level? One approach might be to identify the gap between traditional financial ratings and the OMINDEX? This would start to generate questions about aspects of a going concern on a broader base than has traditionally been provided?

If an organization were financially rated as AA+ but the OMINDEX rating was BBB- then a gap would exist indicating added risk (as demonstrated on the next chart which shows the "risk gap"). This could then be explored for its potential impact as a going concern.

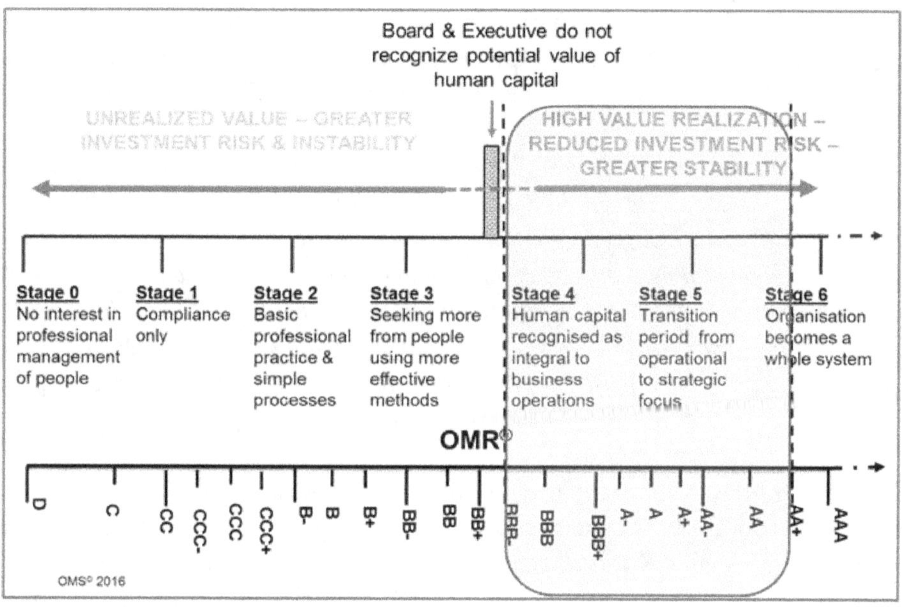

While the business might not "run out of money" there could be concern that, over time management inattention to other capitals - or their enhancing of profits due to depletion of these capitals (maybe like AT&T?).

10.6 Non-Financial Financial Metrics

While this sounds like an oxymoron, it is an important concept in building the intangible accounting bridge to non-financial "integrated" capital measures. There are tools available and others being developed to help provide some level of structure to this "unstructured" reporting. These provide "monetized" values for intangibles that accounting does not recognize. An example would be the reconciliation of brand information. At least two leading global organizations publish annual brand values on a broad range of public companies, and these form a significant part of the social and relationship capital within the <IR> framework. While each company uses slightly different approaches to create their brand value rankings, they could still be incorporated as part of the bridge between financial reporting and relationship (or intellectual capital as required) and reputation.

A key advantage might be that brand values can be early warning indicators of future revenue losses. In many cases a brand declines when it loses the linkage between where the marketplace is going and where their own product is positioned. This shows up in financials "after the fact." An example is Levi's.

Levi's sales peaked in 1997 at $7.1 million and then plunged with the rise of designer labels and fast fashion, with CEO Chip Bergh saying the brand "wasn't even in the consideration set" with trendy young consumers by the early 2000s. To turn the business around, Levi's innovated with new styles, fits, washes, and fabrics (not to mention wearables from Google and customization via lasers), and collaborated with Vetements, Re/Done, Virgil Abloh and stylist Karla Welch. It also smartly capitalized on the "mom jean" trend, bringing back its '90s styles. Last year, the brand saw its best results in a decade, with $4.9 billion in sales.

Identifying the value of the brand and linking this to the financial investments required to sustain the brand would be important investor information especially when social changes start to demand that investments be made to re-position the brand. ISO 10668 "Brand valuation – Requirements for monetary brand valuation" could also be used as a standard "benchmark" to express the value of the intangible asset. This standard has been supplemented with ISO 20671, "Brand evaluation – Principles and fundamentals", to help organizations focus on the challenge facing organizations trying to balance brand and financial management. The Chair of the TC 289 that developed the supplement stated that:

Here is where the potential struggle arises, in Dr Calder's opinion. He believes the crux of the matter is that "finance and marketing don't speak the same language. Marketing focuses on justifying brand expenditures and finance focuses on controlling them". Both need to work together to treat brands, not as an expense, but as a key financial asset.

As stated earlier "brand" can be one of the most significant intangible assets. When one looks at the leading high technology / knowledge economy market values (the FAANG stock), their combined brand value was $725 billion and has continued to climb.

10.7 Transparency, disclosure, and confidentiality

Many readers will be concerned about the issue of confidentiality; there is a balance to be achieved between being accountable to key stakeholders and providing too much information that may impact competitive advantage. This is recognized and will always be a trade-off. However, there is a greater level of public desire for increasing transparency and this must be satisfied. There is already a significant body of information being published. Integrated reports often run over 100 pages, so if anything, the goal should be to report less. If the impact on performance and organizational health and sustainability can be more intricately linked to financial reporting, then the number of other indicators might be able to be reduced. It appears that in many cases, today's integrated reports contain a lot of potentially disconnected and even meaningless indicators that have little relationship to the health of the six capitals? Many are measures of activity rather than outcomes.

The issue of silos was mentioned earlier, and it appears that many reports are the result of silo based thinking - not integrated. It appears that it might be a case that PR departments are responsible for bringing the report together and they call upon Finance of financial Capital, HR for Human and Intellectual Capital (or legal), Compliance for environmental capital, Operations for manufactured capital, and Sales or Purchasing, supplemented by Community Affairs for social and relationship capital? Maybe an unfair observation especially as many are still experimenting - but if true integration is to be achieved and the enterprise looked at as a system, then the primary accountability for integration is the CEO? That is the only person, apart from the CFO who has a truly integrated view of how the whole system works.

One of the other key challenges is being open about what is legal but seen by many as unethical. Specifically, this would focus on tax avoidance. Progress has been made by both the OECD guidelines on taxation disclosure and the inclusion of the tax category within the GRI guidelines. The taxation challenge, is one where organizations, operating in a globally competitive marketplace cannot act in a way that places them in a significantly competitive disadvantage. Decisions on how to balance a fully ethical approach with the need to minimize taxes must remain a governance decision, but organizations need to tell a better story.

Current approaches using the GRI guidelines tend to cloud the tax disclosure issue by combining the issue of tax on profits, which is what concerns the public with taxes actually being paid in each jurisdiction that are paid because there is no planning opportunity - items such as taxes on materials inputs, sales taxes collected on sales and paid to governments and payroll taxes, collected, and remitted. While this information is good PR and helps demonstrate the importance of an organization's economic activity in each jurisdiction, it completely avoids the real issue of income tax avoidance at the corporate level. Possible country level income statements as required by some national securities filings should be made "mainstream" and be prepared in such a way as to demonstrate the intercompany transactions involved (e.g., transfer pricing) and the level of notional tax that would have been paid in each country compared to the actual amount to be paid?

Other issues needed to "get things back in balance" and re-position audits as objective and independent, is consideration of who pays audit fees and whether (like the UK FRC) a levy might be paid to the oversight body. The role of whistle-blowers and their access to auditors might need streamlining and clarification. Maybe the audit committee should be re-thought in terms of additional accountability and representation from a member of an oversight body? Disclosure of relationships might also help to satisfy the need for transparency including provision of information on any interchanges of senior staff between the company and the audit firm (using approaches similar to disclosure of interests over an extended period). Disclosure by the audit firm of total revenues being earned from non-audit activities may also help regulators and others including larger institutional investors focus in on important issues? However, all of these belong in a book on corporate governance. Our focus is on how accounting can regain its balance and enhance its value to management and other stakeholders.

One change that might be considered by the accounting profession is to address unethical conduct more actively by its clients. Whilst there is certain legislation in some US states the rules for handling unethical conduct vary. Firstly, most accounting firms deal with concerns over unethical issues internally through an escalation process. Some further escalation might be valuable to engage oversight bodies at an earlier stage, maybe supported by a lawyer / client type of confidentiality. Secondly the profession needs to self reflect on ethics. Most professional bodies have extensive ethics processes in place to deal with situations where members appear in violation of their code of conduct. The ethics codes of many accounting bodies require members who observe unethical practices to "…remove themselves from the situation…" if they cannot either resolve the issue themselves or resolve the problem in conjunction with others. Unfortunately, many accountants find this an expensive option; if one resigns one cannot tell anybody the reason when applying for another position due to confidentiality - so a person who walks away from an unethical issue faces unemployment, loss of salary and a delay in getting rehired. Many who have mortgages, families and other obligations will find it hard to just "walk away." If professional bodies were serious about members doing this maybe they should consider a fund that will cover a certain level of salary if a member takes this action?

11. Regaining the Balance

The accounting profession has started on the road to change with many professional bodies and individual members involved in initiatives to broaden reporting and engage in climate change aspects. However, this road to change must include addressing the social and environmental issues at the core of ESG but also embrace the "G" part. It is corporate governance, especially as it relates to corporate behaviour in responding both to the natural and environmental issues but especially to the growth of intangibles and the importance of organizational behaviour in organizational sustainability. These aspects appear to remain of secondary importance, yet for organizational sustainability and to be a "going concern" these areas are now critical.

In early 2021 FASB announced that they will be taking another look at goodwill and expense accounting as part of their upcoming work plan; a major issue will be the approach to impairment versus a defined amortization. While these are important, they continue to focus "on the edges of the issue." Intangibles are the principal cause of the creation of goodwill; before the goodwill was crystallized by someone acquiring another organization the costs incurred to create the underlying intangibles were being written off as expenses and depleting equity.

This appears to financially deplete the organizations value, yet when a buyer comes along it becomes evident that these expenses, originally considered to have no identification, ownership or long term value are now realized to have value, and to be an intrinsic part of the business model of the organization being purchased. Accounting "solves the problem" by creating an asset called goodwill so as to "remain in balance." While this, together with annual checks for impairment (or maybe amortization) solves the accounting problem, it hides the understanding "behind the numbers."

Nurturing intangibles is like keeping orchids alive in a greenhouse - their environment is critical to them remaining alive and healthy. For intangibles, the organizations culture is the environment within which they flourish and create value. Change the environment, such as an integration after a merger and often the value will disappear - hence the impairment charges for goodwill that occur annually in the billions of dollars.

If there is no track of the creation and nurturing of the intangibles as funds are being deployed to create them, it is no surprise that the risks involved in post-acquisition integration are often ignored or misunderstood. Accounting is not supporting either the decision making from a management accounting perspective in either seller or buyer organization. Nor is a financial audit providing any material insight into the going concern risk related to intangibles at buyer or seller.

To get "back into balance" the accounting profession needs to find some way to provide better information on how financial resources are being applied to create long term capability in "asset light" organizations. The "balance" involved will require balancing the rigidity of conservative accounting standards with providing important insight into how financial resources are being directed to create and sustain non-financial assets. For integrated reporting, such as <IR> to be effective in expanding transparency and understanding of any organizations business model, accounting cannot view itself as just a protector of their traditional silo but as "bridge builders" between financial information and the other areas of capability. There is no question that the majority of intangible reporting MUST stay separate from traditional approaches to capitalization, however, as protector and reporter of financial capital, providing clearer insight into the use and application of financial resources, especially to the creation and care of critical intangible capabilities must be provided.

When ABC or Activity Based Costing was developed as a tool to align financial resources with process management, only a limited number of organizations adopted the approach. The Balanced Scorecard provided a great opportunity for accounting to bring financial management into alignment with the newer broad based process thinking. Reflecting on the BSC, one can see that as many organizations adopted broad based performance management, much of the financials remained the same. The "internal process" dimension of the BSC was a clear move to the recognition as processes as the building blocks for financial capital consumption - yet while operations shifted in that direction with management systems such as ISO 9001 and 6 Sigma (automotive were already there with tools like the process based FMEA) accounting remained aligned with the departmental / responsibility accounting structure.

Many software developers such as SAP structured their products with the capability to integrate process management but, yet again, many organizations implemented these systems on a "pure conversion" basis, missing the opportunity to view the organization from both a hierarchical (management structure / departmental often used for "roll up's and consolidations) basis as well as a horizontal view looking across departments at the process dimension. Even in governments, where funding is often assigned based on a program / process basis, financial reporting remains heavily biased towards statutory, traditional external needs, limiting its effectiveness for managers engaged in process based decision thinking.

It appears that as th world is moving forward, accounting remains a "lone silo" with limited bridges to the evolving world of non-financial indicators that are intended to report how everything other than financial capital is working. The recent announcement in Europe from EFRAG seems to once again have accounting on the outside. Where are the bridge builders?

The GRI Standards, the most widely used sustainability reporting standards in Europe and beyond, are well positioned to play a key role in achieving the Commission's aims to improve and expand non-financial reporting in the EU. Furthermore, our globally applicable, independent standards can be a bridge to achieving an international solution. The EU has an opportunity to provide global leadership, as the first major jurisdiction to mandate sustainability reporting with the same rigor as financial reporting. GRI stands ready to work with EFRAG and the Commission to make this a reality."
Peter Paul van de Wijs, GRI Chief External Affairs Officer

In 1987, "Relevance Lost" focused readers on the drift of management accounting away from the rapidly changing realities of organizational management. Is the profession in the same place once again - or still? Events seem to suggest that the drift has continued even with legislative changes. Are accountants getting "better and better at what is less and less relevant?" The time has arrived when the profession needs a high level of self-reflection and to ask the question "are we adding value?" The true test of our own sustainability as a profession will be a resounding "yes - we couldn't manage without the information that the accountants provide us with."

Bibliography

Asakawa, Masatsugu., "Transfer Pricing in the New Global Landscape: the OECD's Engagement beyond its Borders" Masatsugu Asakawa, Deputy Vice-Minister of Finance for International Affairs, Japanese Ministry of Finance and Chairman, OECD Committee on Fiscal Affairs.

ASBY, EFRAG., "Quantitative study on goodwill and impairment" Staff of the European Financial Reporting Advisory Group (EFRAG) and Staff of the Accounting Standards Board of Japan (ASBJ), EFRAG, July 2016.

Audit Monk, "A brief history of Accounting" Audit Monk Blog, May 12th, 2017,

Bloch, Samantha., "The US and Corporate Social Responsibility in International Business Transactions: Has Anything Changed?" Denver Journal of International Law and Policy, May 5, 2018

Brooks, Richard., "The financial scandal no one is talking about," The Guardian, 29th May 2018.

Castellano, James. G., "Restoring Public Confidence," AICPA Accountancy Journal, April 1st, 2002.

Crosby, Phil., "Quality is Free,", Signet, 1979.

Darcy, Shane., "The Elephant in the Room": Corporate Tax Avoidance & Business and Human Rights; Published online by Cambridge University Press: 12th August 2016.

Edvinsson, L., and Malone. M. S., "Intellectual Capital," P 168-169, Harper Business,"1997,

Gleeson-White, Jane., "Six Capitals," Allen & Unwin, 2014

Goldsberry, Clare, "Another automotive supplier victimized by General Motors' purchasing strategies", Jul 13, 2016, Plastics Today

Holmberg, Susan., "The Overpaid CEO," Democracy, Fall 2014,

Hood, Daniel., "Trust is just the beginning" Accounting Today. (Study from ACCA, IFAC, and CA ANZ), March 4th, 2019

Hood, David., "Accounting Today," October 01, 2018

Hoogervorst, Hans., "The imprecise world of accounting," from speech by Hans Hoogervorst, Chair IASB, Amsterdam, June 2012:

IFAC, "Materiality in Integrated Reporting" Integrated Reporting <IR>, November 2015

IIRC, "The International <IR> Framework," International Integrated Reporting Council, December 2013

James, Meg., "Nearly 3 million subscribers ditched DirecTV last year. Will AT&T do the same?" LA Times, Jan. 31, 2020,

Johnson, Thomas. H., and Kaplan, Robert, S., "Relevance Lost: The Rise and Fall of Management Accounting" Harvard Business School Press, 1987

Jones, Chris., Temouri, Yama., Cobham, Alex., Tax haven networks and the role of the Big 4 accountancy firms" Journal of World Business, Feb 2018.

Kaplan, Robert. S., Norton, David. P., "The Balanced Scorecard," 1996, Harvard Business Review Press

KPMG., "Unlocking shareholder value: the key to success," KPMG, 1999.

Maister, David., "The Trusted Advisor" Free Press, 2001

Mendleson, Rachel., "Occupy Wall Street Protests' Constructive says Mark Carney, Bank of Canada Governor," The Huffington Post, 14th Oct 2011.

Mintz, Steven., "Accounting in the Public Interest. An Historical Perspective on Professional Ethics," The CPA Journal, March 2018.

Perryer, Sophie., "Top 5 tax scandals," World Finance Magazine, Oct 16th, 2018,

Peters, Sandra., "FASB Turns Up the Heat on Goodwill Impairment Testing," CFA Institute, February 12th, 2020.

Peterson, David., "A Better Way: Redefining the Way America Works," Houghton Mifflin Harcourt, 1991

Rose, Sally., and Hendy, Nina., "How accountants can survive the public trust crisis, Acuity Magazine, 9th April 2019,

Selley, David. C., "The Origins and Development of Materiality as an Auditing Concept," The Canadian Institute of Chartered Accountants, 1984

Shepherd, N., "Governance, Accountability and Sustainable Development: An agenda for the 21st century," Thomson Carswell Canada, 2005

Shepherd, N., and Adams, M., "Unrecognized Intangible Assets: Identification, Management and Reporting," Statements in Management Accounting series., Institute of Management Accountants, 2014

Stanfield, Ken, "Intangible Management: Tools for solving the accounting and management crisis"

Sternberg, William., "Cooked Books," The Atlantic, January 1992

Stewart, T., "Intellectual Capital: The New Wealth of organizations," P 232-233, Doubleday, 1997

Stewart, Tom., "Intellectual Capital: The New Wealth of Nations" Currency Doubleday, 1997,

Trefis, Team Contributors, Great Speculations, "Was AT&T's Acquisition of DirecTV A Mistake?" Forbes Aug 9, 2019,

Van de Vijver., Cassimon. Danny., Engelen. Peter-Jan., "A Real Option Approach to Sustainable Corporate Tax Behavior," Sustainability Journal (EU) July 3rd, 2020.

Welch, Jack., "Winning," Harper Collins, 2005

White, Gwendolen. B., "Perceptions of Accountants: What Are They After Enron And WorldCom?" Journal of College Teaching & Learning, November 2006,

Wikipedia, "Financial audit."

Winick, Stephen., "More About the Business of Scrooge and Marley: An Ethnographic Approach," Stephen Winick who uses this quote from the blog of Ellen Terrell - blog post at Inside Adams December 19, 2019

World Economic Forum, "Countries lose an estimated $125 billion in tax revenue each year. This is why"

Zeff. Stephen A., "A History of Management Accounting: The British Experience," (Book Review) The Accounting Review, American Accounting Association

NICK A. SHEPHERD
FCPA, FCGA, FCCA, FCMC,

Nick has over 50 years of varied work experience including senior general management and finance roles. From 1989 to 2017 he ran his own management consulting and professional development company. Currently he is officially retired but still spends time on research and writing. Nick currently focuses his efforts in the areas of organizational sustainability, human capital, and integrated reporting. Nick has experience working in, and with private family business, public corporations, and governments and NPO's. Nick is currently a Director and Council member of the UK based Maturity Institute.

As a management consultant and facilitator, Nick designed and presented many professional development workshops internationally, and across Canada. Nick was also part-time faculty member at Grenoble Graduate School of Business (GGSB) where he taught modules on Mergers and Acquisitions and Management Consulting; Nick also lectured at McMaster / DeGroote on ethics. Nick led the Professional Standards Committee of the International Council of Management Consultants in developing the competency model that now forms the basis of CMC certification in over 50 global CMC Institutes. In 2007 Nick received the President's Award for Education from the Certified General Accountants of British Columbia. Nick's consulting work included both public and private sector clients in many countries including Canada, the US, the UK, the Caribbean, South Africa, Kazakhstan, Kyrgyzstan, Uzbekistan, and Jordan.

Nick joined CPA Ontario as a Fellow in 2014 following the merger of accounting bodies. Prior to that Nick was a CGA for over 35 years obtaining his Fellowship in 2009. Nick is a Fellow of the Chartered Association of Certified Accountants (FCCA UK), and a Fellow of the Institute of Certified Management Consultants of Ontario (FCMC – Honour Roll), and Past President of the Institute. Nick is Past Chair of the National Certification Committee for all Institutes of Management Consulting across Canada, and Past Chair of the Professional Standards Committee of the International Council of Management Consulting Institutes (ICMCI). He served as one of four trustees for Canada at the International level (ICMCI). Nick has also been a member of Mensa for many years.

Nick is co-author of "Reflective Leaders and High Performing Organizations" written in 2012 with Dr. Peter Smyth. Nick also wrote "Governance, Accountability and Sustainable Development" in 2005, that deals with Governance issues for the 21st century, and the "Controllers Handbook" (now in its 2nd edition) – these books add to a number of other books and articles that Nick has authored, including "Values and Ethics: From Inception to Practice," "The Evolution of Accountability – Sustainability Reporting for Accountants," "Unrecognized Intangible Assets: Identification, Management and Reporting" and "The Human Aspects of Cost Control." Nick also developed several Ethics courses for accountants and consultants nationally and internationally.

Contact Nick at nick@eduvision.ca